having the end of the fly line point toward the fly and doesn't create a ripple when pulled through the water.

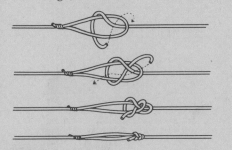

Jam Knot

A good knot for attaching a length of nonofilament leader to a braided baitcasting line. Both lines should be approximately the same strength and thickness.

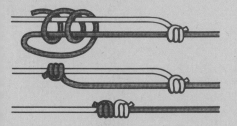

The illustration shows one knot already tied, and the second knot is tied the same way. Then tighten the two knots together.

Dropper Loop

This is a handy knot to form a loop in the center of a leader for tying on a tippet or a dropper fly. First, form a loop about three inches in diameter at the point where you wish to form the dropper loop. Twist the leader around itself several times. Separate the center twisted strands and pull the op-

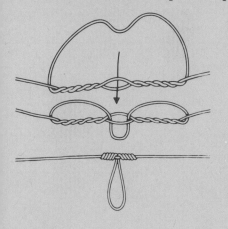

posite side of the loop through this opening. The second illustration shows the knot before it is pulled tight.

Wire Line to Mono Knot

Holding the wire line in your left hand, fold four inches of the end back over the standing part of the line. Run the monofila-

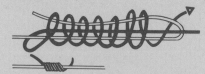

ment through the middle of the bend in the wire, passing it behind the wire and then over it. Make seven close turns around both lines. Pass the end of the mono over the center strand of monofilament and under the top strand of the wire, and then draw up snug. Cutting the free end of the wire would leave a burr that can cut fingers. Instead, bend it back and forth. It will break close to the turns of the monofilament, leaving no burr.

Improved End Loop

A good, strong knot for making a loop at the end of your line. With heavy monofilament, it is difficult to pull up on five turns, so you might have to reduce the turns to

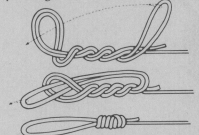

three or four. As in tying all knots, pull it tight slowly so that all coils tighten evenly.

Perfection Loop

Make a loop as shown (A) and bring the end around to form a second loop below the first (B). Bring the end around and lay it between the two loops (C). Hold in place with thumb and forefinger; draw the second, or lower, loop through the first, or upper, loop (D) and pull tight (E). This knot will not slip. It is commonly used at the butt end of fly leaders.

A

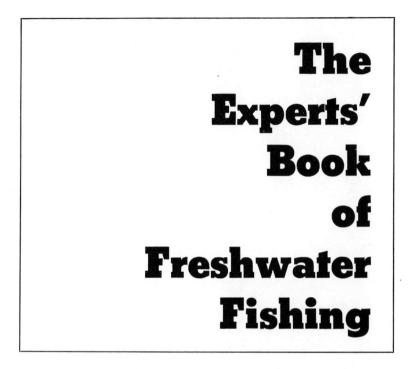

The Experts' Book of Freshwater Fishing

Edited by STEVE NETHERBY

A CORD COMMUNICATIONS BOOK

SIMON AND SCHUSTER   NEW YORK

Cover photograph by Irwin Horowitz. Spinning tackle is Alcedo 2 C/S reel with companion rod—from Continental Arms Corp. Fly tackle is L.R.H. Lightweight reel and "Palakona" Model #5 rod—from Hardy Bros. Ltd., distributed by Harrington & Richardson, Inc. Bait-casting tackle is Ambassadeur 5000 reel and Ambassadeur 8317-A rod—from The Garcia Corporation. All other gear is courtesy of Abercrombie & Fitch. Endpapers are courtesy The Garcia Corporation.

To Jackie,
for her loving support
and long hours at the typewriter.
And to Mel Bookstein,
for his patience and his help.

CONTENTS

Foreword	*By Steve Netherby*	9
Gearing Up	*By Jerry Gibbs*	14
Stream Trout	*By Joseph D. Bates, Jr.*	46
Mountain Trout	*By Norman Strung*	69
Big-Water Trout of the West	*By A. J. McClane*	92
Steelhead	*By Clare Conley*	109
Lake Trout	*By Tom McNally*	131
Largemouth Bass	*By Homer Circle*	151
Smallmouth Bass	*By Jerome B. Robinson*	169
Atlantic Salmon	*By Lee Wulff*	184
Pacific Salmon	*By Larry Green*	212
Muskellunge, Northern Pike, Pickerel, Walleye	*By Doug Knight*	231
Panfish	*By Charles F. Waterman*	266
Epilogue: The Fisherman in Conservation	*By Michael Frome*	286
About the Authors		298
Index		303

FOREWORD

BY STEVE NETHERBY

EVENINGS we'd fish. In summertime Rocky Mountain Colorado, the evenings were long. We'd fish until the sunset was shoved over behind the Front Range and there wasn't light enough to unhook a trout by.

Jackie and I had just left the Navy. We had U-Haul–trailered from Washington State to Colorado "to save ourselves and fix ourselves," to paraphrase a good poet, before we measured ourselves against new careers and the race we knew would come.

At first I worked as a laborer, a jackhammer operator on a gas pipeline, and we'd head for a stream as soon as I'd brushed the granite dust off my jeans and we'd had dinner. Fishing evenings were longest then. They shortened when I took a new job, on the town's only newspaper, and Jackie renewed her teaching credentials. But we still fished. Angling for brown and brook trout in local streams was our one strong link with the elusive "natural life" for which we had come to the mountains, and with the timeless beauties of the high country.

We fished bait—worms and salmon eggs—because that was the way we'd been shown when we were kids and it was all we knew. In our favorite hole, a rock-studded run just downstream from a tiny falls, we always caught enough 8- and 10-inch trout over a week's time to freeze up for a weekend feast and an occasional weekday fry. But the fish, though they weren't few, came relatively far between. It took a fair amount of working (though we never would have called it work) to hook each one.

I remember one fish especially for the efforts he exacted from me. I first met up with him toward the finish of a purple June sunset. I had cast upstream from a tightly wooded bank and was letting my worm bounce with the current along the bottom. Just before the stream began an almost right-angle turn and I began to reel back the worm, my sacrificial offering was sucked by the current around a big midcreek rock.

Suddenly, from the lee side of the rock, my line began to telegraph the frantic wriggling tugging that means fish. And the tugs were heavy—the fish would be bigger than any I'd caught there.

I fed the fish line, hoping to give it time to swallow the worm. Then I struck, hard. But I struck only water.

For six nights after that, my hooks were plundered by that same fish in the lee of that same rock. I tried every tactic I could think of—striking sooner, later, hooking my worms every imaginable way, using hooks of different sizes—but my only reward, each time, was a sickeningly slack line and a hook denuded of bait. I was beginning to feel much like a landlocked Ahab questing after Moby Trout.

On the seventh evening, fishing through a soft summer rain, I caught him. The hook held fast. I played him till all his magnificent fight was gone; then I reeled him, sulking in silent S-turns, toward me. When he was near the bank, I lifted my rod to swing him ashore—and my leader parted from my line as he thrashed one more violent time.

But that evening's best luck was to be mine. As the fish splashed into the water, the leader, still hooked to his mouth, draped itself for a split moment over a half-submerged strand of ancient barbed wire, and I grabbed it. I had my trout.

As I was securing the glistening 14-inch trophy to my stringer line, which already held two 8-inchers—hard-won products of the previous three hours I'd fished there—I happened to glance upstream. At the foot of the small falls, I saw a friend—manager of the camping-supply store in town—fly-fishing.

As preoccupied as I was with my own recent success, my friend still looked grand to me. He was fitted out in chest waders and a fly fisher's vest, waist-deep in the frothy water, whipping sweet, short casts cross-stream. The rain had stopped, and I could see his tiny dry fly riding high through the froth, then swinging into quiet water dimpled by rising trout. I watched until one of the dimples engulfed his fly and he skillfully led a nice brown to a net he had somehow produced. When I talked to him the next day, he told me he had caught six fish, ranging in length up to 12 inches, in half an hour's time.

So after all those seasons of fishing bait, I decided I'd have to try fly fishing someday.

The day didn't come till two years later, after Jackie and I had moved to New York State. Another friend, a commercial real estate broker, invited me to fish with him on a flies-only stream half an hour's drive north of New York City. This friend was not only a talented fly fisherman—he was a skilled teacher, and in that single afternoon he had me casting well enough to catch several of the less wary brown trout that swam there.

Today, fly fishing is my major fishing passion, though I still spend long, lazy hours fishing bait, and Jackie and I have lately taken to fishing spinners and plugs for bass. My two friends added more than they knew to my enjoyment of angling: the first, by showing me that fly fishing could be both esthetically beautiful and effective, giving me the idea to try it for myself; the second, by teaching me to catch trout on a fly.

Inspiration and instruction. I have a strong feeling that this book will be providing these things for fishermen all over North America for many years to come. The fortunate readers of *The Experts' Book of Freshwater Fishing* won't have to wait for chance encounters with knowledgeable fishermen to be inspired to try a new style of angling or to be instructed in how to go about it. And when they hanker for new fish, or new places to fish, they'll find the why, the where and the way within these pages.

And what a council of experts they'll be consulting with! The freshwater-angling editors of *Field & Stream, Outdoor Life* and *Sports Afield*—the country's preeminent outdoor magazines—are here. The Editor-in-Chief of *True* magazine, the Conservation Editor of *Field & Stream,* a department and a field editor from

Sports Afield and *Field & Stream,* editors of some of the nation's leading newspaper outdoor columns and much of the cream of the fishing world's book authors and free-lance magazine writers are represented.

If you haven't come across such a summit meeting of fishing minds before, it's because this is the first of its type to be convened between the covers of a single book. The one ingredient that makes *The Experts' Book of Freshwater Fishing* work is the strength of its original intention: to bring together the top experts in the sphere of freshwater fishing, each to write about the segment of the sport he knows best. I'm convinced that nowhere else, short of a library full of books or in a collection of these men's-magazine articles, will a fisherman discover such a concentrated fund of fishing expertise.

The eleven "fish" chapters that follow are for anglers from beginner to advanced. They tell you where to find the fish you're after, and when. What his habits are and how to identify him. How to catch him on bait, artificial lures or flies. How to choose balanced tackle. In short, they provide all the beginner needs to know to start catching fish right now, along with the knowledge that will enable the fisherman of intermediate skills to begin catching more, and probably bigger, fish. For the advanced fisherman, our master anglers serve up their own distinctive points of view to savor and digest. Perhaps even to argue with.

There are two chapters that are not "fish" chapters per se. In the lead-off chapter, the Fishing Editor of *Outdoor Life* reviews some of the elements of fishing tackle for those who are buying gear or for those who just want to brush up on their equipment vocabulary. In the book's final chapter, the Conservation Editor of *Field & Stream* outlines the crucial role every fisherman must play in conserving a livable environment.

How will you go about reading a book such as this? I have a suggestion, if you want it. First, read the tackle chapter, "Gearing Up." It'll get you speaking the language. Next, read the chapter that talks about the fish you want to catch. Then, read the conservation chapter. Our continent's fresh waters, in addition to providing much of the world's greatest fishing, form one of the most delicate and endangered links in the ecological chain. We have a responsibility to learn how to care for them before we go to them for our sport.

Finally, to get the most from this book, read it from cover to cover. Even if you fish for trout alone—or bass or bluegills or pike— you'll learn something from each of these excellent authors that will deepen your enjoyment of fishing and help you to be a better fisherman.

Better yet, take this book as you take your fishing—in whatever way pleases you best. After all, pleasure is what sport fishing—and fishing books—should be all about.

STEVE NETHERBY

Port Washington, New York

GEARING UP

BY JERRY GIBBS

THE 12:05 from somewhere north rumbled irrepressibly south toward the trestle beneath which I fished. I worked a little two-bladed silver Indiana spinner in figure-8s and slow runs along the cement abutment that supported the trestle and the tracks. The train came closer. Glinting darkly in the noon sun, it was the only thing that had shown promise of positive action in what seemed a long time. There was no bait on the spinner, just a hook, and the lightness of the lure, compared with the rest of my tackle, precluded all casting attempts. The lure was tied to a crude gut leader at the end of a black braided line wrapped around a bait-casting reel with handles that spun as the spool revolved. We called it a knuckle-buster. The rod was as flexible as a Louisville Slugger baseball bat. But I was about 8 years old; what did I know?

So the 12:05 came on steaming and snorting, and blue-gray cinders popped down the embankment, and the vibrations went down into the water. *Whang* went my line out straight. With youthful reflexes I responded in kind, yanking the fish clear from the depths into a glistening airborne arc that took him short feet away on my embankment perch. I pounced. Downslope led to a 2-foot-wide beach. I didn't trust myself to hold the squirming fish

14

in such cramped quarters and wheeled and churned uphill through the cinders. The engineer saw me coming and blew his whistle, which, at close range, sounded like an outraged Hereford. I collapsed at the summit in summer dust, a grimy urchin who had found Nirvana, grinning inanely at my buddy Roger, whose words from below I could not distinguish in the train roar.

"That's a bass!" Roger screeched for the tenth time. "A largemouth bass, I think."

Who cared how big his mouth was? He was a bass. I had graduated from bluegill school. I was a fisherman. I thought.

Had I known the apprenticeship yet before me, the trials through which that heavy casting outfit would put me, I am certain I would have shown more restraint. If I were requested to last through such a similar blundering period of hit-or-miss learning now, I couldn't do it. I wonder how many kids are abruptly introduced to fishing with makeshift equipment that almost guarantees early failure and discourages pursuit of the sport. I know that a great many men and women quit the game before they've ever come to understand its pleasures simply because of frustration over basic technique, which includes developing skill with proper, balanced equipment.

Luck with that bass early in my fishing career was probably responsible for enabling me to overcome an equipment disadvantage that had consistently allowed my boyhood chum to outfish me. We had always gone for panfish. Roger used a beat-up fly rod. He could not actually cast it. The line was tied off at the tip, leaving free about 5 or so feet which he was able to wield with a certain skill. The amount of weight I was forced to clamp to my line in order to achieve a 5-foot cast was astronomical. It also frightened away fish. After the bass, I fished different waters than Roger, dropping bait deeper and coming up with fish—mostly catfish, but they were bigger than the "sunnies" and little yellow perch my friend caught. They were also the success factor that spurred me to continue fishing until I eventually began to understand a simple truth:

If you are going to learn to catch fish consistently, you must start out by catching fish.

The fine points of angling for particular fish species are discussed by the other authors in this book, but the first requisite for following their advice is to be properly equipped. (Keep in mind that I am, by necessity, dealing in generalities here. Authors of chapters on specific fish may differ slightly in their tackle recommendations.)

The initial selection of freshwater fishing tackle is often dependent upon equal parts geography, ego and fortuity. It is gross oversimplification to recommend spin casting, for instance, as the sine qua non for all beginning anglers. The person intent upon gaining admission to an elite fly fishers' association or the man dreaming of collecting top honors in pro bass tournaments throughout the South would find the suggestion worthless. It is better to suggest the character and uses of the various types of equipment, and the fish for which they may be primarily intended. The beginning angler can then, after evaluating his primary needs and intended quarry, make a valid decision as to what is best for him.

Each of the following equipment types will shortly be discussed in greater detail, but it is important to gain initial working definitions.

Fly tackle is the classic equipment for stream and river trout. Contemporary manufacturing techniques have made it adaptable to nearly all game fish in this country—under proper conditions. With this equipment the line is the vehicle through which the fly or bait is cast. The bait is not cast directly from the reel. This is our oldest fishing method and the one requiring the greatest physical coordination. Several major tackle manufacturers have initiated fly-fishing schools of several days' duration or more to introduce the novice to the game and ease him over the early problem period.

Bait-casting—also known as plug-casting—equipment is greatly favored among Southern bass anglers who fish with live and artificial bait. Northern pike and muskellunge fishermen also like the equipment. The lure is cast directly from a revolving-spool reel. Bait-casting tackle has traditionally been assembled as a relatively heavy outfit, but this is not as true today. It is less difficult to master than fly tackle—the chief difficulty being the tendency of the spool to overrun the outgoing line in a cast, resulting in line tangle known as backlash.

With spinning tackle, the lure is cast from a fixed-spool reel located on the underside of the rod handle. The equipment's earliest advantage was in permitting the use of ultralight baits and line, filling a gap between bait-casting and fly tackle. Today, spinning equipment exists that will handle lures in the category once the reserve of the bait-casting enthusiast. The line spool is exposed on spinning reels, and the term open-face reel is commonly applied to them. Ease in mastery of this equipment has made it most popular among recreational anglers throughout the country, who use it on all types of fish from trout to the heaviest species.

Spin-cast equipment is also an application of the fixed-spool principle. The reel may be mounted on the upper or lower side of the rod handle. The rod is similar to those used in bait casting, with frequently one rod playing both roles. The spool, or drum, of a spin-casting reel is enclosed by a cone- or dome-shaped hood, and naturally enough, the unit is commonly known as a closed-face reel. The cone restricts the use of extremely light lures and lines— the latter having a tendency to ball up within the reel cover. Simplicity of operation—the cast release popularly initiated with a push button—has made this tackle extremely popular and usable on most game fish. Beginning anglers often find it the easiest of all tackle to master.

For purposes of quick identification, the fly-rod reel seat is located at the butt of the rod handle. A fixed reel seat with one or two screw-down rings is most commonly employed. Guides—the metal rings along the length of the rod through which the line passes—vary on rod types. Fly-rod guides often consist of one ring guide near the butt, followed by spiral or snake guides and, finally, a ring-within-a-tube guide known as the tip-top. Fly-rod guides are intended to hold the line close to the rod with the least possible weight.

Bait-casting and spin-casting rods have either straight or offset handles. The offset handle is generally preferred for freshwater fishing. It permits the thumb to work the spool easily in bait casting and work the release button on spin-casting reels. Guides on these rods are of the ring type, popularly made of tungsten carbide.

Spinning rods have straight handles with reel seats of the fixed, sliding-ring or older sliding-sleeve variety. The fixed seat with screw locks is most secure but least comfortable. The sliding rings

LEFT TO RIGHT: *Eagle Claw and Zebco bait- and spin-cast rods; Zebco and Eagle Claw heavy-duty spinning rods; Zebco and Fenwick ultra-light spinning rods.*

provide the most comfort with the least weight but can loosen up during casting, necessitating periodic adjustment. The rarely seen sliding reel seat consists of metal rings and sleeve. It is not especially comfortable, but helps prevent reel "feet" from being pushed into the cork of the handle, which is possible on the plain sliding-ring arrangement. Spinning-rod guides are larger in diameter and lighter than those on bait-casting rods. The first and second guides from the rod butt are quite large in order to choke the spinning line and funnel it along into the other guides as it uncoils from the reel. In practice this may extend casting range slightly, but the proper spacing of guides—especially butt guide to reel—is of at least equal importance. There are frequently fewer guides on spinning rods to reduce light-line friction that shortens casts. The guides are very hard, as thin-diameter monofilament may eventually cut into soft metals.

One speaks of fast and slow rods, referring to the time it takes the rod to flex and recover during the cast. This action is built into the rod in terms of stiffness and taper. A stiff rod built to obviate increased weight (the reason for hollow construction) will have faster flex and recovery. A rod that is less stiff throughout is understood to be a slow rod. It is designed for casting of the lightest lures, which do not markedly contribute to flexing of the rod during the cast. Slow rods bend more evenly along the length of the shaft than the so-called fast-tip models, which are favored for the casting of heavier lures.

For years, two-piece rods have been standard. Recently, however, there has been a trend toward the one-piece shaft as giving more satisfactory casting performance. Many anglers seem inclined to put up with the inconvenience of a longer shaft to obtain the more nearly perfect action. In the opposite direction, ferrules, the male and female joints of multipiece rods, are increasingly being designed of the fiber-glass material used in rod construction. One result is a joint more flexible than the metal ferrule; another is the creation of four-, five- and even eight-piece rods that are excellent for traveling anglers. These "pack" rods come in single-purpose (i.e., fly) or multipurpose (fly–spinning–casting) configurations. While extremely practical, the multipurpose rods give something less than ultimate performance from an esthetic standpoint.

We will consider line in the detailed discussion of each individual type of tackle, but some word on hooks is here in order. During his early fishing efforts, the new angler should catch more fish more easily on natural bait, but the size and style of the simple hook on his terminal rigging often make the difference between success and failure.

Good stainless-steel hooks come in a variety of thicknesses, shank lengths, bends, eyes and points. It is necessary to concern ourselves here with the most important basics. It is possible to catch large fish on hooks too small for the job, but attempting to catch small fish on hooks too large for their mouths is obviously not recommended. Straight hooks are most often preferred, but some anglers feel that hooks that are kirbed—offset to the right, viewed facing the eye from the top—or reversed—offset to the left —will not slip from a fish's mouth without sticking. However, these hooks will spin when retrieved. They also take somewhat more power to embed. With small, thin baits they are fine, but when they are employed with live-minnow baits the angle of penetration must be kept in mind so that the hook point does not simply embed itself farther into the minnow when the angler sets the hook into a game fish.

Fine-wire hooks are ideal with fragile bait, or when fish are wary. Such hooks are balanced with light, limber tackle—fly rods, light spinning rods, for example. Straight-shank hooks are perfectly acceptable for a variety of live or dead baits, but the barbed or sliced shank aids in the holding of baits like worms. A long shank is recommended when the quarry is of the sharp-toothed variety (pike, pickerel, muskellunge). The smaller short-shank hooks may be completely hidden in bait such as salmon eggs. They also prevent the weighting down of bait that should float or maintain neutral buoyancy. And they provide good penetration in soft-mouthed species. The barbs on the hook points (especially on trout flies) should be pinched down with a pair of pliers when the fish caught are to be released. This facilitates easy removal of the point. It also makes fish harder to hold while the angler is playing them, but adds to the sport. All hooks must periodically receive a treatment with hone or file to keep them at peak sharpness.

It is often necessary to sink natural and artificial baits or lower their arc of travel underwater. An ever-growing variety of lead sinkers provide the chief means of accomplishing the task, and several types are worth knowing:

Split shot—Small lead balls sliced partway through for pinching

A selection of sinkers. TOP ROW, LEFT TO RIGHT: *keel, worm sinker with propeller attractor, dropper (split shot in nylon sleeve), bottom-walking.* SECOND ROW: *cone-shaped sliding worm, dipsey, dipsey again, split shot with jaws for easy removal, split shot.* THIRD ROW: *crimp-on with rubber insert, sliding bait or worm sinker, sliding fish-finder.* FOURTH ROW: *sliding worm sinkers. The outer two are encased in colored plastic.*

onto the line or leader. Available in many sizes for use when minimal weight is desired. A new variety permits easy removal and reuse on the alligator-clip principle.

Clinch-on—Torpedo-shaped lead with clamp-on flanges or rubber inserts for easy removal and reuse. Slightly heavier than split shot, but designed for use when artificials are to be taken only slightly below the surface on the retrieve, or baits sunk slowly.

Dipsey—A teardrop-shaped sinker with wire swivel and eye at its top. This is preferred by live-bait fishermen when bait is to be free-floating or the line allowed to work through the sinker eye from the bottom and the bait drifted surfaceward. It can also anchor bait at a desired depth.

Cone—Used ahead of plastic worms by bass fishermen. Some models are tunneled out slightly to permit the worm head to fit within. These come plain or painted and coated with polypropylene plastic. One variety is trimmed with a propeller.

Keel—The shark-fin-shaped sinker with bead chain links at both ends and a snap swivel at the end of one chain length. The "fin" rides down. This is used for trolling in fresh water and is positioned ahead of the bait.

Lead strips or wire—Used frequently to add slight weight to flies, bugs and other lures for slow sinking. Pieces of these materials may be cut to give desired weight.

Profile of Spin-Cast Tackle

The day, thus far, had been a success. I was playing guide, and already my wife and 5-year-old son had caught enough small bluegills to convince them that maybe they were going to like this business of fishing after all. Our youngster was standing shin-deep just at the weed line near a large boulder. An angler I did not know passed along the lake bank and immediately queried me.

"That your kid out there?"

I confirmed the fact.

"You know he's right by the drop-off. Goes down to maybe fifteen feet there."

In three wading paces that displayed all the grace of a great white hog in a wallow, I had nearly closed the distance to my first-born when I dropped out of sight. My benefactor on the beach had just finished telling my wife about the *other* drop-off.

All ended well. But upon my return to shore, my wife thrust her new spin-cast outfit into my face.

"Whassamatter?" I sputtered.

"I got excited."

My boy continued to fish—now close to shore—while I tried my wife's reel. It wouldn't budge. Inside, line was wrapped about the gearing like a steel spring. All of which is to say that nothing is foolproof. The spin-cast reel, however, may be the closest thing to it.

A kissing cousin to spinning tackle, spin-cast equipment is built on the fixed-spool principle, but with the line spool enclosed in a hood or housing, as we have already seen.

It has been said that spin-cast tackle fills a gap between spinning and bait-cast equipment. The statement is less true today than it once was, however, because rod, reel and line development have broadened spinning's coverage to include ultralight to heavy tackle. Likewise, the development of more sensitive rods, finer reels and lighter line permits bait casters to work with lures in the ¼-ounce class. Spin casting, therefore, cannot claim to fill a real void; still, the simplicity of the equipment has ensured its continued popularity.

As I mentioned earlier, the design of the spin-cast reel makes it less suited for extremely light, fine lines. Because ultralight lures demand the use of such lines, the tackle is obviously not the right choice for minuscule baits—say, in the $\frac{1}{32}$-ounce category. It is ideally suited for lures in the $\frac{3}{8}$-to-$\frac{5}{8}$-ounce weight class and for fishing natural baits. Line choice should be monofilament in the 6-to-15-pound class. Limper braided line is not recommended as it, like the ultralight line, may "nest" up inside the reel cover.

With spin-cast tackle, as opposed to spinning gear, there is far less of a problem with slack line. Slack, which can cause loops to form on the spinning-reel spool or line to spring off and become kinked or knotted, is avoided with spin-cast gear by a simple maneuver: if line is not rewinding when the handle is initially cranked, simply pull mono from the reel until tautness is felt, then begin cranking once more.

In most reel models, spin-cast equipment eliminates the need to pick up line with the forefinger during the cast, the casting action being controlled by a push button or lever. There are spin-cast reels designed to mount below and above on the rod handle, but most today are of the top-of-the-handle variety. An offset rod handle and bait-casting rod should be used with the top-mount reel. At least one manufacturer produces a spin-cast outfit in which the reel is an integral part of the rod handle. The release button is in the handle and the reel hangs below. It has proved a very popular design.

As with all fishing tackle, the reel, line and rod must balance. While balance is not quite as critical with spin-cast tackle as it is with other types, certain facts should be kept in mind in the choice of an outfit. A heavy line should be matched to a stiff rod. Fine line can be cast with a stiff rod, but if, when the angler is playing a fish, a pull is required that exceeds the line's ability to transmit a bend to the rod, the line will break. The lighter line and reel balance a more flexible rod. With spin-cast reels there is not the great variety in size and weight that exists with spinning reels, but line capacity should be a consideration.

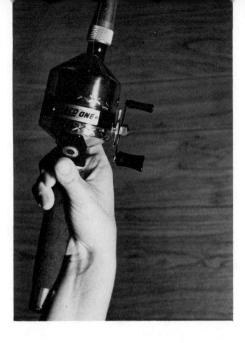

As in bait casting, keep the reel handles up when casting a lure with spin-cast gear.

Spin-cast tackle functions as follows: During the cast the thumb button is depressed and, as the rod brings the lure forward, released. The line spins off the end of a spool, just as in spinning; passes over a drum and spirals around in the hood before passing out through a small hole in its center. Friction on the line as it spins inside the hood cuts down slightly on cast distance, but not enough for most anglers to notice. When the handle is cranked for the retrieve, a pin or pins within the drum extend to pick up the line as the spool revolves. The line is wound onto the spool. On spin-cast reels the spool may oscillate in and out as on spinning reels, or it may not. Those on which it does are made wider and hold more line.

The thumb button causes the pins to retract and moves the spool forward in the hood. A rubber-gasketed brake ring holds the line tight during the period when the button is depressed.

Most spin-cast reels are fitted with an antireverse mechanism and a drag. The former is used to keep the reel locked in position so that line may be cranked in only; the handle may not be turned backward so that line is unwound. It is used primarily when the angler is fighting a fish, so that he can keep on constant pressure. The drag permits a fighting fish to take out line when the reel spool is locked by the antireverse mechanism or held with the handle by the angler. It may be tightened to force a fish to expend the greatest energy in order to gain line. If it is set too tight, a light line may break when a large fish makes a sudden lunge.

There are many ways to set the drag, and experienced anglers can do it by feel with lines of various test, simply by pulling off a section of monofilament. It is better for the beginner to fasten the end of the line to a stationary object, then begin tightening the drag while bowing back the rod. When considerable tension is on the rod and line, suddenly jerk the tip upward as though setting the hook in a fish's mouth. The spool should slip slightly if the drag is properly set.

The main complaint about spin-cast equipment—especially from bait casters— is loss of the ability to feather or feel the lure on target because of a rather abrupt shutoff when the thumb button is depressed at a cast's completion. This fault has been greatly reduced in at least one recent model by the engineering of slow-cutoff capability into the push-button control so that the lure may be slowed in flight rather than having to be completely checked.

The speed with which the novice can learn to cast using tackle of this type will maintain it at a high level of popularity. Among more experienced anglers it finds a place as an alternative rig and is an excellent choice for night fishing to avoid reel-jamming slack that can go unnoticed in the darkness.

Profile of Spinning Tackle

In its wide range of weights and sizes, probably no other tackle type can equal spinning for versatility. The equipment is available in balanced outfits that can handle ⅟₃₂-ounce lures on line testing a delicate 1½ pounds. Or you can choose a husky outfit for lines in the 30-to-45-pound class and lures weighing 3 to 4 ounces.

As it first gained popularity here in the late 1940s and early 1950s, spinning was both praised by those who hailed it as the universal fishing method and damned by those who feared it would cause the destruction of whole fish populations. Somewhere between the extremes lay truth. In the hands of the expert, a light to medium spinning outfit becomes a rapid-fire casting machine, capable of handling a wide range of artificial and natural baits in weight classes beyond its rated capabilities. With it, the experienced angler can extend his casting abilities into head winds. He can use the outfit in small brooks, ponds, rivers and huge lakes. And so can the novice.

The beginning angler will find he can be making perfectly acceptable casts in a fraction of the time it takes to learn bait casting or fly fishing, though the tackle is perhaps slightly more difficult to master than spin-cast equipment. The problem of backlash, caused when the spool on a bait-cast reel overruns the outgoing line, is eliminated in spinning. But if slack is allowed to develop in the spooled line on a spinning reel, excessive loops may shoot off during vigorous casts, resulting in a tangle, or "bird's nest," of monofilament that can hang in the guides or balloon through the tip-top. In any event, it requires the same picking to untangle as does a backlash. The angler can avoid it more easily, however, simply by keeping tension on the line during all retrieves. This he can accomplish by grasping the line between thumb and forefinger of his rod hand while cranking until all slack has been reeled up.

The spinning reel, like the spin-cast reel, operates on the fixed-spool principle. During the cast, line spirals off the spool, which is fully exposed at the front of the reel. The spool does not move, except during the retrieve, when it oscillates in and out to disperse line evenly around its circumference. Because the spinning reel, unlike the bait-casting reel, does not need to overcome inertia to begin moving a spool for a cast, the lighter lures may be used. This is one of the chief advantages of this tackle, especially in heavily worked waters where fish become quite shy of larger baits.

The fixed spool also permits even the novice to achieve long casts quite easily. Two primary factors can cause a reduction in casting distance, however: the use of line that is too heavy for small lures, and permitting the line level on the spool to drop below ⅛ or 1/16 inch of the exterior spool lip.

During the cast, when line spins from the fixed spool, it flies out in relatively large spirals, until they are reduced by the rod's butt guide. These line spirals can slap against the rod, causing friction that also tends to slightly reduce casting distance. To compensate for this, the reel is aimed so that an imaginary line drawn from the spool center passes just below the butt guide. Since reel and guides are mounted on the bottom of the rod, gravity then tends to keep the line falling away from the rod. For this gravitational force to take effect, it is important that the butt guide not be located too close to the reel. This is actually more important than the size of the butt guide.

Instead of the retractable pins of the spin-cast reel, spinning reels accomplish line pickup by bail, manual or automatic pickup-arm mechanisms. The bail is the most popular arrangement and is described as follows: The bail is a curved metal rod or wire that hoops over the face of the reel (the front of the spool). It is connected on one side by an arm or bracket and on the other by a bolt or socket. Both connecting points are located on a revolving cup that spins around the spool when the handle is cranked. For casting, the bail is pushed down and automatically locks clear of the spool. After the cast, the handle is cranked to spring the bail back into place. The bail rotates with the cup to slide the line over until it rests on a roller. The roller is found on all pickup types and can be a true rolling collar but is usually a fixed, polished piece, as the slightest debris can clog rolling action.

Correct position of the hand prior to casting with a spinning outfit. Note that the bail is open and the index finger is holding the line to keep it from spiraling off the spool.

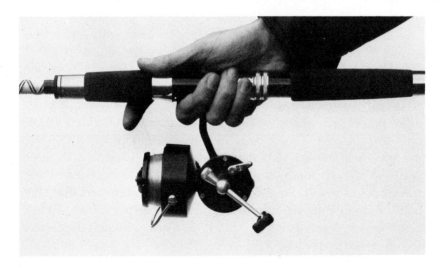

Manual pickups consist simply of a roller on the rotating cup. The angler must pick up the line with a forefinger and place it over the roller before cranking the handle on the retrieve. After a little practice, the operation becomes automatic. The manual pickup is advantageous in that there is nothing subject to mechanical failure. The bail, on the other hand, is rather pliable and can be easily bent in boats or in transit.

The automatic pickup arm can take several forms. It can be a short metal arm that rotates around a beveled edge of the spool's inner face. With this design the arm either disengages or must be moved by backward cranking of the handle prior to casting to free the line. The lower spool–line level required by this arrangement reduces cast distance. In casting, the line is held by one forefinger and the pickup arm is levered back. When the handle is cranked, the arm automatically closes to pick up line. Another type of automatic is actually a spin-cast–spinning hybrid. The reel face is touched by the forefinger, causing the line to swing around to that finger. The line is held normally, then released during the cast. During the retrieve, line is picked up with pins as with spin-cast reels. The reel is semi–open-face.

The spinning reel is fitted with a drag and antireverse lock—the latter, as in spin casting, to be used in fighting a fish or in trolling. The drag is especially critical on ultralight outfits; the slightest hesitation or sticking is usually enough to break the fine lines used with this equipment. The drag must be absolutely smooth in operation under all weather conditions.

Another feature of the spinning reel is the ease with which line spools can be removed. The spool pops from the end of the reel when freed by a push button or simple wing nut. Thus, the angler can carry an extra spool or two loaded with line of different test and rapidly switch as conditions dictate.

The angler can choose either monofilament or braided nylon line for spinning. The former is far more popular. In equal strengths, it is more resistant to wear than the braided. In finer diameters, it casts more easily. The limpness of braided line once made it popular with beginning anglers, who discovered that this quality helped prevent tangling caused by casting faults. Today monofilament is produced in strands that are extremely limp and the difference is no longer so great. Braided line tends to spool more evenly, however, and it does not stretch as much as mono line. It is a matter of the angler's deciding what qualities he demands—and, of course, availability of any given line in his area.

As with all tackle, spinning rods, reels and lines must be balanced. Spinning rods come in one- and two-handed styles. The latter are favored for large fish in big water—steelhead and various salmon, for example. They are geared to handle baits from about ⅞ ounce to an ounce and more. Single-handed spinning rods can handle lures up to 1 ounce, but most wrists will be comfortable casting weights of up to only ⅝ ounce.

In its lightest forms, spinning gear is deadly for taking shy game fish. Once considered a toy or gimmick, ultralight equipment fills a definite need in today's fishing sport. We are talking of equipment of which the rod weighs less than 3 ounces. In this category, lines test in the 1½-to-3-pound class and lures range from $\frac{1}{32}$ to $\frac{5}{16}$ ounce. Surprisingly large fish can be taken on such equipment. Proper technique in fighting; good, smooth-working reel drags and the elasticity of these light lines are responsible. The equipment is practical in stream situations and in lake coves or ponds. It is not designed for horsing of lunker largemouth bass out of brush or working of heavier jigs or spoons in very deep water.

From ultralight, we move into the light tackle category, then to the medium, heavy-duty and finally extra-heavy-duty classes. It helps to know the practical equipment range when one is speaking generally of these classes. A chart of the categories would look like this:

APPROXIMATE LINE TEST (*in pounds*)	LURE WEIGHT (*in ounces*)	*Class*
1½–3	$\frac{1}{32}$–$\frac{5}{16}$	ultralight
4–5	¼–⅜	light
6–7	⅜–⅝	medium
8–12	⅝–1	heavy-duty
14–25	¾–4	extra-heavy-duty

It would be a welcome aid to anglers if more rod manufacturers would list recommended lure-weight and line-test range for a given product on the rod near the handle. Firms are doing this now with fly rods, but few take the trouble with other rod types.

With all its other features, spinning tackle boasts reasonable line-control capability. The line may be slowed during the cast, and completely checked as the bait enters the water, in this manner: the forefinger begins to press toward the outboard lip of the reel spool as the line spirals off, serving as a friction-causing obstacle and eventually producing total brake.

In addition, spinning reels may be manufactured at a lower cost than bait-casting reels of the same quality. The simplicity of design and the need for less critical tolerances are responsible. The cost savings can be passed on to the consumer.

Profile of Bait-Cast Equipment

The pro tournament angler had worked most of the morning without a strike. He was in his middle 40s, built like a football lineman, but his movements were as lithe as those of a hunting cat. For most recreational anglers, concentration would long before have begun to crumble—a fatal mistake in fishing. But the pro was as ready now as he had been when he was fresh and the air was still chill. When the message came, he was ready for it—an electric *tap, tap* telegraphed from the pliable plastic worm working somewhere deep below to the man's reaction center. The pro responded with a hook-setting wrench that must have stretched a neck into the big bass. Its force bowed the thick-butted rod into a classic U, and the man's hands came up over and in back of his head, while his boat seat bent backward until I thought it must break.

I couldn't help laughing. "You like to put it to them," I observed.

The fish thrashed on the surface but was quickly snubbed down.

"Hell, yeah, man," said the angler. "When I hit, I aim t' cross their eyes!"

As I said, the man was a pro. He was also a bait caster.

There was a time when some anglers predicted the demise of bait or plug casting in this country. Spinning and spin casting were supposed to do the older method in. They didn't. On a very superficial level, there is a kind of snobbery on the part of bait-cast enthusiasts toward the fixed-spool boys. It does require more skill

For maximum wrist free-dom when you're using bait-casting tackle, cast with the reel handles up.

to handle revolving-spool bait-cast equipment. As we saw earlier, it is possible for the spool to overrun the outgoing line, producing backlash. However, bait-cast equipment is preferred by many anglers for more practical reasons as well.

Enthusiasts feel that the basic design of the revolving-spool reel is inherently more rugged than that of either of the fixed-spool reels. Though a more complex piece of machinery (thus, in theory, more subject to breakdown, say its detractors), the bait-cast reel has been the favorite for day-in–day-out hard-knocks fishing in debris-filled waters with generations of anglers. In general, bait-cast rods come in short lengths—4, 5, 5½ feet—that are capable of handling heavier lines and lures than spinning rods of the same lengths. The short rods are preferred when much casting must be done in woodsy or brush-choked waters. They give a flatter trajectory to lure flight than the longer rods and send a lure beneath overhangs with ease. Enthusiasts also feel that no other fishing tackle gives quite as much line control as the bait-cast reel, on which the thumb is responsible for "feeling" the bait onto target.

Bait-cast equipment is favored by largemouth bass fishermen—especially throughout the South, where outfits handling lures in the ⅝-to-¾-ounce category and lines from 10- to 20-pound test are most successful. The wider-frame reel is most commonly used here, whereas in the Northeast some bass specialists prefer a narrower-frame reel for lightness' sake. Here, where smaller lures are usually more successful, lighter, smaller-diameter lines may be used. The wide-frame reel is the stronger design, however, and in a national survey would probably prove more popular.

With earlier revolving-spool reels, it was necessary for the angler to "weave" line back and forth across the spool during the retrieve to avoid uneven line buildup. Except in tournament situations, where every casting inch is eked from equipment, the contemporary bait-cast reel is equipped with a level-wind mechanism that, during the retrieve, distributes the line evenly across the spool face.

As the angler gains experience, line control is more and more the task of the thumb riding on one side of the spool flange. Contemporary bait-cast reels, however, are often equipped with mechanical antibacklash control devices which greatly aid the novice in mastering the equipment. Those most commonly include a centrifugal brake and a mechanical brake. The centrifugal brake is merely a thin rod that passes through the main axle of the spool at one end. Attached at each end of this rod are rubber cylinders of various sizes. These spin with the spool, within a thin drum in one side plate of the reel, slowing down the spool's revolutions. The mechanical brake is popularly found in the form of a knob at the end of the spool opposite the centrifugal brake. In effect, it tightens the spool (along the spring-loaded spool axis) against the far side plate in some models, and tightens a braking disk against the spool in others. In combination, both brakes give a wide range of antibacklash control.

Line for bait casting can be braided nylon, braided Dacron or monofilament—either round or flat. The braided lines offer the same advantages they do for spinning. The nylon line is usually manufactured as a floater, while the Dacron readily sinks. Dacron does not have the high stretch characteristic of nylon and is more resistant to deterioration from sun and water. In using a braided line, it is advisable to utilize a monofilament leader, as the braided line is more visible in water and many game fish will shy from it.

More and more bait casters are turning to monofilament as their all-around line. Available in many degrees of limpness and with a range of stretch characteristics, mono can be purchased to meet the demands of many different fishermen. There is even a flat or oval monofilament that some anglers feel spools more evenly than the round. Whatever line is chosen, the quality of the reel must be such that there are no gaps between the spool ends and the reel side plates; otherwise, line will enter to bind the spool or at the very least be nicked and weakened.

In its various weight classes, the bait-casting outfit can handle everything from trout on ⅛-ounce lures through bass to muskellunge, steelhead, northern pike and salmon. A chart of weight classes would look like this:

APPROXIMATE LINE TEST (*in pounds*)	LURE WEIGHT (*in ounces*)	*Class*
4–8	⅛–⅜	extra-light
6–12	¼–½	light
10–20	⅝–¾	medium
18–25	¾–1¼	heavy

The secret of lure-handling capability in bait-casting rods is found in the tapers. Without an extra-light, highly flexible taper, the bait-casting outfit would never be able to handle lures in the lighter classes. Of course, proportionately light line must also be used. Bait-cast rods may be equipped with straight or offset handles. For one-handed casting, the offset handle is more comfortable. Rods in the extra-light class average 6 to 6½ feet in length; in the light category, 5½ to 6½ feet. Medium-class rods are in the 4-to-6½-foot length, with the 5½-footer being most popular. Heavy-class tackle includes rod blanks in the 4½-to-7½-foot category.

Bait casting is properly executed with the rod turned so that the reel handle is on top, despite the fact that many anglers insist on holding the reel with handles to the side. Distance is reduced with the latter grasp.

Profile of Fly-Casting Equipment

One of the supreme ego-deflating moments in the career of any angler might happen as follows: The day is sharply bright, the air perfumed with the promise of spring. Our fledgling Walton has brought his favorite lady, a new fly-casting outfit and a gourmet picnic lunch to the bowered shores of some clear-water river. The lady sits prettily, arms hugging her knees, as he wades chest-deep into the water. The lovely looping curves of the casts he'll soon be shooting out will impress anyone with even a smidgen of esthetic appreciation. But something goes wrong. The rod flashes in the sun; the line goes up and back—but is not recovered on the forward cast. He stands stricken as snakelike coils collapse upon his head and shoulders until he looks like a fantastic living Maypole sinking into the depths. Somewhere nearby a blue jay screams.

There is no tackle like fly tackle for giving truly spectacular responses to angler flub-ups. Anyone starting off with the equipment should be prepared for a few, though with a little practice they are quickly avoided.

Fly tackle is different tackle. With all other equipment one depends upon the lure to carry out the line during a cast. In fly fishing, it is the line that carries out the lure. In fly casting, the power from the casting arm is delivered to the rod, which amplifies this energy and transmits it to the line, causing the line to unfold along its length and finally turn over a length of terminal leader, at the end of which is tied the fly. The angler's timing and properly matched tackle are obviously critical. Timing can be developed through casting practice, but the matched or balanced tackle must be present initially.

Today one purchases an outfit that has been designated by a number referring to the weight of the line. In practice, most anglers tend to translate this number into size or purpose. Through experience, they know that a No. 5 outfit is composed of a light, small-stream rod and line; a No. 6 is a general all-around trout outfit for most Eastern and some Western streams; a No. 10 outfit is good medicine to use in salt water; and so on. To establish these number designations, the weight (in grains) of the first 30 feet of the "working" portion of a fly line is taken. On a tapered fly line, the segment weighed starts at the beginning of the taper.

This is how the categories shape up:

Line number	Weight in grains
1	60
2	80
3	100
4	120

Line number	Weight in grains
5	140
6	160
7	185
8	210
9	240
10	280
11	330
12	380

Fly rods are built to handle from one to three line weights efficiently. The further one gets from the line designed for a given rod, the greater the performance falloff. An angler whose rod is loaded with a line that is too light for its action will need to work it quickly back and forth to extend line. The line loops will be tight, and cast distance drastically reduced. A line that is too heavy will cause the angler to work the rod slowly so that the rod may recover from the great bends the line will put in it. If the rod can recover, it will keep the line moving. Beyond a certain point, however, the line will begin falling. It will slap the water at the terminal end and also near the rod after the forward cast is made.

You will naturally want the fly reel for a light rod and line to be small and light. For the heavier outfits, a larger reel will be desired —not merely as a counterbalance weight for easier casting, but as a storage chamber to hold an increased amount of fine-diameter backing line—usually Dacron. Fly line of heavy or light weight comes in a standard length—commonly 90 feet for regular tapers— but the larger fish sought with the heavier outfits tend to run more and require additional line—thus the backing. For truly long-running large fish, one may wish to look at heavy-duty reels with powerful drags. We'll discuss reels in more detail shortly.

First, let's look at the all-important fly line. Fly lines today come in four basic styles: double-taper, weight-forward, level and shooting taper. The double-taper incorporates a heavy section, or belly, in the middle and tapers down to a thinner tip at either end. It is designed for delicate presentation of smaller flies. The weight-forward line is built with the belly at the front. It is designed for longer casts and for turning over heavier or bulkier flies. The reel end of this line, after about 20 feet of belly, tapers down to a thinner running section. The level line is the most economical of fly lines. It is the same diameter throughout its length and produces short casts. Extra distance can be built into the level line through the leader. A long, gradually tapering leader with a butt section nearly the same diameter as the line will give the level line capabilities similar to those of the double-taper. The shooting taper is headed by 30 feet of line resembling the belly section of the forward-taper, though it is slightly shorter. To the reel end of this line is tied monofilament or special thin-diameter shooting line. There is usually a built-in loop at the reel end of the tapered line to facilitate the attachment of the shooting line. The shooting taper, or shooting head, is used when extreme distances are needed, such as in steelhead fishing.

Today's fly lines have been assigned code letters that greatly simplify identification of type. These are as follows:

DT—Double-taper
WF—Weight-forward
L—Level
ST—Single-taper
F—Floating
S—Sinking
I—Intermediate (dressing is required to float)

Thus, if one were to see a line designated DT-6-F, he would understand that the line is a double-taper No. 6 floater.

The novice is presented with the initially formidable problem of deciding what weight line to choose. When he discovers that rods designed for line of a particular weight are available in a variety of lengths, he may be further confused. Finally, there is the question of line type: should he select a WF line? A DT? The answer, of course, is that no one outfit will perfectly meet all conditions in all waters. An attempt at oversimplification would suggest a 4- or 5-weight line for the tiny or quiet streams, a No. 6 line for medium rivers where both rough and quiet stretches will be worked. Big-water rivers and larger fish call for lines in the 7 size, going up to 8 for bass, steelhead and salmon.

In choosing rod length, it is wise to keep the following in mind: The shorter rods require greater precision in casting and faster work on the part of the angler. They are a joy to use in cramped quarters and wonderfully light for a full day on the water. The longer rods are generally more forgiving, offer better line control both in the air and on the water and are often possessed of a slower casting cycle. The 7½-foot length is considered a good all-around choice for many fishermen.

Another item of vital importance to the fly caster is the leader. The purpose of fly leader is to keep the heavy, highly visible fly line some distance from the fly and fish and to transmit casting energy from the line right down to the fly, which is flipped over in the air and precisely dropped to the water. In order for the angler to achieve these things at their optimum, the leader must be tapered.

There are two main portions of the tapered leader—the butt and the tippet. The butt, obviously, is the thicker section which is attached to the fly line. It is also made of a stiffer-grade nylon. The final end of the tippet is composed of a limper-grade filament. It is possible to get along very well with the better two-piece knotless tapered leaders that can be found in good tackle shops. Still, many anglers prefer to build their own leaders, and for this purpose kits containing spools of monofilament in graded sizes from large to small diameter are available in stores and by mail order.

No matter which type is used, as one fishes, clipping and changing flies, the leader shrinks. With the knotless tapered-type leaders it will be necessary to replace the tippet section with several pieces of leader material in different diameters to obtain the original gradual taper, and even then one will not be absolutely certain his taper is precise unless he uses a micrometer—a rather expensive investment unless used often.

With the knotted-type leaders it is easy to tell when one is running out of a particular section of taper. It is then easily replaced. With the leader kits come directions on building leaders with the proper amount of material. Knotted leaders have a disadvantage in very clear water: the knots are more visible to fish. In weedy water, vegetation may cling to the knots and have to be removed periodically, which is annoying. Getting back to the knotless leaders, even if the taper is not exact, perfectly acceptable casts may be made with all but the heaviest or smallest flies; the middle-range fly sizes causes less trouble with an imperfectly tapered leader.

The angler must experiment with leader types and come to his own conclusion. In areas of length and weight, there are more exact means of evaluating need. Leaders 9 feet long are considered average for trout fishing, and many dry-fly men prefer to go to 12-foot lengths. A 4X tippet (.007-inch diameter) is about average today for trout fishing, but it frequently may be necessary to drop to 5X, 6X or even 7X for demanding fish in ultraclear, slow water. Leaders for bass, salmon or steelhead fishing will be coarser—the bass leader, for example, tapering from about 20- or 30-pound-test monofilament down to around 8- or 10-pound test. In length this leader should approximate the length of the rod.

The leader must match the size of the fly for best casting results; a heavy streamer, for example, will not turn over at the end of a cast with, say, a 5X (.006) tippet. Nor will a No. 22 dry fly work at the end of a 1X (.010) tippet. It will slam down like a little beaver tail and rapidly drown. It becomes necessary to refer to a guide for this matching process. The following fly-to-tippet sizes are recommended, but some overlapping is possible. (The smaller the number, the larger the fly or tippet diameter.)

Fly	Tippet
1/0–2	0X
4–8	1X
6–10	2X
10–14	3X
12–16	4X
14–18	5X
16–22	6X
24–28	7X

The most popular fly reels have traditionally been the single-action type with 1:1 gear ratio. They are available in quality range from sturdy economy models to finely crafted high-priced models. The standard reel is offered in diameters from 3½ to 5½ inches. For light rods and small-stream fishing, smaller models are available. A good reel must have some sort of click mechanism to prevent overrun as line is being taken out. The click mechanism can be quiet or loud. It has traditionally been a kind of status symbol to own a reel that sounds off loudly as a fish runs with the lure. A good solid *whirring* sound is pleasant, but this can reach ridiculous proportions, and I have heard reels that sound as bad as those old party noisemakers, or worse.

Of late, multiplying reels have gained increasing popularity. Reels with a 2:1 ratio (one crank of the handle takes in the equiva-

An avid fly fisherman's reel rack. The two on the right side, bottom, are automatics. Top right and left bottom are multiplying reels. The rest wind in line on a 1:1 basis.

lent of two revolutions of the spool) are handy when you need to retrieve line quickly from the water, getting out slack that could be dangerous when you're fighting a big game fish. Many anglers appreciate the advantage.

With the smaller-size reels, many anglers determine their maximum casting distance with a given line and rod, sometimes allow an extra 10 feet for good measure, then cut off the rest of the fly line's running section. Utilizing backing to fill the spool, they substantially increase the reel's line capacity.

Automatic reels have the advantage of being able to pick up coils of line rapidly to avoid snagging and excessive slack. Natural-bait drift fishermen often prefer this type of reel. Automatics are heavier and do not have the line capacity of comparable single-action reels or multipliers, but often monofilament or backing is utilized with only a short section of heavy fly line for casting. The automatics also lack the drag capacity that can be built into a good single-action reel.

The final choice in fly equipment is in rod material. Actually, for the novice fisherman it is not very much of a choice. Very few anglers taking up fly fishing opt for bamboo rods which are priced in the $200 bracket, unless, of course, such a blank is socially mandatory for admission into some club or other group. The good bamboo rod is truly a magnificent creation. It is primarily hand-crafted of the finest materials. Practically speaking, however, the angler can do the same things with tubular fiber glass that he can with bamboo. Yet bamboo is tough, and in the smaller sizes offers exceeding pleasure in performance, affording the angler more "feel." Though bamboo rods are made in heavy sizes, it is questionable whether the extra expense is worthwhile. I would be loath, for instance, to use a good split-bamboo in salt water—but this is personal prejudice.

Lures

That artificial lures are manufactured to catch fishermen rather than fish is the avid belief of more than one angler's wife. The angler who haphazardly purchases lures solely on eye appeal is living confirmation of this. With thousands of artificials on the market, it is often difficult to know where to begin in choosing a representative selection that will catch fish over a wide variety of conditions. To simplify the task, it is best to consider lure *types*. Though there are lures that may fit into several arbitrary categories, a good working list of lure types would include plugs, jigs, spinners, spoons, plastic lures and bugs. Many of the specific models within these categories combine features of two or three types. Flies, used primarily with fly-casting equipment, are a field unto themselves, a huge one that needs either book-length coverage or the sort of individual treatment you'll find in most of this book's other chapters.

Artificial lures from the above list come in sizes or adaptations that permit them to be used with all previously discussed fishing tackle, fly-fishing equipment being the most limited but more than making up for it with an astronomical catalog of fly patterns and types from which to select.

As we have previously seen, it is important for proper equipment performance that lure weight be matched to tackle. A given outfit may be capable of handling lures in a wide range of sizes and weights, but seasons, local fish preferences and water conditions must be the ultimate determinants in lure choice. When you're visiting a new area, it is wise to obtain information on local lure favorites. Though one basic lure type may be as successful on the West Coast as the East, a small difference in size may determine whether or not one catches fish. For example, a plug in identical finish will catch largemouth bass in the Northeast or the Deep South, but the Yankee angler will most likely find his success increasing if he chooses sizes somewhat smaller than his Southern cousin would select.

Too, it is worthwhile remembering that one can catch big fish on small lures and small fish on lures that are really too large for them, but the latter situation is far less common, except among some of the more voracious panfish.

We'll get into colors for various water conditions later, but first let's look at some of those lure types.

Plugs

Plugs are made primarily of wood or plastic. They are designed to imitate baitfish, frogs or mice or just take the form of an edible glob of something. For fresh water they are popularly available in sizes ranging from $\frac{1}{16}$ ounce to about $\frac{5}{8}$ ounce. Some of the larger models are actually lighter than the smaller ones—a matter of the density of the materials from which they are made. The principal varieties of plugs are: surface agitators, floater-darters, floater-divers, sinkers and floating deep-divers.

The surface agitators include popping plugs with hollow faces. Of these, the short models make a bubbly *plop, plop* sound on the surface, while the longer-faced models *chug*. In this category are the metal disk-faced plugs that cup out water ahead of them as they travel, the plugs with propeller attachments and stick types. Unlike the popping variety, which must be worked with a stop-and-go retrieve, the others can be worked at a variety of speeds. These plugs, which will catch many game fish, are especially favored for bass.

The floater-darters usually come with a V-mouthed front end. They float horizontally or vertically in the water and submerge only a couple of feet on the retrieve. They are ideally suited to shallows fishing, used with a twitching, jerking retrieve that causes them to submerge, dart and resurface. They are good on smallmouth and largemouth bass, pike and pickerel in lakes and quieter river sections.

Floater-divers wobble more violently than the darting-type plugs. They are usually equipped with a front lip or flattened, bent head. They can be worked rapidly or slowly, the faster retrieve causing all but one model to run deeper. They can be twitched on the surface, then brought under and allowed to resurface. They run deeper than the darting type—from 3 to 6 feet or so—and are popular in a metallic silver or gold, black-backed finish. They are successful on trout, bass, pike, muskellunge—just about all game fish.

Sinkers are available in fast- or slow-dropping models. In this category are wobbling, fast-vibrating, spinner-tail and stairstep-lipped models. Sinkers can be cast, allowed to sink to the bottom and retrieved at varying speeds with a jigging or pumping action. On the steady retrieve there are models designed to run at deep and at medium levels. Some models have built-in rattling devices to further attract fish. In the smaller sizes they are especially effective on river species, even in a fairly swift current, but will also work well in lakes.

The floating deep-divers are equipped in front with big metal lips that cause them to dig in and run deep. The more line out, the faster the retrieve, the deeper these plugs run. Some are designed to work around 15 feet, others to 30 feet. There are some deep-divers that belong in the sinker category, but today most float at rest. They are effective in spring, sometimes in fall and also in summer when fish are schooled in cooler depths. Largemouth bass, walleye and muskellunge anglers like them. They are also good for smallmouth bass.

Jigs

Jigs commonly consist of a lead head molded to a hook, though heads made of other metals may be used. The tail is of feathers, bucktail or nylon fibers. Head shapes include round, or ball; oval; slanted; bullet and flat. Though in the hand the lure appears highly unnatural, in the water, worked properly, it quickly gains "life." Jigs are highly effective on game fish from the pan variety to the largest glamour species. They may be used in rivers or lakes. The casting-type jigs with lead heads are available in painted models ranging from dull to quite gaudy. Shiny silver jigs in diamond, teardrop or fish shapes (and sometimes scale finish) are often used through the ice or dropped into submerged tree branches for vertical fishing in which the lure is jigged or *thrumbed*—vibrated up and down. The skirted jigs are worked back slowly or quickly with either hopping action or fast pulls and pauses. It is vital that the hook be honed sharp, because the strike often comes while the lure is dropping.

Jigs are increasingly teamed up with plastic worms or grubs. They can also be used with pork rind.

Another type of lure—the dropping, or tail-spin, lure—could be classified as a plug but is really a jig. It consists of a fish-shaped painted metal jig with a metal spinner on the tail and can be worked like the other jigs or retrieved at a steady rate.

Spinners

Spinning blades are available as individual lures with metal bodies, plain or trimmed with feathers or bucktail. They are also used on wires or swivels to which pork rind or bait can be attached. Finally, they come as trim on lure types already mentioned or as the popular safety-pin–type lure with skirt and rubber tail so popular with largemouth bass fishermen. There are tiny spinners in $\frac{1}{32}$-ounce size designed for fly-rod use and large blades for huge lake trout. Spinners are used to cast to known fish-holding spots or may be trolled when an angler is prospecting for fish. The large multispinner tandem trolls to which plugs or natural baits are attached are popular in some areas. Spinners can be worked more slowly than spoons and are at home in streams, rivers and large impoundments. They are effective for nearly all fish at some time or other.

Spoons

The concave metal lures known as spoons come, like spinners, in light and heavy models, wide and narrow, painted, plain or hammered metal. They are available trimmed with bucktail or feathers, with single or treble hooks. Spoons of equal weight sink at different rates depending upon the width of the blade. Spoons with a wider blade area will drop more slowly, ride higher. Effective on most game fish, spoons may be used in rivers or lakes. One variety of spoon, the wobbler, is molded in a wiggly shape which gives it a somewhat faster vibrating action as compared with standard concave models. The wobblers are good for river work in deeper riffles and pockets but can also be used effectively in lakes.

Spoons can be cast, trolled or jigged vertically near submerged brush or through the ice.

Plastic Lures

Plastic or vinyl lures are molded to imitate worms, grubs, frogs, maggots, eels, shrimp, baitfish and other foods. In the late 50s and early 60s, the plastic worm revolutionized black bass fishing. Today, it ranks as the favorite lure of largemouth bass tournament anglers—primarily as a bottom lure. It can also be used as a midwater lure or on the surface. The plastic lures are not limited to bass; plain or in combination with lead jigs, feathers, bucktail, spinners and spoons, they have been used to catch species from trout to catfish. A recent innovation is the artificial scenting of these lures, and the trick seems to encourage fish.

Plastic lures can be jigged, retrieved at a steady rate or drifted in streams and rivers. They are effective until water temperature drops below 50 degrees.

Bugs

Bugs in cork, balsa, foam rubber, plastic or deer hair are primarily fly-rod lures, but can be used on very light spinning outfits when a bobber is incorporated to give casting weight. On hooks from a No. 4 to a No. 6 there are poppers and bugs designed for bass. The hollow-faced popper is a popular model, but the bullet-head type is good for casting in vegetation-choked waters, as it does not pick up plants as rapidly. Hair and cork bugs on hooks sized 8 to 12 are about right for trout fishing. Panfishermen using the swimming foam-rubber spiders and bugs generally like them in sizes 10 to 12. Again, it is vital that bug hooks be extremely sharp for sure setting.

Color

The best lure colors depend on weather and water conditions, time of day and regional factors. For instance, silver spinners reflect light from a long way off; they are popular all over the country in water conditions that are not extreme. In ultraclear water, however, they may be too bright and spook fish. As water becomes muddy from rain, copper- and bronze-finished spinners and spoons are often preferable for the same reason that many anglers—especially in the South—like a gold or yellowish-green plug in muddy water. It shows up better—not necessarily reflectively, but in silhouette. Black works the same way. In the South, solid black on plugs is not as popular as it is in the Northeast or Northwest. But on plastic worms it consistently ranks high, right next to purple. Black is often popular during very cloudy periods, both as a contrast hue when viewed against a silvery surface from a fish's-eye view and as a silhouette, phantomlike against a dark bottom.

The perennial red-and-white combination is an excellent choice. Against a darkish bottom, the white part stands out, and viewed from below, the red shows up well, not as red but darkish. You have two things going for you. Yellow is extremely popular on plugs. Even viewed from a good distance underwater, it holds its yellow color and stands out well. The flash-scale silver and gold colors are two of the best all-around finishes. Even when the lure drifts out of sight in the mist of underwater visibility, the lure's action will cause flash to get through, thus attracting fish from a distance until they can see the lure itself. Fluorescent finishes on plastic lures and solid plugs are sometimes quite effective because they pick up the sun's ultraviolet rays, which penetrate deeper than infrared rays. They do not glow in the dark, however. They are worthwhile trying on cloudy days and when fish are deep. Some anglers swear by luminescent lures or those to which luminescent tape has been fastened.

While the foregoing is usually consistent, there are plenty of times when fish violate general conclusions, leaving one with the belief that the only thing sure in fishing is uncertainty. But that's part of the mystery and excitement of the sport—and brother, that's fishing.

STREAM TROUT

BY JOSEPH D. BATES, JR.

OLD HANDS at the game know that too many people go trout-fishing without first learning the ground rules. They may frighten trout by walking too near or by bad casting. They may fish in the wrong places or perhaps use flies on top or in midwater when trout are hugging bottom. They may use the wrong methods or lures for the situation at hand. These and other errors may cause them to return home troutless.

Knowledgeable anglers, on the other hand, can glance at a brook or stream and immediately tell where and how deep trout should be lying. They save time by concentrating on the hot spots. They know whether to drift dry flies on top, to fish nymphs in the current or near the bottom or to try streamer flies, or lures, or baits at the correct level. They understand the basic rules that govern a trout's habits, and so they catch fish.

In this chapter we'll acquaint you with many of these basic rules of stream trout fishing and tell you ways to take advantage of them. Utilize what you learn and you'll catch more fish. You'll also discover for yourself the challenge, the fun and the charm of fishing for trout.

Getting to know the trouts is a major factor in knowing how to

46

Fine day, fine small brook. Atmosphere is half the lure of stream trouting. (Erwin Bauer)

catch them. The (Eastern) brook trout really isn't a true trout. It belongs to the family of chars, which also includes the lake trout and the Dolly Varden. The true trouts are the cutthroat, the rainbow and the brown (or "Loch Leven"). Here we are concerned only with the brook trout, the brown trout and the rainbow trout; others are discussed in other chapters.

Brook Trout

Considered the handsomest of all the trouts, the "brookie" is usually the easiest to catch. Positive identification can be made by the bright red spots ringed with blue on its sides and the dark, wormlike lines on its back and its dorsal fin. The lower fins also are distinctive: pink or reddish, striped with white and black on their forward edge. Males in fall spawning colors are even brighter than the average brookie, with coral-red lower sides shading to black above a white underbody. In some areas brook trout (and some other species) have pink flesh, or flesh tinged with pinkish yellow. This is due to the food they eat: mainly crayfish and other crustaceans such as daphnids (freshwater "shrimp").

Once common only in the Northeast, the Eastern brook trout has been widely transplanted. It inhabits small streams, cold-water ponds, lakes and rivers where water temperatures are near 58 degrees. As temperatures drop, trout seek the bottoms of pools and become increasingly logy and hard to catch. As temperatures rise, they seek cooler sanctuaries in cold-water brooks and streams or in springholes. Some springholes well up beneath the surface and are difficult to detect. Others flow or drip down from banks and usually can be spotted by the lusher vegetation they sustain.

Thus the first tip in locating brook trout is to pay careful attention to water temperatures, using a thermometer or an electronic

Some streams call for short, accurate casts. (Illinois Department of Conservation)

temperature probe. Look for areas (or levels, as in ponds or lakes) where water temperatures are nearest 58 degrees. In warm weather, trout may find this temperature on or near the bottom, so surface and near-surface fishing will probably be unproductive except perhaps when the air is cool early in the morning or late in the evening.

Anglers in the Northeast should remember this important temperature tip on opening day and early in the season when mornings can be so frigid that lines freeze in rod guides. It makes no sense to be streamside at crack of dawn unless the plan is to fish bait deep in pools. Even then, why not sleep later and go fishing around noon, when water temperatures are a bit warmer and air temperatures more comfortable? Trout will be more active then.

A late-season trick is to remember that brook trout are fall spawners. Fish in lakes with feeder streams will leave the lakes to go up the streams for spawning, and they may collect near the mouths of the streams before ascending. I remember fabulous fishing days late in the season near the mouths of streams entering lakes in Maine. The biggest trout were usually caught then; more trout were caught then; and the fish were fat, full of fight and very beautiful in their brilliant spawning colors.

Another trick, useful here and there, is to mark the dates of migrations of baitfish. Smelt, for example, run up rivers and brooks in early spring to spawn. Trout and other fish know this and collect at the mouths of streams to wait for them. In spite of the vast hoards of smelt, the hungry game fish take streamer flies or bucktails and other lures avidly. Why should they bother with artificials with so much food around? Perhaps because they are tired of it and want something different.

Another idea for locating trout in streams is to think of their requirements in terms of those also needed by people. We like temperatures of about 70 degrees, and we seek environments in about that range. Trout like the 58-degree area and seek it, even if they do tolerate water somewhat warmer or colder. We like to be near a food supply, and so do trout. Their supermarket is the current which brings food down to them. Thus, in moving water, look for trout along the edges of currents rather than in slack-water areas. They rarely venture into slack water, but may do so if more food can be found there. We also like protection, such as from wind, rain and enemies. Trout seek protection from enemies and from water that flows too fast for comfort. Their protective covers include the quieter water above and below rocks, the sanctuary of ledges and overhanging banks, the shade of streamside bushes and trees that have fallen into the water.

Adding this up, we have a surefire formula for finding trout in waters they inhabit: favorable water temperature, feeding lanes and protection. Look for spots that offer all three, and trout should be there. These are the "trouty" spots, and we can save a lot of fishing time by ignoring the others.

There are a few more trout-finding tips, too. Trout will leave areas of protection (usually in early morning or late evening) to cruise over food-bearing shallows such as rocky riffles or the tails of pools. This is usually over gravel or small rocks, because nymphs, crustaceans and small baitfish are found there. Knowing they are exposed and away from protection, these fish are very shy. Anglers lacking the cautious approach and the delicately landed lure will only see them scooting for cover.

Trout also leave cover when an insect hatch is on, or when nymphs are rising to the surface preparatory to a hatch. They are less shy then and may be boiling the surface in a feeding frenzy. Such occurrences aren't common everywhere, but where they are, emergence dates of insects can be predicted locally with reasonable accuracy. This fishing usually calls for artificial nymphs (such as when the fish are "tailing"), or for dry flies (such as when they are "dimpling"—or sucking in the naturals). The idea is to "match the hatch"—which a few writers seem to have tried to make into some sort of occult science. It may pay to be scientific about it, but any reasonable imitation of the natural in size, color and presentation usually gets results. Little streamers or bucktails, properly fished, often do so too.

Trout often aren't overly fussy about food. They are usually bottom feeders, but frequently take naturals and imitations on the surface. Favorite foods are waterborne nymphs, insects and baitfish; also earthborne creatures such as grubs, beetles, caterpillars, ants, grasshoppers, worms and night crawlers. A trick in summer is to see what kind of food predominates. When streams pass through fields where grasshoppers are hopping, for example, the very best lure may be an artificial hopper!

Streams flowing into salt water or very large lakes may contain anadromous brook trout in season. The season is the fall spawning time, when these "salters" enter the rivers. Salters are usually bigger than resident fish, and may be silver-colored when they first start upstream. Good lures for them include artificials that imitate crayfish or shrimps—or bucktails that simulate resident baitfish in size and color.

Rainbow Trout

So much of what has been said about brook trout applies to the others of the "big three of troutdom" that comments on rainbow trout and brown trout can be short. The rainbow, partly because it is a leaper, is considered by many to be the greatest game fish of the three, even though the brown trout may be harder to catch. The rainbow is distinguished from the others by its pink or crimson lateral stripe, which varies in intensity. The sea-run rainbow, most highly prized of all trout along the Northern Pacific coast, is the famous steelhead. Rainbow trout like faster water than brookies or brownies do, so they are often found in the swift glides and riffles of big streams, as well as behind boulders in white-water areas. They enjoy somewhat warmer water, about 62 degrees. When surface temperatures are agreeable, they may be boiling for flies on top or following bait in shallow water. When surface temperatures are not agreeable, look for them down deeper.

Rainbow trout fishing reaches its peak in the fast rivers of the Northwest, where it is sportier and where the fish usually run bigger than in the slower streams of the Northeast. Nymphs and nymph-bodied wet flies often are weighted (at times with common brass pins) to make them hold well down in fast water. Ideally, they are fished from the open to the brushy side of the river, with the cast made directly across or slightly upstream. They are allowed to "dead-drift"—to swing in an arc at the end of the cast—whereupon they are retrieved slowly against the current.

In low water, the most effective way to handle nymphs or wet flies is with a floating line, thus providing a visible and sensitive link between rod and fly. The slightest touch then can be observed and quickly answered by a slight lift of the rod. In medium water,

Drifting nymphs through likely lies is one of the most fascinating ways to fish for stream trout. (Erwin Bauer)

a floating line with a sinking tip may be more practical for fishing the fly deep. In high water, a sinking line may be necessary to get the fly down—but most anglers consider this a last resort, because the fly is difficult to lift and more tiresome to fish.

Dry-fly fishing on Western rivers usually calls for flies that will float high and dry for extreme distances in swift currents. Such flies are made to ride high on their hackle tips and are more readily taken by trout as well as being more visible to anglers. Matching the hatch isn't necessary, because the fish are used to seeing a wide variety of large aquatic insects and windblown terrestrials. Deer hair is very popular for high-riding floaters such as the Goofus Bug, the Irresistible and the famous Wulff patterns.

The development of high-riding and relatively unsinkable dry flies for fast-water fishing reached its current peak in the art of weaving of hair hackles as pioneered by George F. Grant (Box 3606, Butte, Montana 59701), who has published a book on the subject. He also has been responsible for innovations of a similar nature in Western wet flies and in nymphs such as his Stonefly Creeper and Black Creeper, which are only two of many examples from his skilled hands. Such noteworthy improvements in fly construction occur rarely and are well worth investigating.

Rainbows are the least selective feeders of the three species being discussed. Bucktails and streamers are favorite fly-rod offerings, because big fish usually take these baitfish imitators more readily than the small patterns which simulate flies and nymphs. Small spoons and spinners are productive with other tackle, and bait works as well here as for other species if it is fished properly. The quiet and cautious approach is less important in the fast water usually preferred by rainbows, because they see anglers less easily in it. In other respects, what has been said about brook trout also applies to rainbows.

Brown Trout

The brown trout is a European import. Its eggs were first brought here from England in the early 1880s. Other eggs later came from Germany and Scotland. These strains merged essentially into one and ended the speculation as to whether importation of the fish was a boon to anglers or a piscatorial calamity.

The brownie thrives in some waters that are too warm or otherwise unsuitable for brook trout and rainbows. On the other hand, it is more of a cannibal, living largely off the young of its own and other species. It grows satisfyingly large, is a worthy contender on the end of a line and generally is fussier about lures and harder to catch than the other two members of the big three of troutdom. Brownies have dark backs shading to amber-colored sides and white bellies which vary from yellow to tan as they mature. Their sides bear large brown or black speckles, including a few of red or orange. Fins vary from brown to yellow, without the vivid barred markings of the brook trout. Tails are slightly forked on young fish, but are more nearly square on older ones.

Brown trout (especially big ones) consume an amazing variety of foods, including insects, any other fish they can catch and swallow, mice, frogs, crayfish and even small birds. This doesn't mean that almost any lure or bait will take them; quite the opposite is generally true. They are at least as wary as the other trouts, and usually far more selective. For these reasons, there are legions of anglers who take more pride in catching trophy brown trout than in their trophies of any other species. Browns of trophy size are usually considered to be those in the 10-pound range, although much larger ones are taken here and there, and in some places "bragging size" is much smaller. It is generally conceded that the big ones, being cannibals, should be removed from the water.

Brown trout addicts take their favorite fish with the fly rod and the fly—usually the dry fly. Since brown trout are normally found in clear pools and runs of slow streams, this calls for the sneaky approach—the long, accurate and delicately presented cast—and considerable expertise in choice of the fly. Matching the hatch makes more sense here than anywhere else. Dry flies are usually size 14 or smaller, and one goes smaller if in doubt. Favorite flies vary widely, depending on location and season, but dull patterns in insect colorations usually do best. In summer, and at other times if you're in doubt as to pattern, a grasshopper imitation can be as good as any. Nymphs and streamer flies or bucktails often do well, especially when nothing is hatching, but they have to be properly selected and fished. The selection of nymphs is less important than their proper action in the water, because several varieties and sizes are usually indigenous to any locality. The selection of streamers and bucktails depends on the size and type of baitfish and on their general coloration. Sometimes far-out patterns such as deer-hair mice and mothlike lures ordinarily used for bass bring savage strikes.

All this doesn't mean that brown trout fishing is purely the fly fisherman's game. Big brownies are often caught on spinners and spoons, or on worms, shiners and other baits. It doesn't mean that brownies are always cautious and selective, either. I have seen them curiously following a lure to leader length when the angler was standing streamside in plain sight. A final jiggle of the lure often hooked the fish!

Brown trout fishing often is excellent when streams are cloudy and rising after a rain, because the fish are on the feed at such times. It is good for all trout when the air warms after a period of cool weather. Since brown trout are usually nocturnal feeders, the ideal time to try for the big ones is late dusk. Brown trout spawn late in the fall, and the big ones often work up into smaller streams then.

The Importance of Water Temperatures

We have noted that the three species of trout being discussed are normally found where they have protection (or can be near it), an easily accessible food supply and suitable water temperatures. Since the first two requirements may be found at various levels, temperature is the key. If we want to be fussy about it, the following table will help:

	Optimum Range	Ideal Temperature
Brook trout	50°–65°	58°
Rainbow trout	60°–70°	62°
Brown trout	55°–70°	63°

Fishermen roaming brooks and streams can't confine themselves to locales with ideal water temperatures, so the figures given above are more or less academic. Trout aren't always quite that fussy either, and their ideal temperatures do vary a bit, depending on the environment to which they have become accustomed. For practical purposes it can be said we'll find trout and find them most active where water temperatures are between 50 and 70 degrees, even though the more exact figures sometimes can be useful. Surface or near-surface fishing should be good in this range.

When water is colder, trout will feed less actively and should be found deeper, or along shorelines or in riffles where the water temperature is higher. When water is warmer, trout will seek springholes, brook mouths or shaded parts of streams. When water is very cold or very warm, the solution is usually to fish bait down deep. When you're fishing lakes and ponds, a knowledge of water temperatures at various levels is of special importance, because trout will be along shorelines at depths where optimum temperatures exist. Anglers who pay little or no attention to water temperatures shouldn't wonder why they don't catch trout; the fish are nearly as sensitive to comfort as the anglers themselves!

How to Read the Water

The simple knowledge of how to "read" the water in streams is a valuable key to locating trout. We noted earlier that trout seek protection from currents that are too fast for comfort, yet they want to be in moving water near the food supply it brings to them. The trick here is to fish the edges. What is an edge? A simple way to discover the answer is to stand in the current and watch it as it swirls around your boots. The water flowing around both sides of a boot is fast, but the water immediately downstream of it is slower because the current is obstructed by the boot. The water immediately upstream also will be somewhat slower because the current has to split to go around the boot, thus leaving a small, quiet spot upstream. This quiet water is, of course, much larger when the current flows around a rock.

The difference in current flow around an obstruction is visible. Note the line extending downstream on each side of the boot which separates the fast current from the quieter water immediately downstream of the boot—or the same difference in current flow around a midstream rock. This dividing line is called an *edge*. Not wishing to combat the current flow, trout will rest just inside the edge. Edges on both sides of protruding rocks are visible, but those around submerged ones are not. They are there, nevertheless, and can often be detected by the boil on the surface caused by the rock. While trout will usually be lying inside one of the downstream edges, one or two may also be in the cone of quiet water immediately upstream. If a rock is near the shore, the streamside edge may be better than the landside edge, because it is deeper. In such places trout enjoy the three main requirements they seek: comfort in quieter water, concealment offered by the rock and the swirling surface around it and nearness to the food supply provided by the current. They can dash out to pick up food and quickly return to the resting place.

The abundance of rocks in most trout streams offers a wide selection of edges to cast to, of which the larger rocks usually provide the best. But edges are found in other places too.

When a ledge or a large rock protrudes from the shore, it offers an edge. Since ledges may be recessed underwater, thus providing ideal concealment, they may be worth special attention.

The current flow from an entering brook or stream also provides an edge—sometimes a long one. If water in the main stream seems warm, the cooler water of the entering stream provides another reason for trout to be there.

The current flow around an island joins to form an edge below the island if the water is deep enough. A tree that has fallen into the stream may provide an edge as well as concealment. All such places are "trouty" ones, but there are more.

Undercut banks are excellent lies for trout, offering the fish concealment as well as terrestrial foods falling from the growth above. Overhanging brush provides the same thing. When the sun is on the water, the fish should be lying along the shady side. Patches of leaves that cover the bottom camouflage trout lying over them, and the fish know it. These are all important examples which indicate others, such as weed patches growing in the current. Many streams, because of their chemical content and other factors, are very weedy, thus providing concealment as well as food. Trout may be anywhere amid the weeds, because such streams usually flow slowly. In an attempt to avoid snagged hooks, anglers usually cast to rises in open spots, often using very small dry flies.

Of course, trout don't always stay along edges and in the other places that have been mentioned. They may come out of hiding to search for nymphs in rocky riffles or near the tails of pools. They may feed voraciously on or near the surface of pools when an insect hatch is on. Such feeding periods can usually be observed. When they are not, the hiding places should be explored, either on or near the surface or, if necessary, down deeper.

Anglers who understand these principles of reading the water and of being guided by water temperatures save valuable time by ignoring places that should be troutless and concentrating on the hot spots. Sometimes a very few hot spots provide all the action anyone needs!

How to Fish Streams

While what has been said offers an introduction to stream fishing for trout, a few other notes are also important.

When streams are fairly deep, too many anglers hopefully fish the surface or the middle depths and ignore the bottom. Don't fish middepth without reason, because trout almost always will be feeding on top or lying on the bottom—usually the latter. If they are feeding on top, the action will be seen. If they aren't, the trick is to work the bottom—especially the places that have been noted.

Why are trout more often on the bottom? First, they are normally bottom feeders. Also, the bottom offers better concealment. Current flow along the bottom is slower than at middepth or on the surface, because rocks and other obstructions slow it down. Water near the bottom also may be cooler—a factor that may be important in summer.

Since trout seek moderate flow in streams, a few comments on current flow seem appropriate. The fastest flow is down the middle, below the surface and above the bottom. Flow is slowest along the bottom and more moderate along the sides, because obstructions slow it down. This is another reason for not fishing middle depths. The current may be too fast for trout, and there is less food there than elsewhere. Of course, many streams, or parts of them, are shallow enough to eliminate middepth considerations, because lures fished below the surface (or even on it) will come close enough to the bottom for trout to rise slightly to take them. On such streams, relatively useless middepth areas may be found in pools.

When water temperature conditions are ideal or near-ideal, trout (which are more active then) may travel considerable distances to take lures. But when water is outside the optimum temperature range, or when it is discolored, lures must be fished at the fish's levels and close to their noses. This means dragging bottom, which contributes to hang-ups. As an old angler used to say, "If you don't get hung up once in a while, you ain't fishin' right!"

How to Fish Brooks

Since brooks are streams in miniature, we now know the basics of fishing them. Most brooks fall within three general classifications: meadow brooks, brushy brooks and rocky brooks.

Meadow brooks often meander through farmland and may be

so narrow one can step from bank to bank. One should be careful of this, because the thick turf may conceal a wide and deep run gouged out by the current—sometimes to the extent that the sides of the bank collapse and fall into the brook. Such places may conceal large trout, because they offer shade and protection, water that stays clear and moderately cool and an abundant food supply augmented by insects dropping from above.

Such places demand the stealthy approach—quiet walking and often crawling to casting position. It helps to scout for good casting spots first and to fish the stretch later. A long rod is helpful, because some fishing is done by dapping, or dropping the bait gently onto the water, rather than casting. In casting, the trick is to drop the lure onto the edge of the grass and then to twitch it very lightly into the water.

Meadow brooks often contain sharp bends, with deep runs along the outer sides of the bends. A lure drifted or tumbled through the run should coax strikes. Often, such brooks also contain small pools, probably with an overgrown bank. Sneak up slowly to quietly fish the pool, especially under the bank.

Small, clear streams require a stealthy approach. (Erwin Bauer)

One friend of mine favors a seemingly insignificant meadow brook no one else bothers with. Experience has shown him how to fish it, and he invariably returns with a few very respectable trout, after having carefully released many smaller ones. His favorite fly is a black-and-orange clipped-deer-hair dry pattern imitating a bee —used, of course, in midsummer. He crawls to casting position and flips the floater into the cleft amid the grasses for a very short float. The lure is often taken instantly. Another favorite pattern imitates a grasshopper.

Brushy brooks call for a different technique. The angler uses a very short rod and wades the brook, poking the rod between the branches and usually letting out line while lure or bait drifts downstream. Every rock big enough to have an edge is fished; also every deep glide, every undercut bank and every small pool. Admittedly, this is frustrating and challenging fishing, but it has one thing going for it: the average angler won't bother with it, thus leaving the fish for you.

For many years I had a spot like this—a dense growth of alders and willows in a swampy area all other fishermen walked around. Unknown to them, a fallen log had made a sizable pool where trout collected. Kneeling quietly there, I would take a fish with almost every flip cast.

Some brushy brooks are wider and less overgrown than others, which makes things easier. One of the tricks is to find the supposedly inaccessible places. Trout collect in them because they think they are safe; and they are less shy than others that are fished over too often.

Rocky brooks may drop through woods or run through open mountainous areas, such as in Western states, where drops can be fast with rushing white water. The principles are similar. Look for deep runs, for areas of moderate flow behind boulders and for deep pools. Since many Western brooks are very cold, lures should usually be fished close to the bottom.

Wet-Fly Fishing

Wet flies include short-haired or feather-winged imitations of insects and the longer streamer flies or bucktails, which simulate baitfish. The two general types are fished very differently.

Wading a stream allows you to cast a fly free of interference from shoreline brush and branches. (Milt Rosko)

Since the short-haired or winged imitations usually represent drowned insects (but can be taken by trout for nymphs or something else), they are fished by dead drift, the cast being made cross-stream or slightly upstream, depending on the force of the current. The current shouldn't be allowed to pull or whip the fly. This you can usually avoid by "mending" the line; that is, by flipping the rod tip in an upstream direction to put a temporary upstream curve in the near part of the line on the water.

Dead drifts are cast to drift the fly along edges and other spots where trout are presumed to lie—this sometimes being aided by the taking in or letting out of line. On completion of the drift, the fly is allowed to hang momentarily downcurrent and can be twitched a little in case a fish has followed the fly and might take it when it is given a change in action. (This often works, but we don't know exactly why—unless the imparted life suggests an active nymph.) On completion of the cast, the fly is retrieved by short twitches until enough line has been regained for another cast.

Since streamer flies or bucktails simulate live baitfish, they must be given the short, darting action with which a baitfish swims. It helps to observe baitfish in the water and to imitate them with a fly of similar size and coloration. Sometimes bright "attractor" patterns are used. If they coax action without a strike, one switches to an "imitator" pattern and repeats the cast. Here again, the fly *usually* should not be allowed to whip. However, if a fish shows interest and doesn't take, a speeded fly may make it do so. Experiment with different fly speeds, because sometimes the fish prefer a slow fly and at other times one that is fished much faster.

Match line size to the power of your rod. The tapered leader is usually about as long as the rod, but can be as long as desired, with tippet size proportionate to that of the fly. In thin streams a floating line should put the fly down several inches, which may be deep enough. If not, a floating line with a sinking tip will fish it a foot or so deeper. As I mentioned before, the sinking line, or a fast-sinking one, is used only when necessary to get the fly nearer to the bottom.

Nymph Fishing

Nymphing is much less of a science or an art than some angling writers would have us believe. One can go to the bother of investigating the undersides of wet rocks to see what size and type of nymph may be clinging there, and then imitate it with an artificial, or perhaps he can observe nymphs crawling in shallow water. Since nymphs in streams are usually of several types and sizes, exact imitation isn't very important. In fact, you can quickly make an excellent caddis-case imitation by pulling bunches of deer body hair around a hook and clipping them off close and fairly rough. The way a nymph is fished is much more important than what it resembles. Some are weighted; others are not.

Nymphs are fished in two principal ways. One is by dead drift, as in fishing of the wet fly. This simulates one caught in the current. Another way is to simulate an emerging nymph—that is, one gradually rising from the bottom to the surface to shuck its skin preparatory to emerging as a fly. With this method, you must allow the nymph to sink and then twitch it upward by the slowest and shortest jerks possible. No matter how slowly the nymph is fished, it probably isn't slow enough.

Since trout usually take nymphs very delicately and spit out imitations quickly, most of the trick in using them is in hooking the fish. If a floating line or one with a sinking tip is used, watch it carefully for the slightest twitch, striking lightly and immediately. To aid in this, a bushy dry fly is often tied in up on the leader, as an indicator. If the dry fly is suddenly pulled under, or otherwise acts unnaturally, it probably signals a strike.

Dry-Fly Fishing

A great many anglers eventually become addicted to the fly rod and ultimately to dry-fly fishing, because it presents a challenge accompanied by very productive fun. The challenge is less in selecting the proper fly, or in "matching the hatch," as it is often called, than in being able to drop the fly lightly in the chosen area so that it will float free of drag. The fun is seeing trout rise to the fly, because the action is on top and visible, rather than being hidden down below. It is productive because dry-fly fishing often takes trout when other methods fail.

Because modern light fiber-glass all-purpose rods handle dry flies nicely, specialized dry-fly tackle is not essential. Specialists may go to rods with faster tip (or "dry-fly") action because it is superior for making the many false casts necessary to dry the fly in the air. Leaders are at least as long as the rod and are finely tapered, partly because the flies usually used are very small.

Flies for trout of small or moderate size usually range between sizes 12, 14 and 16, with 14 being a good average. Popular ones include the Adams, Hendrickson, Light Cahill, Quill Gordon, Red Quill and Royal Coachman. Good dry-fly hackle feels prickly when pressed to the lips.

You can make the turle knot, generally used to tie leader to fly, more secure by stringing the fly on the leader and tying an overhand knot in the very end of the leader, then tying the turle knot and working the two knots together into one.

Anglers who tend to splash terminal tackle down onto the water can land the fly lightly by aiming the cast a few feet above the water so that fly and leader drop naturally onto it. Leaders, of course, must be straight, and they should sink. You can straighten a leader by pulling it through a small, folded piece of rubber (such as inner-tube rubber) or leather to provide the friction heat which removes the coils. Commercial preparations are available for sinking leaders, but rubbing them with mud or fish slime helps. Some anglers use a floating line with a sinking tip, because the tip pulls the leader under and usually won't drown the fly. Others, who use a floating line, add a tiny bit of lead midway on the leader. (This isn't approved by "purists.")

Matching the hatch may help, but the importance of this has been overemphasized. Fly size and presentation are more important. All-purpose dry flies are available which adequately match a variety of insect hatches. We have noted that terrestrial imitations such as bees and grasshoppers are extremely effective in season— their "season" being warm weather.

Since we have learned where trout usually lie or feed in brooks and streams, where to cast the dry fly is no longer a problem. The problem often lies in getting a satisfactorily long, free float— chances for this usually being improved by mending of the line. Skittering the fly (particularly if it's a skater type) is often worth a try. If the dry fly pulls under, fish it in carefully anyway. Dry flies fished wet often coax strikes.

Light Spinning

Spinning and spin casting are two different techniques which are often confused. Spinning calls for an open-face reel on which the uncoiling line is unimpeded by a cover on the front face of the spool. This affords longer casts with lighter lines and lures, thus providing more fun for anglers who remember to keep the line on the spool tight at all times.

Spinning fishermen have the most fun and get the best results by using the lightest tackle adequate for the job. They may need monofilament lines testing between 4 and 6 pounds to throw relatively heavy lures of ¼ ounce or more long distances on big rivers, but light or ultralight gear is more fun and takes more fish on

A varied selection of spinning lures is often the key to a creelful of trout. (Milt Rosko)

smaller streams and in brooks. Smaller reels and lighter rods, used with lines as light as 2-pound test or even finer, are available for this purpose. This light gear affords long casts with lures in the ⅛-ounce category—ideal tackle for small trout, and for much bigger ones when obstructions aren't much of a bother.

Three principal types of lure are ideal for this: spinners, wobbling spoons and tiny plugs. Each type has its purpose.

Spinners are best for near-surface fishing in streams having slow or moderate flow. Light ones like the C. P. Swing are excellent for short casts in thin water. Heavier ones such as the Mepps do better for longer casts or for going deeper in stronger currents. They should always be fished under moderate tension.

Spinners are cast cross-stream or quartering downstream to swing with the current. To cover all the fishable area, start with shorter casts and extend to longer ones. By letting out or retrieving line, you can guide spinners into edges and the other trouty spots which have been discussed. They are ideal for fishing long, flat stretches of slow-moving water running over stones and for working pockets between and around rocks. Try them in riffles in case trout may be feeding there.

Wobbling spoons can be used in the situations above, but they are more suitable for deeper water, such as deep glides and pools. They don't need to be fished under tension. In pools, for example, they can be cast out and allowed to flutter down to or near the bottom, after which they can be worked up and dropped back as often as desired—as when you're fishing a jig. If the current is moving, this sort of action can cover a wide range at all depths. Here again, start with shorter casts and extend into longer ones. Drop the wobbler upstream of rocks so that it can sink and flutter deep along the edges. Use it to cover areas near the bottom.

Wobblers of the same size come in various weights. For example, the Wobble-Rite is made of thick metal to sink quickly in pools and deep in faster water. Being very compact, it can be cast longer distances. It would snag if fished in thin water or over weeds. On the other hand, the Dardevle is a thinner, longer wobbler (enameled in one color with a contrasting stripe: usually red and white) which won't cast quite as far or sink as quickly. This is an all-purpose lure for shallower areas. There are also very thin wobblers which can't be cast far, but which are ideal for working downstream in fast currents. When water is very fast or deep, wobblers can be cast upstream or quartering upstream so that you can make them sink quickly to cover areas near the bottom.

Spinners and wobblers can be baited, but this usually isn't necessary. When fishing is poor, try putting a piece of a worm on one of the treble hooks, or use a tiny pennant of pork rind or a similar strip cut from a fish's belly.

Most spinners and wobblers come with treble hooks; this is due more to their European ancestry than to any ability to hook fish better. Trebles don't hook any better than singles, and perhaps not as well. They are harder to unhook from a fish's mouth, catch frustratingly in the meshes of nets and usually cause the death of small trout which should be set free. For these reasons a growing number of anglers—particularly trout anglers—are replacing treble hooks with singles. Many manufacturers now offer wobblers and spinners with single hooks, and more of them should.

The third (and usually less useful) principal type of spinning or spin-casting trout lure is the plug in miniature sizes. This type of lure is better for bass and other species than for trout, but it often works for trout when nothing else will. An excellent example is the famous Flatfish. This isn't a good caster in its smaller versions, unless you add weight by pinching on a split shot or two a foot or so up on the line—a trick that also makes the lure fish deeper. Tiny plugs like this and others (particularly of the crawler type) sometimes work well for big cannibal trout such as brownies in the trophy class because they imitate food such as mice and frogs.

Catching Trout with Bait

Many fishermen prefer to use bait for trout and never progress to artificial lures—perhaps because they don't think they need to. In spite of what "purists" may say, bait fishing can be developed into an art. Bait and a fly rod offer a deadly combination for working runs and glides in brooks and streams from the bank or when you're wading. When a worm is used, hook it once under the collar for a lifelike presentation, rather than multiple-hooking it into an inactive ball. Grubs, hellgrammites, crickets, grasshoppers and many other baits to be found streamside are also effective for fly-rod trout fishing. These baits should be drifted naturally, rather than dragged in the current. A split shot or two a foot or so above the lure may be necessary to make them fish deep enough. If you're using spinning or spin-casting tackle, you may need this weight to cast them out. You can drift baits down a pool or a deep run by attaching a small float on line or leader at the desired distance above the lure.

These small baits are suitable for any light tackle, but spinning gear is more for larger morsels such as live or dead baitfish. A very productive method is to use a live shiner under a float, with a split shot or two to keep it down, and to drift it over likely spots where the water is deep enough. Hook the bait just forward of the dorsal fin so that the hook passes through *above* the backbone. This way, the bait should remain alive for some time. To cast a baitfish, hook it upward through both lips. Tumbling a shiner down fast water, or fishing it through quieter water, is a deadly way to catch big trout—especially brown trout.

One trophy-size brownie no one could catch met his doom when he took a live mouse. The fisherman put the hook through the mouse's back skin, set the little animal on a small board and drifted it down the pool to where the big trout lay, paying out line from his spinning reel until the lure was over the right spot. He then engaged the reel and pulled the mouse off its raft. The swimming mouse didn't go far before the big brownie took it.

Unfortunately, the days when a fisherman could fill his basket quickly and distribute the catch among neighbors are long gone in most places. The practice of conservation is necessary even in wilderness regions. Smart anglers now fish for trout more for fun than for meat, harvesting a big one or two and carefully letting the others go free. Thus, in some fishing areas, several anglers have the fun of catching the same fish.

Many streams, or parts of them, are restricted to fly fishing. This shouldn't upset the bait casters or the spinning addict, because most waters remain open to any method. The cult of fly fishermen is growing by leaps and bounds—rightly so, I think, because the fly rod and the artificial fly offer the peak of angling sport.

MOUNTAIN TROUT

BY NORMAN STRUNG

THE MAN who goes after mountain trout can count on more than just the catching of fish. His will be a memorable combination of adventure, discovery and sheer beauty that, in truth, is in a world all its own.

Although taxonomists might argue, I like to call any trout species that lives within an alpine environment a "mountain trout." Rainbows, brooks, goldens and cutthroats all fit into this category. What sets them apart from their more common kin is the fact that they live in high country, amid the snowcapped summits and glacial valleys of the mountainous West.

These fish are native to, or have been introduced to, suitable waters in every state from the Rocky Mountain States west. The factors that make these waters suitable are functions of location and elevation. In my adopted state of Montana, waters holding these fish lie at or above the 6,000-foot level. As you move farther south down the Rockies, the low limit of the fish's range rises. Colorado's alpine environment begins at about 8,000 feet; in California, you've got to get up around 10,000.

Although altitudes may differ, the characteristics of mountain trout country remain the same. Up there, the air has an arctic clarity about it, the sky is split by jagged, dominating peaks that

dwarf even the imagination and there's an overriding sense of solitude that becomes the day. It has other unique aspects, too: the
growing season is quite short; lakes and streams are iced in for
nine months each year. Vegetation is largely limited to grasses,
scrubby willow and conifers, and it's sparse. What little soil there
is lies thinly dispersed over a bed of solid rock. The environment
can only be described as Spartan.

This general lack of fertility and the short growing season have
a direct influence on the fish that live there. There's a marked absence of low-country terrestrial insects commonly thought of as
important sources of trout food: worms, crickets, grasshoppers and
the like. Aquatic plants, and those insects associated with them,
are sparse too. As a result, the growth rate of most mountain trout
is slow, and their size, on the average, is less than you might expect of their lowland brethren living in fertile, food-rich waters.

Though their size might be small, they have ways of compen-
sating the angler. Like the highlands they inhabit, mountain trout
exhibit a vigor and a wild, untamed nature that other fish just
can't match. Their strike isn't just a tug; it's a searing lunge. They
don't just break water; when they come up it's a combination pole
vault, pirouette and hurdle. When a mountain trout chooses to
fight deep, he doesn't merely pull. He dashes, he dives, he vibrates
in a desperate attempt to break free. I'd rather duel with a 12-inch
rainbow at 8,000 feet than a 2-pounder in the Madison River.

But that moment of contest isn't the only lure that keeps calling
me back to the high country. Necessary to tempting these fish is
an absorbing and intriguing body of specialized tackle, technique
and offbeat savvy just as unique as an alpine meadow brook and
the trout you'll find in it. For starters, any angler venturing into
the mountains would do well to familiarize himself with some
basic geology.

Although there are many maps available of the high country
(Forest Service, BLM, U.S. Coast and Geodetic Survey), they
don't always list every lake within their boundaries. Then too,
there's a chance you might wander into an area for which you have
no map. In any case, knowing how to recognize areas that could
conceivably hold a lake will help you find fish.

It isn't purely a matter of following water, either. The source of
many mountain streams is a melting snowbank or glacier. Con-

versely, some of the largest, most productive mountain lakes I
know of have no apparent outlet. Their excess waters flow under
a rubble of boulders and scree, often emerging a mile or more
away.

In the absence of a map, the most reliable indicator of the
presence of a lake is a terminal moraine. Virtually every lake that
lies close to the clouds was formed by a glacier. During a colder
age, snow fell on snow—never completely melting, and compacting
into a thick mass of ice. Rather than building straight up to the
clouds, the ice displayed fluid properties, flowing slowly over the
terrain like thick taffy or molten lava.

The glacier was hardly soft, though. Its leading edge acted like
the blade of a bulldozer, pushing a great mound of rubble ahead
of it. When the climate changed and the weather began to warm,
the glaciers gradually melted, retreating to higher elevations.

But there remained that pile of boulders, gravel and dirt that
they had pushed ahead of them. It now acted like a plug in the
valley the glacier had traveled, trapping waters that melted off
the warming ice. That pile of rubble is known as a moraine—the
waters behind it, a true glacial lake.

Moraines are reasonably easy to recognize, even from below. In
the topsy-turvy tumbledown of rocks and peaks, moraines stand
out as level ridges, seeming almost man-made in their geometric
perfection.

Behind many of these moraines will be a sheer rock mountain-
side or headwall that has the appearance of having been scooped
out with a huge, round spoon. In fact, on a grand scale, this was
effectively the case. The glacier was the spoon; the dished-out area
it left is called a cirque.

When you find both moraines and cirques, the presence of a lake
between them is nearly a sure thing. Another good bet is that there
will be several other such lakes in the area.

Mountains in glacial country generally tend to form a bowl—
a rough semicircle of peaks that slope down into a central valley.
Glaciers undoubtedly once were active all around the edges of that
bowl, feeding into the central valley and leaving numerous pockets
of water as they melted away. So if you find one lake unrespon-
sive to your fishing wiles, take a walk over the nearest ridge. Its
sister might be more kind.

Remember, however, that not all mountain lakes hold a stock of trout, and this is yet another matter not indicated on maps. So along with geology, it pays to know something about fish biology when you're packing in to the peaks.

Freeze-out is a major factor in high-country fishing. When the long winter months arrive, a sheet of ice plugs a mountain lake like a cork in a bottle. Oxygen can no longer be introduced to the water by wave action and surface contact with the air. To a large extent, the lake must subsist on whatever oxygen is contained in the water at the time it is closed up.

The situation is further complicated by the presence of aquatic plants. When the lake locks in, the plants growing there die and begin to decompose, using up available oxygen in the process. If there are enough decaying plants to command all of a lake's oxygen, the fish that live there suffocate—"winter kill" is the common term. The lake is then "frozen out"—voided of fish life.

There are a few rules of thumb for determining whether the lake

A glacial moraine—an immense pileup of rock and boulder debris bulldozed into place by an ice age glacier—dammed up this sky-high lake.

you've come upon is subject to winter kill. Depth is one. The deeper the lake, the less chance for freeze-out. This is a matter both of sheer volume of water and of plant growth. Aquatic vegetation won't take root where sunlight can't reach it. However, even a large lake with many deep spots can freeze out if it has an over-abundance of weed-producing shallows. A tributary stream is a very good sign for a fisherman, particularly if it carries a large amount of water. Chances are it runs all winter long, and even if it does so under 10 feet of snow, it picks up some oxygen to add to the lake waters below.

You can find clues along the shore too. Generally, the presence of aquatic insects that take a year or more to complete their life cycles is a good sign. Caddisworms, or "rockworms" as they're often called, will usually be the most prominent residents in a living lake. The sight of a minnow signifies a near-sure thing, and of course, the swirl of a feeding fish is an open invitation to start rigging your rod.

There is, however, one more factor to be considered before you pitch camp next to waters you've determined hold fish: many of these lakes hold huge populations of dinky trout.

The situation arises from a number of causes. Lack of predation is one. Here's how this can come about: Many productive lakes are subject to periodic freeze-out; it's not a yearly phenomenon, just the result of that one unusually severe winter in thirty. Rather than allow these normally productive lakes to lie dormant, fish-and-game departments will restock them, but economy and logistics dictate that they do so with fingerlings. As these fish grow, they do so at the same rate. Our 2-inch fingerlings are all 6-inch trout in a year or two.

In a lake full of same-size fish, there are no lunkers to keep the small ones in check and thereby provide a natural distribution of sizes and weights. Tied directly to this matter is available food; there won't be enough of it to grow large fish. The little ones already there, living on bare subsistence, keep eliminating any possibility of a surplus, and the size stratification that results when certain fish find their way to more food, to become bigger and stronger than their cousins, does not occur.

Finally, the fish's species has some bearing on stunting. A stunted population most often occurs when the initial stock is brook trout. Because they breed in the fall and are quite prolific to boot, brookies are a highly productive strain. As long as they have optimum water conditions—and an alpine environment suits that requirement to a T—they're very resilient in their survival capabilities. They're also competitive to the point where they'll eliminate other species of trout that could offer some balance.

How can you tell when you've come on a population of stunted fish? When you take a trout a cast and none of them is much bigger than 6 inches, you've got one good indicator. The size of their heads in relation to the rest of their bodies is another excellent determinant.

When fish grow, their body structure is influenced by the food they get—or the lack of it. But heads tend to accomplish near-normal development even when there's a severe nutritional deficiency. So when you note fish with large heads and small bodies, stunting is practically a sure thing.

Remember also that the converse is usually true. Even if you catch nothing but smallish fish, if their bodies are fat and firm and their heads small in proportion, the signs are more than good that you've got a healthy, normal population. Chances are there are a few soakers roaming those waters, too.

To a large extent, the angler after mountain trout is a specialist, moving in a world apart from that of the prosaic trout fisherman. There are no hatches of green drakes, no universal gluttony for worms after a heavy shower, no rich slick of lowland streams. These fish are a product of the same environment that spawns the grizzly bear and the cougar, and their preferences and habits reflect that unpredictable heritage.

With them there are no absolutes, no easy formulas, and therein lies a great deal of their charm. But some basic techniques for fishing the high country can be discussed, and the best way is by dividing the waters to be fished into categories. Lakes are, obviously, lakes, but streams fall into two distinct types: the meandering alpine brook, and the wild, tumbling mountain stream.

The mountain streams are the first of the types you'll encounter, probably along the trail you're taking into the high country. They'll run in the bottom of a deep valley and carry quite a bit of water at a steep gradient.

These streams are the result of contributions made by upper

water sources: glaciers, snowfields, springs and the overflow of lakes. They're characterized by large boulders, frequent palisades and falls and a rather direct route to the lowlands, where they'll join a major river.

Because they flow so violently, fishing them with classic technique—long casts, drifted bait, etc.—is difficult if not impossible. What's more, standard lies for feeding fish are largely absent; the entire watercourse appears to be a torrent of raging white water.

The fish are there, but in places where you might not expect them. Look for action anyplace you find relatively calm, slow-moving water. Right up next to the bank is a consistent producer. Even if the water looks swift, the drag created by bank roots and rocks will temper the current inches under the surface. The reverse eddies formed on either side of falls are hot spots too, and so are pockets behind rocks.

Usually, these spots will be located in tight brush, or will be so small in total area that they preclude conventional casting. They can be worked with very short, rapid casts from a fly rod, but more productive is the use of bait—worms, salmon eggs, grasshoppers or corn—and what I call "cane-pole technique."

This is nothing more than fishing with a static line 4 to 6 feet long. Pinch a ball of shot that's just heavy enough to reach bottom 6 to 8 inches above your hook. Get back from the bank or hide in a spot of shade, drop your offering into a hole and let it move slowly around the bottom. If you don't get a nibble in thirty seconds or so, move on to the next hole. Large pockets and eddies might deserve more probing, but in no case should you spend more than a few minutes at any one spot. Trout in a stream of this type are single-minded. They either bite immediately or refuse to bite entirely.

Meandering meadow brooks lie at higher elevations. Eventually, the rather steep trail you're following will top out into a land of broad, grassy meadows. These are the lower limits of the alpine region.

Because of the relative flatness of the terrain, streams that run through a basin of this type will tend to wander around lazy curves. Their surface will be glassy-smooth and their waters as clear as the mountain air. Bank brush will be largely absent, depths will be relatively shallow—in short, these streams virtually shout perfect fishing conditions for the feather merchant.

Because of their characteristic clarity, meadow brooks require the sneaky approach. Stay well back from the bank or hide behind brush or a boulder.

Because of the water's characteristic clarity, long, light leaders and distance casting are most productive. The easiest way to work these places is by moving downstream, letting the current do part of the job of placing your fly. Wading, of course, is out, but it's not really necessary. You can stand well back from the bank without having to worry about tangling with a tree.

Virtually every inch of both banks will be undercut by the stream; look for fish there. Another hot spot lies at each bend. Currents will have carved out a hole there, and two or three trout should be inhabiting each one. When you take a fish from any lie, move downstream at least 10 feet. The splashing that's bound to accompany the battle will put down every trout within that radius.

Spinning, while not so productive as fly fishing in this situation, will take its share of fish. Here too, the best approach is to work downstream, keeping well back from the bank. Accuracy is extremely important; you've got to be able to hit a good-looking hole right on the button, and with a fairly long cast.

Rather than trying to cover a lot of water in a hurry, get used to making several casts that will thoroughly probe each likely lie. Trout in these brooks seem most enticed by a lure from the time of splashdown to 5 feet into the retrieve. By working over the water with clocklike precision, you offer that kind of exposure to every potential lie.

The mountain and the meadow streams have one thing in common: the times at which they're most productive. Midday might occasionally turn up a few trout, but early morning and late evening will always be the most reliable periods for fishing.

This is not true of the highest waters in which mountain trout live: glacial lakes. These places just aren't predictable. Although logic would seem to say that any fish that lives most of its life under a sheet of ice should jump at the chance for an easy meal, it isn't the case. Lake-dwelling mountain trout can seemingly go for days without a feeding period.

You'll pick up enough fish to justify your labors, but full-scale feeding binges aren't predictable. They're worth waiting for, though; when you're in the right place at the right time, the fishing comes close to fantastic.

I can remember one busman's holiday I took with my partner in the guiding business. We were camped at Solitude Lake, high in Montana's Spanish Peaks Wilderness Area. Although we hadn't fished so hard that we were red-eyed and fevered, we'd put in a fair amount of time lakeside. In two days, we'd taken enough fish to eat, but no significant numbers beyond that.

Then, on the afternoon of the third day, it started. First a dimple, then two, then five; then the whole lake seemed alive, boiling with feeding trout. I don't know how many cutthroats we caught and released in the hour-long spree. In retrospect, it seems a hundred, but thirty is probably a more accurate number. Then it was done, just as quickly as it had started. After the fish were off feed, we were hard pressed to coax so much as a hit.

When high-mountain fish go on that kind of a binge, you can

catch them on anything—even the cliché bare hook. When they're less cooperative, however, there are still some things you can do to pique their interest.

Concentrate your fishing efforts around the lake's hot spots. These include inlets, outlets and sharp drop offs that border good-sized shallow areas. The flowing water at inlets and outlets both introduces and concentrates insect life. I've also got a hunch that trout enjoy the feel of water moving around them and like to lie in these places much like a sunbather.

Drop offs that border shallows are quite important to a mountain trout. The shallow water warms fast, and the warmth in turn produces insect activity. Trout will cruise in deep-water safety just off these food factories, picking up whatever meals they can find. When the sun is off the water, I've also seen them venture right onto the flats, where, if you're careful, you can stalk them like bonefish.

Whatever type of lure or fly you're using, make your presentation slow and deliberate. Trout in lakes seem to require a long time to make up their minds.

They also tend to look toward the top for their meal. This isn't an absolute, of course, but I'll usually try to tempt them with a floating line; a light, shallow-running lure and a bobber-and-bait before I go to fishing deep.

Beyond these generalizations, there are some specifics worthy of note in terms of individual species. Of the four types of mountain trout, each is subtly different in its habitat, its habits and the techniques to which it responds.

Brook trout behave a bit differently from the norm in an alpine environment. At lower elevations, and in their native East, they're a favorite of the fly fisherman because of their preference for insect life. In the mountains, however, I've found this species to be the most predatory.

If you fish a lake with mixed species, you'll find the brookie first to strike a retrieved lure. Ditto streamer flies and live bait. What's more, brookies are the regular feeders; when other species of mountain trout decide to play hard to get, you can often count on the cooperative brook trout to take up the slack.

This isn't to say that brookies will refuse a fly; they'll gladly become involved in any insect hatch. But their leaning toward a meat diet throws the odds for success in favor of the angler who tries lures and bait first when he knows he's in brook trout waters.

Cutthroats are my personal favorites when I fish the high country. They don't fight with the dogged determination of a big brookie, or the aerial flair of a feisty rainbow, but their delicate habits, relative uniqueness and delicious flavor out of a frying pan makes them substance and symbol of what I'm after when I'm roaming the mountains.

Cutts up there are decidedly insectivorous and quite selective in what turns them on. They're a susceptible quarry for the fly fisherman who's used to working with a light leader and capable of making long casts.

These fish also favor foods that lie under the water. On more occasions than I'd care to count I saw swirls, spotted flies on the surface and, understandably, rigged up with a matching dry. Most of these assumptions produced nothing but exercise; I cast my arm off until I realized the fish were nymphing—taking immature insects just under the surface seconds before they emerged to their

These glistening cutthroat trout were caught with packed-in fly tackle. Cutthroats tend to favor underwater flies.

adult stage. They simply weren't interested in the flies that waited on the water.

As confusing as they might be, cutthroats do have a real weakness for those tiny crustaceans known as freshwater shrimps or "scuds." When I don't have any clues to what they might be feeding on, I always try scuds first.

Golden trout are the rarest of all mountain-dwelling species, and as a result virtually every one you catch rates as a trophy.

Contrary to popular belief, goldens were never common throughout the Rockies but, rather, native to a very small drainage system in California's Sierra Madre.

Thanks to transplants, they now inhabit a respectable number of lakes throughout the high mountains of the West, but they're still not so common that you can expect them to be a regular part of your catch. Generally, if you want goldens, you go to a lake known to have them—a fact that is usually well publicized.

These trout like their food truly on the tiny side. They show a preference for No. 16 to No. 20 midges and nymphs, but can also be enticed to strike a thumbtack-size ultralight lure.

Goldens aren't particularly good fighters, and their flesh isn't nearly so tasty as that of other high-country species. It has an oily, slightly soggy consistency where other fish are flaky and delicately moist. Goldens are also rumored to keep poorly, spoiling easily on the pack out. I can't attest to this; I've either eaten them at the lake or thrown them back.

Rainbow trout are more common in outlet streams than in glacial lakes, but it's this species that will grow the largest when present in a lake. The biggest high-country fish I ever caught was a 5½-pound rainbow (measured on a pocket scale).

In streams, look for 'bows near the white water. They'll lie in a relatively slow-moving slack and dash out into the foam to pick off food whipping by.

Lake-dwelling rainbows like to cruise the shoreline, swimming just above the point where the bottom melts from view.

Rainbows aren't quite the meat eaters that brookies have proved to be, but they're certainly more interested in minnows and worms than are cutts or goldens. This points in the direction of a throw-everything-you-got-at-'em attitude when you know you're fishing rainbow water and the trout seem uncooperative.

Trout like to lie off the edge of a shallows, picking off hatching insects.

Grayling aren't a true trout, but they deserve mention at least in passing. They're present in many of the alpine waters in the Rockies, and are identified by a huge, sailfishlike dorsal fin.

Grayling are very much like cutthroats in their food preferences, fighting characteristics and feeding behavior, with two exceptions: grayling will feed freely on surface adults; and their initial strike is quite fierce—a 2-pounder will practically yank the rod out of your hand.

Like the fish and the lands they live in, the equipment you'll need to tackle the trout and the terrain is rather unique. First, there's the matter of how you get around.

Transportation in the mountains means one of two things: your own two feet or a packtrain. In either case, a backpack is the best way to carry your equipment.

When you're loading pack animals, the bag of a backpack amounts to a soft, compartmented suitcase. It can be shaped to conform to the back of a mule and lashed in place or slid into the pocket of a pannier. When you're walking, the advantages of a modern pack and frame over other ways to carry gear should be obvious.

All modern backpacks that make toting a load relatively easy have several things in common. The frame or packboard should be made of a light welded metal, usually aluminum. All your running gear—straps, belts and the pack bag—will serve your needs best if they're anchored to the frame with removable stays or clevis pins.

Shoulder straps should be wide and padded with tough, bunch-resistant foam to prevent them from digging into your arm. Any pack worth its weight should also have a waist belt; it's this device that makes for most of the comfort in a modern pack. When drawn up snugly around your hips, it transfers much of the weight from your shoulders to your legs, the part of your body best suited to bearing a load. Like shoulder straps, waist belts should be wide, padded and bunch-resistant. They do their job best when they also incorporate a positive-locking, adjustable quick-release buckle.

The second major component of your backpack is the bag. Bags come in two sizes, full- and three-quarter length. The full bag offers the advantage of complete weather protection for all your gear. The three-quarter type gives you a space outside the bag to lash some gear directly to the frame. Generally, I prefer the full bag for my fishing trips, the three-quarter for my hunting trips. The frame that goes with the three-quarter bag is ideal for packing out meat.

Apart from size, there are several other things to look for in a top-notch bag. Lots of pockets are one, and I'd say five is a practical minimum. There will be many items you'll want to get at while you're on the trail: maps, a candy bar, a slicker—and of course, your fishing equipment. When all this stuff is packed into one or two compartments, finding individual items is a tedious procedure. Also available to the angler/backpacker are bags with long, vertical compartments on the sides. These provide a ready place to tuck your cased rod.

The bag itself should be waterproof. Not rubberized, but a heavy, tight-weave synthetic that sheds water under all conditions but total immersion. In addition, the pockets should have drip lips over their zipper closures to prevent water and dirt from entering.

Bags should also be easily removable from the frame. When you make camp, a bag hung up in a tree makes a perfect dresser; the frame, propped up against a log or rock, provides support for your back that's close to easy-chair comfort.

A tent is also a wise investment, and under all conditions I favor a fully enclosed, screened and ventilated mountain tent. Pitch-anywhere plastic tarps might be inexpensive, but a heavy storm will drive rain under the eaves. Then too, they offer no bug protection, and mosquitoes, no-see-ums, horseflies and deerflies are a lot more profuse in the high country than most novices imagine.

The best size is debatable. The bigger the tent, the more weight it will add to your pack. But sometimes size is a welcome comfort. Generally, I take a big 7½-pound tent when I'm fishing in the mountains from June to mid-July. This period amounts to spring up there—a time when day or two-day storms are a real possibility. In August and early September, I take a small 4-pounder—about half the floor size of my big tent. That's the dry time of the summer, and weathering a passing shower in a tiny enclosure is at least bearable. This isn't true when you have to endure an all-day rain.

Clothing should be chosen with lightness in mind. My usual selection includes one complete change of warm-weather clothing, a wool sweater, a quilted set of insulated underwear, a nylon ski shell and a rain slicker. Worn in various combinations, this kind of selection affords you latitude to adapt to virtually any weather condition, including bitter cold, which is always a possibility in the mountains.

You'll need other equipment, of course—eating and cooking utensils, sleeping gear, a light and food. In general, I'd recommend buying this stuff from manufacturers who specialize in backpacking equipment, rather than rounding up mismatched gear from your home. A cook kit is a good example why. If you packed your own pots, pans, plates, knives and forks, chances are you'd end up with a potpourri of sizes and shapes with no relation to one another. By buying a backpacker's cook kit, you get a large pot with a tight-fitting lid that doubles as a frying pan plus a coffee-

pot, a small soup pot, cups and plates. All this stuff is made to fit
inside the one large pot. What's more, the kit is made of very light
aluminum, so you save space and weight. Equivalent foresight and
careful design go into commercial camp lanterns, grills, small
cookstoves and the like.

Fishing equipment for the mountains, like your living and walking equipment, needs to be a highly specialized, totally integrated
package. At the top of the list is the rod you choose.

"Pack" or "trail" rods are by far the most practical. These are
four- to six-section rods that break down into an 18- to 24-inch
bundle. When deciding on the best length for the broken-down
rod, keep your pack in mind. The rod should be able to fit inside a
full-length bag, since there's no place to lash it to the frame. Even
on a three-quarter bag, the rod shouldn't be so long that the case
juts out significantly on either side of the frame. Unless it can be
rigged vertically, you'll find it constantly hanging up on brush and
tree trunks.

Another item I personally favor is a soft, rather than hard, case
for the rod. The case should of course be reinforced with a stout
stay to prevent rod breakage, but its otherwise conforming nature
makes for more efficient use of packing space.

The rod should be a combination spin/fly rod. This dual function is usually achieved by a cork grip that comes apart. It breaks
right at the point where the spinning-reel seat meets the forward
section of the cork grip. Turn it 180 degrees, slip the ferrule back in
place and the reel seat is on the very butt end of your rod—the
standard location on a fly rod.

Be positive any rod you buy for the mountains offers this
changeable-reel-seat feature (though the changeover doesn't have
to be achieved in exactly the way I've described). I've seen some
products that claim to be "combo" rods with a fixed reel seat, and
when this is the case, either spinning or fly fishing is going to be
intolerably difficult, depending on where the fixed seat is located.

Length of the assembled rod is an important consideration, too.
Mountain waters are characteristically gin-clear, and long casts
are often necessary, particularly when you're working with feathers. The most popular size is 6½ feet, but I personally prefer 7 feet
because of the reach those extra 6 inches afford.

Purists often criticize these rods as being neither fish nor fowl—

either too stiff because of the many ferrules, or not coming quite up to snuff as either a spin or a fly rod because they're expected to do both jobs.

Sure, I'll admit they're a little mushy for driving a heavy fly line, and a little stiff for casting an ultralight lure, but when you consider their small size and dual application, you've got a good argument for a little give-and-take. Then too, you can get the most out of a very pleasant package if you'll buy a trail rod with glass-to-glass ferrules. The extra flex they add to a rod makes them come impressively close to first-class shafts designed with a specific application in mind.

Reels are just as important as the rod you choose. Simply because of the weight factor, lean toward the smallest reel available that will accommodate your line and still balance well with your rod.

Of the two reels that I use, my fly reel is a single action "trout" model that weighs 6½ ounces with line. My spinning reel is a 6-ounce reel—slightly larger than ultralight, but not quite up to standard freshwater weight. I chose this maverick because ultra-light reel weights don't quite create the balance I personally like in my 5.6-ounce rod. Arriving at this spinning combination entailed some puzzling problems on my part. At first, I tried an ultralight, and it seemed to balance well enough in my hand. But in practice, my normal casting accuracy just wasn't there. I eventually discovered that my threshold of balance with that little reel was so critical that the addition of a quarter-ounce weight threw the whole thing out of whack. The slightly heavier reel solved the problem admirably.

The spinning-line weight I favor is 4-pound-test. While water clarity might justify 2-pound-test, this stuff is just too gossamer, too delicate to be handled with a 7-foot rod. I also tote along an extra 100 yards of line in case I lose enough to cut down on my casting reach.

Fly-line weights that balance well with typical trail rods are in the 5 and 6 category. Instead of just one type of fly line, though, try taking a floating line and cutting it in half. Splice it to half a sinking line. Spool it on your reel, and by unspooling and respooling, you're in good shape to handle both a dry-fly hatch and fish feeding deep on nymphs or minnows. Several companies offer this back-to-back package, made at the factory in a variety of tapers.

By its very nature, fishing far from the reaches of civilization presents a major problem. You can't drop by the tackle shop to pick up an extra pack of hooks when you run out. The temptation, then, is to overstock—to take more equipment, especially terminal tackle, than you'll ever need.

It isn't really necessary though; the theme is still integration.

Two 6x10-inch plastic boxes will carry all the lures, hooks and flies you need to match any hatch or satisfy any whims of a fish's feeding behavior. Make one box essentially for spinning gear.

The number of hooks you tote along is no problem. They're light and occupy little space. I usually take about fifty, unsnelled, in sizes from 8 to 12.

Pack two water-fillable clear plastic floats. These double as top-water bait-fishing rigs and—by substitution of a fly for a hook on a 4-to-5-foot leader—a means to cast a fly with a spinning rod, just in case you're not too familiar with classic fly techniques.

Lead is heavy, so I go sparingly on the stuff. One vial of BB-size split shot and one of .22-caliber-size split shot is all I ever take. By adding or subtracting pieces of shot, you can quickly achieve light or heavy weighting.

Snap swivels are important too. The lighter a line is, the more prone it will be to twisting. Four-pound-test can get downright kinky.

Lures should be limited to sizes from ⅛ to ⅜ ounce. Trout in the high country are accustomed to very small meals, so large lures are unnecessary burdens. I also favor those spoons and spinners that are quite thin, with stamped-out rather than precast blades.

Thin blades and bodies mean a lot of action at relatively slow speeds, and this presentation has proved quite effective for mountain fish. The only problem this type of lure presents is the depth at which it works. Because of its high ratio of surface area to weight, it tends to hang quite close to the top.

If you suspect fish to be working deep, you can remedy this problem in a hurry by adding sufficient pinches of shot to get the lure down to where the action is. One nice thing about using this approach is that even deep-running lures will still retain their frantic appeal.

While colors seem to make a difference to trout that live in low-

This fine mess of fish—one rainbow on top, the rest brookies—fell prey to one of their special weaknesses, a small spinner.

country rivers and lakes, I don't find a parallel in the mountains. What seems to count up there is finish. Lures that are predominantly gold, copper and silver make up my basic selection. The only colors I occasionally lean to are a dash of red or a few spots of black. Rather than carrying a tackle-shop selection of color patterns, you might consider the creativity that lies within a tube of bright red lipstick and a black grease pencil. These two unlikely items are always components of my pack-in tackle box.

Another way to add attraction to a piece of hardware is by way of the flies you'll have with you. If fish don't seem receptive to the jewelry you're throwing at them, try removing the treble hook and replacing it with a fly. Again, this is a trick that hasn't worked spectacularly well in the low country, but it has produced some monumental catches above 6,000 feet.

Your choice of flies needn't be so trim and interchangeable as your bait- and lure-fishing gear. By their very nature, flies are light, compact and crammable into very small spaces.

One general rule of thumb, however, is to keep them on the small side. Dries and wets will produce best when they fall between No. 12 and No. 16 sizes. Occasionally, you'll run into a frantic hatch of No. 18 and No. 20 midges. Nymphs and streamers can be a bit larger, up to No. 8, but I still find those tied on No. 12 and No. 10 hooks more appealing.

The patterns I've found most productive are drab rather than colorful, paralleling to a certain extent my convictions about lures. Flies I've learned to lean on include a basic selection of dries in black, gray, ginger and white shades. The Blue Dun, Grey Sedge, Ginger Quill, Adams and Quill Gordon patterns all deserve special mention.

My selection of wets is roughly the same in color distribution and especially significant patterns here would include the Gold Ribbed Hare's Ear, Leadwinged Coachman, Black Gnat and Blue Dun.

Although these are all essentially monochromatic, that dash of red has occasionally come through; I carry both the Red Ant and the Royal Coachman in wet and dry configurations.

Because I'm hardly a purist, I seldom use streamers. When I

Mountain trout, such as these mature brook trout, can surprise you and turn out pretty big at times. (Erwin Bauer)

think the trout are in a meat mood, I opt for spinning lures. I have taken trout on the few patterns I've tried, however—mostly Muddlers, Spuddlers and their variants.

On the other hand, I've taken most of my high-country fly-caught fish on nymphs. Here, the drab-color rule includes insect green. Woolly Worms and imitations of freshwater shrimps and mayfly nymphs that are predominantly of this color have knocked 'em dead. So have caddis patterns; this insect is an extremely important component of a mountain trout's diet. Other favored nymphs include the Spruce Budworm, the Breadcrust, the Dragonfly and a fabrication of my own, to date unnamed, that consists of a No. 16 hook, a slate-gray dubbed fur body, a natural-wool dubbed thorax and a grizzly hackle tied palmer style.

While that rounds out the tackle selection you'll need to catch fish under most conditions, a few words might be in order about when to use what.

Generally, if you can see fish cruising in a lake or stream, it's a sign they're interested in insects. If they're topping, this obviously points in the direction of dries. If the surface is smooth, try wets or nymphs. Although it hardly works all the time, I've found that when the fish are working close to the top, wets are the most productive. If they're hanging deep, just inside that pale where visibility melts away, nymphs are the place to start.

When there's no sign of fish or activity, I'll try working nymphs on a deep-sinking line first, then plumb different depths with an assortment of spinning lures. When all else fails, I'll go to bait.

Beyond tackle and techniques that have proved their worth in the mountains, there's some support fishing equipment you might consider toting along. I've found that it makes fishing easier and, most important to the packer, travels light.

Perhaps the handiest item is a fishing vest. All the tackle outlined here can be carried in a vest, giving you the advantages of a tackle box without its drawbacks. Because you wear a vest, your hands are free, and you don't have to worry about leaving it behind when you move on to the next water. Then too, a vest is soft. It will take on whichever shape fits best in the pocket or compartment of your pack or pannier. You can stow it in a place where it's always handy, and quickly get to your tackle when you come to that unexpected, inviting pool.

A light plastic stringer will keep your catch alive and fresh, and it takes up far less space and weight than a conventional creel.

A 3x4-foot piece of cheesecloth or insect netting is the best bait-getter you can use. Stretch it between two willow switches; then hold your makeshift net downstream from a rock. Overturn the rock and the net will trap a selection of aquatic life suited to live-bait fishing or close examination for matching with feathers. This cheesecloth will also seine minnows in a lake and trap grasshoppers and crickets. What's more, the cloth when wetted will make a cooler. Wrap your catch in it, lay the bundle in a breezy, shady spot, and natural evaporation will keep it icebox-cold until dinnertime.

Waders aren't necessarily out for the backpacker, but choose the cheap, thin plastic kind that are worn in conjunction with tennis shoes. Their total weight will be under 3 pounds, and the tennis shoes can double as knockabout camp loafers. You will, of course, have to be extra careful around prickly brush and snags.

A few other things that don't weigh much but might throw the fishing odds in your favor include leader sink, mucilin and a small multipurpose pocketknife.

I carry a knife that weighs exactly 2 ounces, so light as to be unnoticeable, yet in its compact frame are included one small and one large standard-bit screwdriver, a phillips-head screwdriver, a wire stripper, two cutting blades, a hook file, a leather awl and a bottle-and-can opener. The knife isn't only handy around camp: its tools are perfectly suited for minor reel repair, and in that capacity it's saved an outback fishing trip more than once.

As in any other form of fishing, the successful alpine angler is going to be the guy with practice, perseverance and savvy: the man who knows both his equipment and his quarry, and who has the good judgment to alter his technique as conditions warrant.

But in the same breath, I'd be less than honest if I said any system was foolproof. I've been skunked more times than I'll admit, and anyone who straps a pack on his back and strikes out after mountain trout had better include that possibility in his plans.

To translate this into practical advice: Don't depend on fish as a food source. View them as a wonderful potential change from an otherwise blah dried-food diet—but make sure you've got a good meal stowed in your pack for every night you'll be on the trail.

Not catching a thing is hardly enjoyable for a fisherman, but even if it does happen, simply poking around the peaks has a few things going for it that just aren't available to the more casual angler.

On those nonproductive days when the finicky fish refuse even the most carefully constructed offerings, just lay your rod against a convenient pine and take a short hike up the nearest hillock.

Eye the tallest peak. Trace the jagged skyline of the surrounding mountains. Measure the depth of blue in the lake below you and fill your lungs with a draft of pure, clear air.

You'll find you haven't been skunked at all.

BY A. J. McCLANE

ONE MORNING, Dan Bailey and I were floating the Yellowstone River in a rubber raft. We stopped on a gravel bar to make some coffee, and while Dan was puttering around, I caught eleven trout behind one boulder. Most of them weighed about a pound—but we landed about thirty later that afternoon, and some of these weighed between 2 and 3 pounds.

The next morning, Joe Brooks and I stood side by side in a spring creek and worked our dry flies over a dozen big trout that rolled and splashed like porpoises as they ate their way through a cloud of duns. The browns and cutthroats that stayed on long enough to be released were much larger than you ordinarily see. I don't know how many fish we caught, but Ed Zern took twenty-two in a riffle below us.

Then there was the evening on the Missouri when I talked Bill Browning into trying a spot just off the road, and in less than an hour I had five browns up to 4½ pounds without moving more than 20 feet. These aren't big trout for the Missouri; when conditions are right, you can graduate into the 5-to-10-pound class. There's no point in telling you about the good days on the Jefferson and the Willow, Beartrap Canyon and Henry's Fork of the Snake, because you can always beat figures—but you can't match the pervading sense of space and abundance these Western waters offer. Montana is a case in point.

A good way to enter Montana is to drive through West Yellowstone and then go up to Virginia City. The Daltons are still on Boot Hill, and so are Club Foot George and Haze Lyons, and the town sleeps as though there had been nothing before and nothing since. Just over the Ruby Mountains to the west are the Ruby, Beaverhead, Jefferson and Big Hole rivers. Beyond these, going toward the Bitterroot range, are the Clark Fork, Blackfoot, Flathead and dozens more. To the east are the Gallatin, Missouri, Yellowstone and Madison flowing through the scaly-hided, straw-colored earth that is the fourth-largest state in the Union. You can drive 535 miles in one direction and 275 miles in another and still be in Montana. With a total population of 682,000, all of Montana holds fewer people than a Midwestern city such as Cleveland, Ohio. That's why her thirty-one major rivers are the last great stronghold of American trouting.

Road markers will tell you where General Custer made his stand, and how gold was discovered in Bannack, and where Lewis and Clark camped, and how twenty-four gunslingers jigged at the end of a rope in the winter of 1864. But the makers of signs won't have to tell you that one out of three Montana citizens is a trout fisherman. You will be technically advised by everybody from the barber to the bartender, and the information will usually be accurate. There is little synthetic entertainment in Montana. You either hunt or fish—and either way you have the best of it.

Any Eastern fly fisherman making his first trip West is apt to think that Rocky Mountain fly tiers are really a bit over the hill. After dealing with double-domed trout on rivers like New York's Beaverkill and Ausable, a visitor viewing the local patterns in Livingston or West Yellowstone might be shaken down to his felt soles. Some of the flies in fashion are the size of a hummingbird and have no more character than a hank of hair wrapped on a hook. However, practical members of the sombrero set learned long ago that big trout won't usually rise to a bit of fluff; to coax one to the surface requires a monumental reward. True, the micros developed for gentler rivers have their place here also, but in the West extremes pay off.

When delicate Eastern flies fail, turn to a horse-size Western favorite.
(Erwin Bauer)

Several years ago, we floated a pair of double-enders down the New Fork in Wyoming to a long stretch where the river runs deep and foamy under a cut willow bank. Bill Isaacs and Larry Madison stopped at the first gravel bar, and I rowed another half mile to the next pullout with Elmer George. It was early in the morning, but there was already a nice hatch of small blue mayflies on the river. They looked fairly close to a No. 14 Dark Hendrickson, so we went to work on the nearest risers that were popping away in midstream. We fished for about three hours, then took a coffee break. Elmer said he'd released about twenty trout, but his biggest fish hadn't been much over 10 inches, and most had been 8- or 9-inch rainbows. I had had the same results. This isn't *bad* fishing, but the New Fork holds much heftier trout. I had tried a Quill Gordon, a Blue Upright and a Blue Quill, hoping to find a better match with the natural, and Elmer had gone through the same procedure.

There was a time when I'd accept the fact that the big ones just weren't feeding, but Western trout have their quirks. I tied on a No. 6 Goofus Bug which looked about ten times larger than the ephemeral insects dancing in the air and waded back into the stream. After I'd covered a short distance along the willow sweepers, the surface exploded and I was fast to our first good fish of the day—a brownie of better than 2 pounds. By noon we had released a dozen trout in the 16-to-18-inch class.

When Larry and Bill came downriver to join us for lunch, they reported a similar experience. We all agreed that while "matching the hatch" is a basic tenet of fly fishing, and without question a sound piece of advice, it is often true that it takes a veritable puff-ball—wholly unlike anything flitting in the air—to catch trophy trout in sagebrush country. The reason is probably no more profound than the fact that big fish normally hold closer to the bottom than small trout, and in heavier water, where only a substantial food item would make swimming to the surface worth the effort. During the early-July salmonfly hatch, large fish do stay near the top to nail those fat stone flies as they zoom over the water depositing their eggs. Almost instantaneous strikes are common then; the fly seldom floats more than a few feet if it's going to be taken at all. But the exception doesn't prove to be the rule.

The lore of dry-fly fishing is full of adjurations to keep the artificial riding high with no hint of movement save that imparted by the current. This is the recognized principle, and worth remembering. So before my preoccupation with big flies and downstream casting appears eccentric, let me say at the outset that my purpose in writing this piece is to offer some practical observations about Western angling which may be helpful when more orthodox techniques fail.

I have in years past spent entire summers and the fall season out West, and it was early on when I discovered that my stylized Eastern methods might just as well have been expended in a bathtub. The weather that summer in the Rocky Mountains was freakishly cold, with melting snowdrifts in the peaks until late July. Many of the major trout streams never did reach a fishable level for the purist. The celebrated stone fly hatch on the Madison occurred at a time when the river was a raging torrent, and the more acrobatic anglers hooked fish by hanging on to a clump of willows and lean-

ing over the water; but landing a tigerish brownie in those foam-
ing rapids was something else again. There was only one mayfly
hatch of any significance on the Green River, and the successive
broods petered out before the stream even approached its normal
flow. The delayed haying season, which resembled clipping hair
from a bald man, didn't expose enough grasshoppers to stir the fish
into their usual frenzy. But despite the constant high water, I had
fine dry-fly fishing.

I kept a careful set of notes that season on the hatches that occurred and my results with respect to what was emerging at the
time, and I collected hundreds of aquatic insects for later identification. It still makes interesting reading, but I have to admit the
great majority of large trout (which I count from 18 inches, or better than 2 pounds) fell to the Dry Muddler, Goofus Bug, Irresistible and Joe's Hopper. None of these flies resembled the significant emergences that may have been in progress. I missed the
salmonfly hatch by a week. My fishing that summer was confined

*The trout in Western rivers, such as Wyoming's Madison, run big and
wild, like the rivers themselves and the country they pass through.
(Erwin Bauer)*

to the New Fork and Green in Wyoming and the Madison, Yellowstone, Big Hole, Missouri and Beaverhead in Montana, with a couple of visits to Henry's Lake. I fished eighty-nine days in all, for a
total of 1,233 releases—with the largest trout a brown of 7 pounds,
5 ounces. There were several blank days, to be sure, but we also
experienced sixty- and seventy-fish days on some of the floats. I
know that if I had included streams of a different character—like
Montana's Spring Creek near Townsend or the Spring Creek feeding the Snake in Wyoming near Jackson Hole—it would have been
a different picture entirely, with No. 16 and 18 Light Cahill, Adams,
Mosquito and other miniskirted patterns taking the honors.

Unquestionably, getting a good, high float in fast water is of
prime importance in raising big trout. This also applies to low-
silhouette patterns such as Bird's Stonefly, Muddler, Joe's Hopper
and Sofa Pillow. It's when the fly is skimming along the top in a
lifelike fashion that trophy fish respond. If it hangs half-suspended
in the surface film, the ratio of strikes goes down rapidly.

This requires prime materials in the fly and a reliable flotant, as
well as a long leader and short, accurate casts. Even a scraggly
deer-hair fly should be tied with the finest gamecock hackles.
Light-wire hooks are also an advantage on patterns with hackles
ranging up to 1¼ inches in diameter. Many anglers feel that wings
are not important on large dry flies, but they're a great help for
visibility to the caster working in rough currents or poor light. Although deer hair is little used in the East, it is virtually a *must* in
the West.

Deer-hair flies had their genesis in Oregon. Undoubtedly frustrated by trying to float a dry pattern on the tumbling waters of
the McKenzie, Rogue or Willamette, some unknown tier resorted
to hollow-celled mule deer hair. When used in a wing, the hair
caused the fly to pop up to the surface after being sucked under.
The first of these patterns was the Bucktail Caddis, a palmer-tied
fly with its wings sloped back along its body. The Light Buck
Caddis and the Dark Buck Caddis have been around since Hector
was a pup.

Then someone discovered that the wings could be tied down
both fore and aft, and this evolved into a whole series of dry flies,
epitomized by the Horner Deer Hair and later the Goofus Bug, on
which the body and tail are formed of deer hair pulled back over

the hook shank and secured at the bend. The same idea was applied to nymphs such as the Henry's Lake pattern and the Shell-
back, but these have to be weighted.

I have caught trout on large dry flies when there wasn't a sign
of an aerial hatch and in examining their stomach contents found
the fish literally stuffed with bottom organisms such as snails,
nymphs and sculpins. Apparently they just couldn't resist a big
floater. When Georgetown Lake in western Montana was in its
prime, the red-sided rainbows gave us a fit on our deeply sunken
shrimp imitations. The trout were in the shallow portions of the
broad weed beds, and for several hours the fishing was hot. Then
it stopped. There were no surface rises until I saw a dragonfly dart
over the water and perch on some emerged vegetation. A trout
swirled nearby, evidently frustrated by its disappearance. I tied
on a fluffy No. 6 Muddler, dropped it next to the weed patch and
had an immediate strike. The fish took out my entire fly line and
was into the backing before he rolled on the surface and displayed
about 24 inches of crimson stripe—and was off. Disappointing, perhaps—but the one opportunity to take a trophy trout had come
with the outsize dry fly.

Deer-hair patterns are not the only type of fly that will bring big
trout to the top. Variants such as the Light and Dark patterns
originated by Roy Donnelly (which are tied with mixed-color
hackles two sizes larger than regular for any given hook number)
work extremely well at times. Because of the air resistance caused
by the large diameter of the extended hackles, it is almost impossible to bring a variant down heavily on the surface of the water.
It is a great boon to the mediocre caster, and ideal for difficult
trout. The fly does not imitate any particular insect, although it
may suggest one, but it does have some of the ethereal qualities of
many aquatics, because it is delicate and rides high on the water.
The key in its design is the lightness of the hook. A light-wire hook
permits the use of minimum hackle, and when that hackle is long
the hook will stand away from the surface, provided it is supported
by an equally long tail. Furthermore, it falls easily to the water
and has less tendency to drag on complex currents; it literally
bounces over them. This ability to move almost independently is
no small part of its attraction.

The variant is most effective on water that is glassy or reason-

This rainbow's end came when he rose to a shaggy wet fly. (Erwin Bauer)

ably flat. In very fast runs the bulkier clipped-hair-bodied flies float better, and their larger impression against the surface is undoubtedly more useful in tempting trout to the top. However, on many rivers the problem fish are in the moderately swift places where artificials are easily distinguished from the real thing. There is a great deal of this type of water on the Firehole, for example, and also on Henry's Fork of the Snake. The stiff, long, sparsely dressed fly is a brilliant suggestion of insect life under these conditions.

It is usually difficult for the amateur fly tier to find the quality spade and saddle hackles which are necessary in dressing a variant; a rooster doesn't grow more than a half dozen of the former, and commercial skinners are inclined to trim off the saddle hackles. For this reason, many of the popular patterns consist of two different mixed spades, such as ginger and grizzly or mahogany and grizzly. To get maximum flotation, do not make a body on the fly, but wind the hackles around two-thirds of the shank length of the hook.

Some years ago, and just before his passing, I fished with a fine gentleman and author, Claude Kreider. Among other things he was a skilled rod builder, and with his home-glued sticks Claude laid out a beautiful dry fly. It was my first visit to the Firehole in

Yellowstone Park, and the river was alive with feeding trout that day. There was a brown mayfly hatch in progress, and the fish were greatly in evidence. A dozen widening rings in front of us caused me to joint my rod with trembling fingers. Under the sod bank right at our feet a handsome brownie rolled up to suck in a dun. We had found the Firehole at its best, and there was nobody else on the river for at least a mile. I pawed hurriedly through my fly box and found a No. 12 Mallard Quill with just the right shade of hackle to match the natural. Then I noticed Claude tying on a huge cream-colored variant. I knew he usually wore glasses, but my naive observation about what was in the air and being accepted fell on deaf ears. Claude gave the variant a good oiling, then tossed it out with wiggly S-casts—and proceeded to catch trout. I did too. The difference was that he took a 4-pound rainbow and a brown of about 2½ pounds, while I raised merry Ned with yearlings. It wasn't long before I was borrowing his variants.

There was no magic in his performance. Claude had fished the Firehole many times, and after slaughtering the innocents over a period of time, he began to experiment. He began by fishing a given hatch with flies that seemed to match the naturals, keeping note of his success. Then he tried various outsize floaters on the same water. Even during a hatch of small ephemerids, trout—especially big trout—came for the large flies. Convinced by repeated experiments, he began to fish them exclusively. The big fly has proved particularly valuable on swift Western rivers because it floats high even on deep swirls and riffled stretches of water. On such broken water, with the trout's vision more or less obscured, the trick is to keep a "lively" fly dancing on its hackle points.

The big-fly story is, of course, contrary to accepted dry-fly principles. It might also be added that *how* the fly is fished is often diametrically opposed to standard technique. On rivers that run at a full gallop, I cast the big dry across and downstream about 90 percent of the time.

There are two problems in high-water dry-fly fishing. The first is the effort expended by the angler in working upstream, wading against the current and flailing the water ahead with fast casts and quick float-backs. The fly is seldom "fishing" for more than two seconds before the line is sucked under in the turbulence, and it takes a powerful amount of casting to get even an hour of actual hook-in-the-water time. There is also the energy saved by the trout; being much less enthusiastic than his angler, the fish is not about to rise from his quiet hold on the bottom through 6 or 8 feet of rushing water to chase the momentary presentation of a dry fly. The stomach contents of trout during high-water periods reveals algae, snails, the occasional bottom-hugging forage fish such as the sculpin and, of course, nymphs. It is a very sensible diet. Yet a trout can be made to hit a floater if it's left to dance over his head in a *lifelike* manner.

A positive action is the only thing that separates a walking dry fly from one that is dragging. While our textbook definition of drag (a condition that causes a floating fly to pull against the current in an unlifelike manner) is reliable, it does not imply that you have to keep the fly working at the current's speed all of the time. The thought of moving a dry fly almost paralyzes the pious hand—yet in high, bouldery water it is the *motion* of surface foods that compels the trout to feed. To forget the lore of the mayfly for a moment, many meaty winged foods such as stone flies (which are strong, active swimmers even against a current), dragonflies and grasshoppers are more common to Western rivers than the delicate ephemerids. It's difficult for me to believe that a 3- or 4-pound brown trout with jaws like the claws of a lobster is not conditioned to aggressive feeding. For all the mayflies that appeared on the New Fork last summer, the fish would starve to death. The trick is, of course, to convince a big trout that what he sees is real.

Ordinarily, the angler accomplishes this by casting a slack line and letting more line out to delay drag until the fly runs over the fish. But sooner or later the fly is left pulling against the current anyhow. Furthermore, if you are using a forward-taper line, or even a mediumweight double-taper, it's difficult to make a retrieve that trout will respond to; the line is practically anchored in the flow once it has been extended. The better method—and its subtleties can be quickly learned in practice—is to cast quartering crossstream with a slack line, the exact angle depending on the spot to be covered. Wade as deep as prudence dictates above the potential lie, and after you have fished a normal dragless float the fly will reach a point at which the trout either accepts or rejects it; in the latter case, you must now draw the floater back for a new cast. When you're working directly downstream, this invariably requires

Rock Creek, Montana, was the home of this 5-pound brown before he fell prey to a Muddler Minnow. (Erwin Bauer)

pulling it over the fish—a motion that is going to either excite a strike or put the trout down. You will rarely get a second chance, as you might in upstream casting when the fly dances away on tippytoes. This is the moment when a fine-line point, long leader (preferably 12 feet) and correctly hackled fly make a critical difference. On slick water in particular, coarse terminal gear is going to create a wake and spoil the whole illusion.

Raise the rod slowly and begin twitching gently, bringing the fly upstream in short, pulsating strokes. If the fly is standing up on its hackles and the fish doesn't respond after it has moved a few feet, lower your rod and let the fly drift near it again. A keen fish sense helps at moments like this, but gradually you will learn to gauge the fly's action according to the response of the trout. Occasionally you might try skimming the fly away at a steady speed. As last-cast reeling has repeatedly proved, a positive and continuous flight often triggers blasting strikes.

Although mayfly lore more or less conditions our thinking in terms of delicate ephemeral flutters, the fact is that many other insects such as the big stone fly can swim like hell against a swift flow. Nature designed the stone fly for highly oxygenated tumbling riffles, and its skill as a sprinter is classic. In most cases I imagine the trout mistakes the big artificial for a stone fly, but grasshoppers, dragonflies and moths also disturb the surface greatly.

Learning to cast a slack line is very easy. Correctly executed, the slack-line cast is aimed directly down to the position of the fish, but it should float about half that distance. In other words, if the trout is holding 40 feet downstream, you should drop the fly about 20 feet in his direction and cover the difference by shaking more line out. There are several ways of making slack-line deliveries. The easiest for most people is to false-cast in the usual manner and, on the final stroke forward, stop the rod at a 45-degree angle; then when the line begins to pull-shoot, simply wiggle the tip from side to side. This lateral motion will create little curves in the outgoing line. Play with this for a few minutes and you'll find that you can make narrow or wide elbows of slack with no effort. For most purposes, seven or eight small curves should be enough.

When you drift the fly down on a fish, don't get the slack concentrated in one big belly. It will be caught broadside in the current and cause drag. As a tactical advantage, the initial presentation should be made in a perfectly natural float. After the cast is fished out, you can begin animating the fly against a dragging line. So the rod wiggling must be timed to distribute the curves through the length of the cast.

I stood next to Bob Hardwicke on the New Fork while he teased an Irresistible over a deep pool that had been thoroughly fished by a number of people earlier in the day. Bob, an attorney from Fort Worth, Texas, had never walked a dry fly before (at least not intentionally), but he got the hang of it within a few casts. There was a slight upstream breeze, and after the fly made its float and he raised his rod between the eastbound air and the westbound current, the fly practically stayed in one spot for a minute, hopping up and down. Bob had just said something about how it was like fishing a bass bug when a 4-pound brown literally tail-walked, marlinlike, over the water and slammed the Irresistible. On another occasion, while I was fishing with Fenwick's casting champion, Jimmy Green, he raised the same trout three times before it finally nailed the fly. Then there was the day Phil Clock struck three big trout, one after another (Ted Trueblood and I could hear the fish hit the water a hundred yards upstream), and I stepped on my own rod tip while trying to release a husky brown that wrapped the leader around my ankles and dashed downstream.

It goes without elaboration that big fish can't be teased to the top in high water with coarse tackle. Ideally, this is best done with the lightest line and longest leader at your disposal. A No. 4 double-taper joined with a 15-foot 4X leader is perfect. The fly must be tied on a fine hook with stiff hackles so that it bounces buoyantly on the surface; it doesn't matter whether it's a Blond Wulff, Irresistible, Ginger Variant, Blue Upright, Royal Coachman, Adams, Muddler or Joe's Hopper—it must ride high. A No. 10 is about right for most fishing because it's large enough to attract big trout, yet small enough to cast and handle easily on a fine leader. When you're making 25-to-30-foot casts—which is practical when you're hip-deep in a turbulent stream—the line will seldom touch the water after you have made the float and raised the rod.

This angler flew into Alaska's Battle River for a chance to cast over big rainbows. (Erwin Bauer)

For subsurface fly fishing, no Western tackle shop is completely inventoried unless it stocks a variety of Woolly Worms. Although synonymous with sagebrush country, the Woolly Worm made its reputation as an Ozark bass fly back in the 1920s. However, it was first described by Charles Cotton in the 1676 edition of *The Compleat Angler*, so the idea is an old one. In our Central and Northern bass states, anglers believe that it simulates a caterpillar commonly called a woolly worm or woolly bear—hence the name. However, it may suggest a variety of insect forms, and the contrast movement of the palmer-tied hackle certainly induces strikes. The cylindrical chenille body usually ribbed with tinsel (following the hackle stem to reinforce the hackle feather to prevent it from tearing loose) is dressed with the hackle reversed, with the fibers pointing forward so that they sweep back and forth when the fly is in motion. Straight- or curved-shanked, weighted and unweighted, Woolly Worms are tied in all body colors, but olive, yellow, black and brown with grizzly or cree hackles are late-season favorites.

Everybody has his own pet method of fishing the Woolly Worm, but I seem to get the best results by working the fly in a quick pulsing movement which makes the hackles pump. The idea is to retrieve not rapidly, but rather in short hops along the bottom.

For streamer flies I highly recommend the Marabou Muddler, Dave Whitlock's Multicolor Marabou and that old reliable, the Spruce. These animated-wing patterns are deadly when fished deep, especially late in the season. Generally, the fly is cast slightly up- and cross-stream, causing the submerged streamer to swing down in a curve. By jerks of the rod tip as the fly follows the natural path of the line, and stripping of short lengths to exaggerate the action of the feathers, the fly is worked back across the current. For my fishing, which is mostly on big streams at this time of the year, I prefer to use a sinking-tip line and sometimes a slightly weighted fly as well to make certain the streamer is fishing close to the bottom. With a sinking-tip line, about the first 15 feet sink, which in a current means that the fly will go down 4 or 5 feet rather quickly. Naturally, if the cast is mended and allowed to drift it will sink even deeper when necessary.

Equally important in this method is the size of the fly used. A No. 4 sounds Gargantuan on Eastern streams, but it's only a starter on vintage trout water. In the West, don't hesitate to use No. 2s and stock patterns such as the Yellow Muddler, Troth Bullhead and Whitlock Sculpin in sizes up to No. 3/0. These large streamers should be fished more slowly in the fall. In other words, after you've made the cast and retrieved the fly a few feet, let it sink again and idle around in the bottom currents. Trophy trout are not fooled by something resembling an overstuffed bullhead that moves around too much.

Western trout fishing is to a large extent done by boat, although this is principally a means of transportation to reach remote spots. The ideal hull for big, rough rivers is the McKenzie River boat, or double-ender. Double-enders are built in many parts of the West. They are sensitive to the oars, can turn on a dime and can be held in currents that would sweep a canoe or raft over the rocks. Once you get the hang of changing direction in rapid currents by spinning the bow, and learn how to pull out of trouble, it's as easy as walking. It *does* take practice, and if you can't read the surface of a fast stream, don't attempt anything wilder than the local brook.

The important thing about a double-ender is that despite its similarity at bow and stern, the man on the oars must face downstream, because the hull is controlled by rowing against the current. It doesn't travel like a rowboat—bow first. I forgot to mention this to Elmer George when he wanted to learn how to operate one. Poor Elmer took off in a chute of white water on the upper Green River, and before I could get my jaws unhinged we were going about 20 miles an hour spinning like a top. The current shoved us at a deep undercut where the river makes a right-angle bend, and for a hundred bone-bruising yards we denuded that bank of overhanging willows. When we finally came to a crunching stop on a gravel bar, the durable Mr. George sat there staring at a bladeless oar. "Hell," he said, "I shoulda' worn my spurs." A sense of humor helps, but a sense of direction works better.

Casting from a freely drifting boat is mighty pleasant. You sit in the bow, passing from the shadows of tall timber to a shoring of sand and hardwood where the mule deer, bright in the noon sun, come down on sharp-pointed hooves to drink and feed, and around the next bend a great flock of greenheads are waiting to jump and surprise you; but always you watch for the signs of rising trout along the banks, the ledges and the main current. The mechanics

Even when you get there by boat, wading is often the most productive way to fish a big river. (Erwin Bauer)

of fly fishing are simple. With your shooting line stripped in coils on the floor you can cast quartering downstream, and since the boat is moving at the same speed as the current, the fly will float without drag. In a day's time you can cover an amazing length of river, including places that a wading angler couldn't touch.

One thing that makes float fishing especially productive is that most rivers have a limited number of access points that a man on foot can use. An angler can walk or wade only a limited distance, and as a result long stretches of water are often relatively unfished. Even where a boat livery exists, a one-day angler can't cover too much river. It's also true that while many streams are paralleled by highways, there is frequently a considerable mileage that runs away from the road. Such places may provide excellent angling.

An advantage of float trips lasting two days or more is that you can comfortably be on the water early and late. This makes a big difference in summer angling. Most motorists find it difficult, if not impossible, to arrive on location at dawn or to stay on the river until dark. The leisurely pace of floating not only extends your range but permits you to be on the productive pools at key hours.

One afternoon, Oregon biologist Bob Borovicka and I were floating the Deschutes. Although I had been careful to quarter my casts along the bank, I once let the fly swing around below, and an old horse of a brownie turned with it. He wanted that Muddler so bad he could taste it, and just about the time he opened his mouth we drifted right over him. I don't recall ever seeing such a big trout outside a museum. The point is that when fishing from a boat on running water and making long casts, you have to anticipate where your fly is going to work in relation to where the boat will be. Casting directly downstream is probably one of the most common errors made by novice floaters. I have found that cross-stream casting is a great deal more effective, because the boat is always going away from the fish. But the real art in floating big streams is in knowing when to use the boat and when to use your waders.

Intelligent use of the waterproofs will pay off in more fish for the following reasons. First, when you're floating, your fishing speed remains constant. Second, you seldom have the opportunity to observe the reactions of your quarry. Third, you pass a large percentage of good water before you have a chance to cover it. And finally, you are in no position to make corrections in your technique. An experienced guide will anchor or wedge his boat at likely-looking places to eliminate some of these problems, but during the greatest part of the trip you are a floating island of unprofitable sanctity—unless you get off your seat and meet the fish on your two feet.

Obviously, you can't step into a couple of fathoms of running river, but I've never seen the big stream yet that doesn't have shallow vantage points or banks that offer a stable platform of operation. Even the Thompson of British Columbia has gravel bars that any experienced angler can wade, and that river is so big it would scare you. On rivers with boggy banks, like the Deschutes, the Teton, Michigan's Au Sable and most Southern streams, you can pole your boat up into the grass and, after fishing the area within casting distance, move downstream another fifty yards or so.

STEELHEAD

BY CLARE CONLEY

FOR A LONG time I have listened to Florida fishermen extolling the virtues of the tarpon, claiming it is the best of all game fishes; but pound for pound, a 15-pound steelhead is as strong as or stronger than a tarpon—and a lot more fun to catch. The reason a steelhead is more fun to catch is that it requires more of the angler. Most often this fishing is done by walking and wading rather than by standing in an outboard motorboat, and frequently it forces fishermen to be out in cold, wet weather. Obviously I don't think that sportsmen should have everything easy. I have found that the more difficult things are and the more of a challenge they are, the more fondly you look back on them.

That's enough philosophy. Let me show you why I like steelhead and what I mean by challenging. Ted Trueblood and I were fishing on the Salmon River in Idaho just a short distance upstream from a sawmill. We had found a slot in the river bottom where the fish would hold, and if we waded deep enough and cast far enough we could get to them. It was one of those maximum-effort jobs that frequently occur in steelhead fishing. It was late enough in the afternoon for the sun to be off the water. We were fly-fishing at the time, and my arm felt as if I had made five hundred casts that day—which I probably had—and I hadn't taken a fish yet.

Steelheading often forces the fisherman out into cold, wet weather. But the prize is usually worth the pain.

Ted was ahead and downstream of me, in the slot, and he had hooked and lost a fish, which always gives steelhead fishermen enough enthusiasm to make another five hundred casts. Anyway, as I worked down the river yard by yard, stopping to cast every 6 or 8 feet, it finally happened that my fly stopped. Nothing more than that, but to a steelhead fisherman that's enough. Ninety-nine times out of a hundred such an occurrence signals a snag, but on the one-hundredth it means steelhead. And so I struck, bringing my rod up firmly, tightening the line. Instantly I could feel a fish surging against my pull, and from experience I knew that something was about to happen fast.

I had to get out of the river, so that I could run on the bank if I needed to. This was not easy. I was up to my waist in moving water at the end of a downstream-projecting underwater bar. I had to inch my way back upstream and diagonally to the bank. Life is not simple for a steelheader.

Meanwhile, back in the river, as Zane Grey would say, the fish decided to take off for parts downstream, and a steelhead with the current helping can leave the scene in a hurry. My reel handle raced backward, paying out precious yards of line, and I had to make matters worse by going in the opposite direction—upstream —to get out. The fish was at least a hundred yards away by the time I got to the bank after once nearly going over my wader tops trying to shortcut. Don't ask me why the steelhead decided to stop. Otherwise my story would end here.

On the bank, I wound in line and ran at the same time. It's important to keep a tight line on steelhead, but it is also impossible to play one that is almost directly downstream from you in a fast river. By the time I caught up to the fish, he was refreshed and ready to go. He raced around and broke water a couple of times and then decided to go downstream some more. Now, anyone knows that you can't keep up this kind of thing very long without having trouble show up one way or another.

Downstream was a moderately shallow riffle; then there was a small pool across from the sawmill. Below that, the river turned and tumbled into a deep pool at the base of a cliff on my side. If the fish got into that deep pool, there would be no way to land him; I would have to break off, because I couldn't drag him back up the rapids to where I could reach him.

But he was on his way, and I was helpless to stop him before he had gone over the riffle into the small pool. The situation looked bad. The steelhead still was strong, and I had gone as far as I could go. Around and around the pool he raced, and every time he started downstream I thought he was gone, so I put on all the pressure I could. After what seemed like an hour, and probably was only 15 minutes, he began to weaken, and at last he turned on his side in the shallow rocks in front of me. Before anything else could go wrong, I hauled back on my rod, slid the steelhead to the water's edge and booted him out onto the rocky bar I was on. (That's right, I kicked him out—standard procedure in steelheading.) And as I did, lumberjacks I didn't even know were watching shouted yells of approval from the windows of the mill.

How much did the steelhead weigh? Nothing special for a steelhead—just 12 pounds—but exciting and challenging, and that's why I like these fish.

Time has come to lay on you some background about steelhead, so if you'll bear with me I'll get it over with and into more interesting things. The steelhead is simply a rainbow trout that is hatched in fresh water and works its way downriver to spend three or four years in the ocean before coming back to spawn. Steelhead grow a great deal faster than nonmigratory rainbows, because the ocean has a lot more food. To illustrate: A 5-pound trout is considered a nice fish, but a 5-pound steelhead is really nothing to talk about. It's rather small. To get much attention from fellow steelheaders your fish must go 10 pounds, and 15 pounds is even better. And if you break 20 pounds, you have a right to brag and even mount the fish. The world-record steelhead, caught in 1970 by a 9-year-old boy in Alaska, weighed 42 pounds 2 ounces.

In appearance steelhead have the standard trout/salmon look, and the quicker they are caught after leaving salt water the more pronounced are the silvery bottom half and dark, iron-gray upper half. As the fish stay in fresh water the upper part fades somewhat and the lower half becomes more grayish; then a light, pinkish stripe appears down the midside. Because they must go varying

Kicking your fish ashore is an accepted way of beaching these hard-won trophies.

distances to reach their home spawning beds, steelhead are in freshwater rivers for varying lengths of time, and so they may become quite "dark," in steelheaders' parlance, before they return to the ocean. Steelhead become very grayish all over after spawning and, again in steelheaders' language, these "downstreamers" are not considered as much fun to catch or as good to eat. Steelhead, like Atlantic salmon, do not die after spawning, although all the Pacific salmon do. Spawning may take place within a few miles of the ocean in small streams, or a fish may swim a thousand miles up the Columbia, Snake and Salmon rivers to reach its spawning bed.

The basic range of steelhead is from San Francisco north to central Alaska. Over what is left of their original range, they are found in the states of California, Oregon, Washington, Idaho and Alaska and the province of British Columbia. Transplantings of these fish have spread them to many places, the most noteworthy being the Great Lakes, especially Lake Michigan. Incidentally, many steelhead are taken by trolling in both Lake Michigan and the Pacific Ocean, and although I do not wish to put down large-boat trolling, it nevertheless is big-water trolling, and it is a far cry from what I mean by steelheading on rivers. Later on I'll list some of the better steelhead rivers in each state and province.

Perhaps one of the best features of steelheading, at least in the West, is that the fish are found in many rivers, and most of the rivers are accessible and available to the public. Steelhead streams occur in five Western states, and almost all these waters are public. All you need is a license and a steelhead punch card—a means of keeping count of your daily and yearly limit. Generally the daily limit is two or three fish, and in some states you are supposed to keep the first fish you land and not return any fish after playing them. In steelheading, as opposed to Atlantic salmon fishing, no guide (except perhaps in British Columbia) is required—a better deal for the average fisherman because it keeps costs down.

In all honesty, it is important to point out one other aspect of steelheading. You may fish for steelies for days or even seasons without so much as hooking one. This does not mean that the fish are not there. It just happens sometimes. For the most part it is true that you will not hook many at any one time. There will be exceptional days when you may have a dozen on, but you also may have a dozen days of hard daybreak-to-dusk fishing without hook-

ing a fish. Another thing about steelheading is that the more steelhead you catch the more you are likely to catch. Experience is a
great teacher in this sport. And, finally, if you can start your steelheading by fishing with someone who has experience, you will improve your chances greatly.

I vividly remember catching my first steelhead at the mouth of
a small creek in the Snake River in Hells Canyon on the Idaho–
Oregon border. It was a puny little thing, not more than 3 or 4
pounds, but it was my first after at least twenty trips and thousands of casts. Up to that time I had fished beside friends who had
caught dozens of fish right where I was casting. They were fishing
exactly the same as I was with the same lure or bait, and neither
I nor they could see what the problem was, if in fact there was
one. But after I caught that first steelhead it all got easier, and I
took my share from then on.

On the other hand, I have a friend, Herb Carlson, who rather
on a lark one day tossed his lure into the mouth of a culvert on an
irrigation ditch that carried water from a nearby river. Out of the
culvert raced a 5-pounder that grabbed the lure. While others
stood by in shock, Carlson proceeded to land the fish.

Another friend, Willard Cravens, one day had a new rod and
reel he wanted to try casting. So he went to the nearest water, a
slough on a river about 300 yards from his house. The slough was
never particularly good for any fishing, but it was certainly more
suited to bass, crappies and bullhead than anything else. He was
casting a small bass plug when, to his surprise and to the everlasting surprise of anyone else who knew the piece of water, a steelhead grabbed the plug. Needless to say, we tried casting for steelhead there several times after that—without success.

Regardless of the crazy ways these fish sometimes get caught,
there is a real technique to taking steelhead consistently. They are
caught on all kinds of equipment, but except for the differences in
casting and a slightly more sensitive means of feeding line to a
drifting lure with a bait-casting reel, spinning and bait-fishing
techniques are the same. And so in this next section we'll deal with
spinning and bait casting together.

In discussing the selection of tackle, please remember that I am
talking about an average outfit that will work properly on most
steelhead rivers—rivers from 30 to 75 yards wide mostly—with a

Fishing with spinning tackle demands essentially the same techniques used in bait casting for steelhead.

strong current but not raging rapids and with deep pools and bends. For this type of steelhead water the best rod is 8 to 9 feet long and should easily cast lures ranging in weight from ¼ ounce to ½ ounce. The rod length suggested here may seem long, but a rod of this length makes distance casting easier, and it gives you a height advantage when you're trying to keep your line from dragging on the center of the river while your lure drifts along the far side.

Nylon monofilament line is the only kind to use, no matter whether it be on a spinning or a bait-casting reel. The weight of the line can be varied somewhat, but I'd choose 15-pound-test most of the time. With the proper rod such a line will cast a long way, and it still has enough strength to salvage many snagged lures. But if light, small lures are necessary, I recommend 10-pound-test; if the river is full of big rocks and stumps and you are casting a heavy lure, then 20-pound-test is better. After all, the idea is to fish, not keep a tackle store in business with your trade alone. And when you get down to it, the strength of the line does not land the fish. If you play a steelhead too hard because you have strong line, he will usually either tear off, straighten a hook or break open a snap swivel. So line strength is a factor mainly in getting free from snags and casting where you must. Don't get the crazy idea that using a light line for steelhead is somehow more sporting. Also, carry several hundred yards of line with you at all times. Steelhead streams have a way of using it up fast.

Finally, keep plenty of line on your reel. I was fishing with Ted Trueblood once on the Quinault River of the Olympic Peninsula in Washington when this precaution was especially important. Just after we arrived at one of our favorite fishing "holes" (for some reason they are most often called holes instead of pools) one morning, Ted hooked a strong fish. He got the strike at a rather unusual place for us in that it was at the head of a rather uniform chute of semifast water. This chute was probably 200 yards long and was without the normal riffle-and-pool combination that tends to keep fish from running wild downstream. One good thing, however: the chute was made up of round river rocks the size of grapefruit and smaller, so snags, for the most part, weren't a problem.

The one exception was the stump end of a tree that was stuck midway down the chute, exactly in the middle of the river. Naturally, when Ted's fish felt the hook it took off downriver. Ted saw his problem right away, and for a while it looked as if he could get the fish in before it got to the stump, or at least keep the fish on his side of the stump when it went past it. But the steelhead had a lot of fast river water carrying it and no place to stop. The inevitable happened. The steelhead went down the river on the far side of the stump and continued on downstream.

Ted was stuck. He could feel the fish was still on, but he couldn't follow downstream. So he just stood opposite the stump and did the only thing he could: he fed line to the fish a little at a time and hoped that somehow a way out of the dilemma would present itself. By the time Ted had fed out probably a hundred yards of line, the fish reached slower water near the end of the chute and stopped. That was the first break. But how could Ted get off the stump?

At first he considered just breaking the steelhead off and getting on with the fishing; but after what must have been half an hour of messing with the steelhead, that seemed a shame. Then, what appeared to be a crazy answer to this problem struck me. I would cast my lure, a spoon, out below the stump and snag Ted's line, and while he fed more line out I would reel in his line with my outfit. When I had his line in hand, I would cut his end loose. He was to reel his end back from around the stump and then retie it to the length I was holding, at the far end of which was the steelhead.

On the second cast I hooked his line and our little drama began. In came his line, and I'll never forget the burning-your-bridges feeling I got when I cut it. Ted worked like lightning. Quickly he reeled in his end of the line and tied the fastest blood knot that was ever tied with cold, shaking hands. What a relief it was when he started tightening up the line again and found that the fish was still hooked. But he still had a hundred yards of line to wind in as he worked his way downriver to the fish. By now, however, we felt that luck was on our side and we could do no wrong. At one point I had to wade out as deep as I could around the end of a log that projected into the river and hand Ted's rod around to him. Once past that, however, he played the fish in and landed it—one of the few times that landing a steelhead seemed anticlimactic.

The selection of lures for steelhead fishing with spinning and bait-casting equipment is wide, and the lures themselves are frequently wondrous to behold. Many of them are designed for steelhead alone, although some have crossover uses in other kinds of

In a photo taken several years ago, Ted Trueblood, a frequent fishing companion of the author's, shows a bragging-size steelhead taken on bait-casting gear.

fishing. Of this latter group, the two outstanding categories of lures are spoons of the Dardevle type and diving, swimming trout and bass plugs.

Red-and-white spoons used in steelhead fishing are usually not over 3 inches long, and most often they are 2 to 2½ inches in length. Although they are not especially long, they are often much heavier than conventional lures. It is true that the standard ¼-ounce spoon will often do the job, but more often a ⅜-ounce spoon in the same size will be better, and you will understand why this is when we get into how they are fished.

There are also many other versions of spoons not in the shape of Dardevles that will catch fish too. They all have the wobbling spoon's cupped shape, but they are often short and stubby for their weight. In other words, they pack a lot of weight into a small spoon. There are, in fact, so many varieties of spoons used that it would be hopeless to try to describe them all.

Spoons of many colors are used, including brass, copper and chrome-finished, but the standard red-and-white-stripe is always a strong favorite. Curiously, I have fished red-and-white spoons until almost no paint remained on them and they still caught fish, so it makes a person wonder at times just how important color is. I have nevertheless spent a lot of time repainting lures to restore them to something like their original finish. More often than not, though, a steelhead angler doesn't have a lure for long enough to worry about the paint's being worn off, and you'll soon understand that better, too.

In this business of color, however, there is one kind of finish that is strongly favored, and it does seem to catch more fish. It is the fluorescent finish. Spoons for steelhead are frequently painted fluorescent red or orange. Since I can't read a steelhead's mind I can only guess why this is, but I believe that fluorescent lures are brighter on dull days, and they can be seen better anytime in murky or "colored" water. Another possible reason is that fluorescent colors look to a fish more like a gob of natural roe, or fish eggs. That they are brighter goes without question. Whether they look like roe or not only the fish know.

Spoons of the store-bought variety designed for other kinds of fishing represent probably 80 or 90 percent of the lures employed for steelhead, but plugs are sometimes used. The plugs must be of a shape that casts well, and they must dive quickly and deep. This narrows the possibilities. Billed plugs such as the Heddon River Runt and the Hotshot catch steelhead too, but they are best in shallow streams. Often they require that some lead be put on the line to sink them deep enough, and this does not make the casting or fishing of them any easier. Again red and white is favored. Plugs are easier to handle in trolling for steelhead than in casting for them.

Of manufactured lures designed specifically for steelhead fishing, the Cherry Bobber and all its kin are some of the most popular. The original Cherry Bobber had a balsa body varying from ½ inch to 1 inch long and shaped like a teardrop, the big end being toward the hooks. This body was painted fluorescent red, and just ahead of it was a single-bladed spinner which wobbled and sometimes spun around the body. Many variations have been born of this original lure, but the basic principle of it is in all of them. Being light, the lure floats, so it is fished with lead on a dropper up the line a foot or so. The idea is that the lead touches the bottom and the lure floats up a short distance, avoiding snags. The idea works, and a lot of fish have been taken on these lures since they were invented fifteen or more years ago.

Finally comes the yarn fly, which you can either buy or make yourself. Flies of this sort consist of nothing more than a tassel of red, orange and sometimes yellow or chartreuse yarn. This yarn can be purchased at most knitting shops and tackle stores that have steelhead equipment. Or, if you are a fly tier, it is a simple matter to wrap the yarn a dozen times around a small, flat stick about an inch or a little more wide. Then slide the whole thing off and tie one group of the folded ends at the head of a No. 2 hook. With that done, cut the other folded ends off equal to the length of the hook. Don't make the flies too bulky. It has always seemed to me that the sparser ones work better.

Another popular way of making these lures is to snell-tie a foot or 18 inches of monofilament to the shank of a hook with an upturned eye and pass the long end of the line out through the eye. Prepare your yarn by wrapping it around two fingers, take it off your fingers, and pass it underneath the monofilament just where it goes out through the eye. Pull it halfway through. Then double the yarn, by pulling both sets of ends toward the bend of the hook, and clip off the ends. The yarn is actually not tied in; it is just held there by the pull of the monofilament against the hook. It looks as if the yarn would not stay in place, but it does. The advantage of this second method is that it leaves a leader on the hook, which comes in handy.

I have also seen steelhead taken with baits of night crawlers, smelt and shrimps, but the most popular of all is eggs—steelhead or salmon eggs—as fresh as possible. Roe is really the best possible natural bait for steelhead. Just why they take it will remain an everlasting puzzle, because steelhead are not supposed to feed when they are in freshwater on a spawning run. Eggs can be bought in jars, and clusters are the thing to buy in this case. The choicest of all, however, is fresh roe, and any dedicated egg man will go to great lengths to get the real thing fresh from the fish.

All female steelhead and salmon have two large skeins of eggs which are about 8 or 9 inches long, 2 inches wide and an inch thick. The eggs are all clustered together, and it is a simple matter, although a little messy, to cut them with a pair of scissors into bite-size chunks about an inch wide. Naturally, they need to be preserved and toughened somewhat, so these pieces are then dredged with a preservative and stored in a refrigerator until the time comes for fishing. The preservatives that are handiest are sugar and borax. I prefer borax, because it makes them tougher.

The best way that I have found to put eggs on a hook is to embed a hook into the mass and then wrap a number of turns around them with red thread, being careful not to break the eggs. The thread is then tied off at the head of the hook. The thread just gives the eggs a little more durability for casting, because when they are cast without anything holding them on they fly off with frustrating frequency. Again a snelled hook, as mentioned in connection with yarn flies, is a big help, and often eggs are put on yarn flies. The theory is that if the eggs don't get the fish or if they fly off, at least the yarn might catch a steelhead. No use having a bare hook down in the water.

There are two methods of fishing this equipment—drifting and "plunking." Drifting is the more popular, and it consists of drifting the lure—not floating in a boat, as it might sound like. Steelhead, when working their way up a river, move through the riffles and rapids and rest in the pools. They lie in deep water when resting and if possible stay out of the current behind an obstacle such as the lip of a ledge, a boulder, a log or anything that breaks the movement of the water. Sometimes they will move about in a pool in which the water is slow enough, but most often they just hang behind the protection of some debris and rest. This accounts for two things that give steelheaders fits. The fish are deep near the bottom, and there are usually a lot of snags. Steelhead rivers, like Charlie Brown's kite-eating tree, are lure-eating rivers.

Drift fishermen like to find places on streams where the river makes a bend that is sharp enough to have caused the water to scour out a deep channel against one bank. Sometimes other reasons cause such channels to form as well. In the channel the water is slower along the bottom. Starting at the upstream end of such a pool and on the opposite side from the deep water, the drift fisherman casts his lure or bait as far across the river into the channel as he can, often close to the far bank. Then, depending on the depth and speed of the water, he allows his lure to sink to the bottom before tightening up the line. When the lure or bait is just bumping and pecking along the bottom, he holds his rod tip high and keeps his line just tight enough so that the lure swings in an arc back across the river along the bottom. If there is one trick to steelhead fishing, this is it. The lure must be within a few inches of the bottom, and if you don't feel it moving along ticking the bottom often, you are fishing too high and you'll catch few fish. Obviously the technique produces a lot of snags, and steelheaders become very tricky about getting free, but they also lose a lot of lures. But then who wouldn't, happily, for a 10- or 15-pound fish?

Over and over the angler casts, letting the lure sweep back across each time. Little by little he moves down the pool, covering every inch of it with his lure. Frequently several steelheaders will be fishing the same pool in a line, slowly inching down the stream, and it is considered very poor manners to jump in ahead of anyone working his way down. Newcomers start at the end of the line upstream and probably have as much chance as anyone of catching a fish. Hip boots or waders are a must, and felt or chain soles are a tremendous help, because the footing in fast water is often poor at best. Many anglers use wading staffs in the really difficult water, and some also wear life vests. Oh, yes, steelhead anglers have been swept off their feet and drowned.

Spoons are usually and preferably fished with no lead on the line, because that way you can feel them better. Yarn flies and Cherry Bobbers require lead. For these, lead or solder wire of about ³⁄₁₆-inch diameter is usually chosen. A straight piece of this lead is cut off to a length that will provide just enough weight to take the fly or bobber to the bottom and let it ride along just ticking the bottom, but not dragging. If it constantly scrapes, it will move too slowly and snag frequently. The beauty of lead is that it can be clipped with pliers to adjust for the best weight in each hole, and it costs very little.

The best tie-up for terminal tackle using lead I have found starts with a yarn fly on 12 or 18 inches of leader. Tied to the other end of this leader is a small barrel swivel with a loop at each end. The lead is slotted slightly about a quarter inch from one end with a knife blade so that it has a ring around it, and a piece of leader is tied to the lead with a jam knot. At the other end of this lead-sinker leader another, tiny barrel swivel is tied. The open end of this swivel is threaded onto the line from the rod, and then the fishing line is tied with a clinch knot to the open end of the swivel from the lure. When it's done this way, the lead is free to slide on its dropper up and down the fishing line, but it cannot go past the lure swivel and down to the lure. The whole setup costs next to nothing—and you'll see why that's important when you start snagging up. Another reason it is good is that virtually all the knot tying can be done at home. Only one knot puts the whole thing together when you're fishing.

This same terminal rig is used by egg fishermen. I mention this even though egg fishing is the method I least enjoy. Actually, it is a very effective way to catch steelhead. It is just the mess and bother that goes with it, and I am too lazy to go to the trouble. It requires a belt to hold your bait can, a rag to wipe your hands on and frequent rebaiting. But I have seen good egg fishermen catch fish when I couldn't, and then I started using eggs. I know good egg fishermen can catch fish better than lure tossers when conditions are bad. But when conditions are good, lure fishermen will keep up with them. Eggers do some amazing things sometimes, though.

The two best egg fishermen I've ever had the pleasure to fish with were Lucky O'Neill and Malachi McMahon. One was a motel

operator and the other a blackjack dealer in Las Vegas. I fully believe either of them could catch a steelhead out of a barrel on the
bottom of the Columbia River. They seemed to have radar at the
ends of their lines. One day Trueblood and I were fishing with
Lucky. Midday came and nothing much had happened. More and
more we were wading out of the stream to sit on the bank and
drink coffee. Ted and I were talking about going somewhere else
while we watched Lucky fish a little side chute off the main
stream. Of course, we knew that no steelhead in its right mind
would come up that little dead end when it was so much easier
to swim up the main body of water into the pool we had been
working.

The chute was so small that Lucky couldn't work it the usual
way, so he was just tossing his bait in at the head of the little
pocket and feeding line as his rig drifted straight down the current
—the worst possible way to tell what is going on at the other end
of the line, because feeding line leaves it slack and it takes tension
to feel a fish take the lure.

As we watched, Lucky casually said, "Throw your lures in.
There's a steelhead in there." To me that was hard to believe. A
poor piece of water, fished in the hardest possible way, and he said
a steelhead was there. While I questioned the whole thing, Ted
did just what Lucky suggested. In a second his little yarn fly was
drifting down the pocket of water, and sure enough, he hooked a
fish, which he proceeded to land.

I was still in a complete state of amazement even after the
whole thing was over. I couldn't get over the fact that Lucky had
known the fish was there, and when I asked him about it, he said
offhandedly that he had "felt the fish mouth the eggs, but not take
them," and he thought it might strike a lure. One thing about steelhead fishing: the minute you think you know a lot about it, someone like Lucky shows you just how much you don't know.

One other thing that should be pointed out in relation to drift
fishing for steelhead is how to recognize a strike when a fish does
take the lure. Much as I would like to say that steelhead hit like
the proverbial "freight train" so often described in fishing literature, the fact is that they seldom hit in this manner. Once in a
while they do, and at those happy times you are usually involved
with summer-run fish when the water is in its warm cycle. But

their most frequent manner of taking a lure makes you think the lure has just stopped in its swing across the current. It can be just a snag, which it is 99 percent of the time, or it can be a fish, so the only thing an angler can do is strike every time the lure comes to a halt. This means that often you set your hook solidly in a rock or a log, but once in a while it is a steelhead. The only safe thing to do is strike every time the lure pauses. Very few anglers are as proficient as Lucky O'Neill at recognizing the difference, and so we just strike back at everything. As they say, "It's the only way to go."

There is another way of fishing for steelhead that is totally different from drifting, and it goes by the picturesque name of "plunking." This is a method used in the big, slow-moving pools where a river runs more like a gigantic canal than a stream of riffles, bends and small pools such as those I have described. (You can also fish such water with a spoon by constantly reeling in line after a cast to keep the lure from stopping on the bottom.)

In plunking, lures like the Cherry Bobber which float up off the bottom must be used. Again, lead is used to sink the lure to the bottom, but in this case the rig is just cast out into the slow-moving water and allowed to sink to the bottom. There the lead anchors it, and the lure floats up a little and stays in one place with its spinner blade fluttering in the current to catch the eye of any passing fish. Frequently the bobber is made more attractive by being baited with eggs or worms. Along with fishing of eggs, it is the closest thing to bait fishing that normally takes place in steelheading. While waiting, the fisherman often props up his rod in a forked stick; otherwise, he just sits down and holds it and waits.

Plunking doesn't require a lot of casting or really much of anything except patience, but a lot of fish are caught this way from water that the average drift fisherman will pass up because it seems too slow. For me, plunking doesn't have enough activity; but who am I to say that any method that's legal and catches fish isn't good? The Cherry Bobber was originally designed for just this kind of fishing along the lower Columbia River.

Finally, there's fly fishing. Because I like to fly-fish and to fly-cast, to me it is the best. But it is just another way, though sometimes it really is the best. If the time comes when you want to try your hand at it, then I would suggest a 9-foot "bug-action" fly rod.

Such a rod when flexed carries the action, or bend, down about two-thirds of its length. For steelheading, it should be rated by the manufacturer for a No. 10 or a No. 11 line.

Because the casting is always to long distances, the line is a weight-forward, or WF in the code system. Preferred by some is a shooting head backed up by a monofilament shooting line of about 25-pound test. Monofilament, when properly handled, will shoot out the head, leader and fly farther than anything else. And when the monofilament tangles, it will tangle like nothing else, too. So "you pays your money and you takes your chances."

It is often said that anyone who can cast a fly 60 feet can catch a steelhead. Quite true. The trouble is that anyone who can cast 90 or 100 feet will catch a lot more fish. With modern fly-fishing tackle, the average steelhead fisherman will probably cast 80 to 90 feet. Some will cast 100 feet, but beware—those who brag about their 100-foot casts are many; those who actually cast that far are few. A very few will actually cast 110 and 120 feet. In my book they are fantastic.

Distance casting of this kind, in addition to requiring either a weight-forward line or a shooting head, is achieved by the use of a "double haul" in casting the line. The first haul, or pull, comes as the line starts toward the caster, and the second is made as the line starts forward for the cast. Combined with the double haul are various means of handling all the line that must be shot out. Some, myself included, hold several loops of running line in their mouths, and as the forward cast is made the line is allowed to peel out of their mouths. This method keeps the running line from extending downstream in the flowing water. On the other hand, casters have been known to lose false teeth, bridges and even real teeth.

The line itself is also different from the standard trout fly line. Because the fish are deep in moving water, a fast-sinking, or high-density, line is most often used. With such a line, a steelhead fly fisherman casts across the current and slightly upstream so that by the time the line swings by in front of him it is on or near the bottom. Then the fly is fished much the same as a drifter would fish a lure—right along the bottom in a swing. When the line has finished the swing and is pointing downstream, it is stripped in as fast as possible for another cast.

I would like to tell you of a few fly patterns that are used every-

An angler prepares to grab his fly-caught steelie behind the gills. A fly fisherman does well to buy his flies near the river he plans to fish, since favorites change with seasons and water conditions.

where successfully for steelhead, but the fact is that there are favorite patterns for almost every stream a person fishes, and favorite flies for the various seasons and heights of water. There are hundreds of steelhead flies, a majority of which are brightly colored with reds, whites and oranges, but there are many dark patterns which are also good. A fly fisherman is best advised to buy his patterns locally near the river he intends to fish and either copy them by tying flies or buy plenty—because he, like the spoon caster, will lose many.

For what it is worth, my favorite pattern is the Fall Favorite. It is a streamer fly, like most steelhead flies, with an orange polar bear wing, red feather hackle and oval silver-tinsel body. Tied on an extra-heavy-wire No. 2 hook, this fly has proved itself in the waters I have fished, but it is not good everywhere.

One of the biggest problems for the fly fisherman in steelhead fishing is the wind. No matter whether you are left-handed or right-handed, it always seems to come from the wrong side. You have no choice but to learn to live with it. Just one word of caution: Wear polarizing glasses when you can. They make seeing a rocky bottom much easier when you are wading; and if by the odd chance a gust of wind drives your fly into you as it passes, it will not hit you in the eye. I have never hit myself in the face, but I have been hit in the back of the head, in the neck and on my back and arm. There is nothing quite like the anguish you will feel when a heavy steelhead fly moving a hundred miles an hour hits you in the neck. It teaches you like nothing else how to keep the fly away from you at all times.

When fly fishing for steelhead is good, it is out of this world. Generally that means that the water temperature is above 45 degrees and not dropping. Fifty or even 55 degrees is even better. The water should also be clear or reasonably close to it. Dropping water temperatures seem to turn the fish off, and although steelhead can be caught in muddy water, it is generally by the fishing of bait, as in plunking.

The best steelhead fly fishing I ever lucked into resulted in an article by Ted Trueblood called "Shangri-la for Steelhead." In it Ted told of all the exciting things that happened to us during a period of two weeks on a certain river. The fishing was truly great, and we were there alone. To make it even more unbelievable, we were fishing most of the time within sight of a large U.S. highway, but nobody seemed to take notice of the 10-to-20-pound fish we were catching. And naturally we weren't advertising it. The kicker in the article was that Ted would say only that the river was within 500 miles of his home in southwestern Idaho, and that fishermen should find it for themselves.

For several years following that episode both Ted and I were plagued, badgered and hounded to reveal the whereabouts of the river, but we had pledged each other to secrecy. Guesses ranged from rivers in northern California through all of Oregon, Washington and southern British Columbia. Of course, the river was eventually located by steelheaders who figured it out, and it is not a secret anymore. It was the Salmon River near the town of Riggins in west-central Idaho, not more than 150 miles from where Ted lives.

It was one of those freak chances that are all too rare for steelhead fishermen. We just figured that the fish ought to be there then—and they were. It was October, the water was still warm, the skies were clear and the river was full of fish. We had miles of pools to fish, and the stream banks were untrodden.

I can't begin to remember the number of fish we landed, but it was a great many, and we lost many more. Every stretch of river was a new adventure, because we had to prospect each spot. Neither of us was acquainted with the river there, but Ted had a good eye for steelhead water. So many things happened that it's hard to pick the most outstanding one. I had a fish go downstream through a rapids so fast that it straightened my hook. We kept only enough fish to eat, and because we had a fish in camp, Ted had to release the biggest fish of the trip—which he landed after an epic fight with many jumps. It had to be at least 20 pounds.

Late one afternoon I remember driving to the edge of a new stretch of the river which was wide and flat, with large underwater boulders. We had only an hour or so before dark and so we plunged right in, wading with difficulty. Within a few minutes Ted hooked and landed a fish. Then I got one. Next we had two on for a brief moment. We were excited and yelling back and forth to each other. Finally we hooked two fish at practically the same time. They ran wildly across the huge pool, jumping intermittently. And finally, the moment I recall the most vividly happened. Both fish, not more than 20 yards apart, jumped high into the air at exactly the same instant. I can still see them frozen in air against the dark far bank. Such moments are rare indeed. In that hour Ted and I each landed six fish.

The best seasons for steelhead fishing vary according to the river, and many rivers have both winter-run and summer-run fish. One limiting factor is warm water. If a certain river, generally one that comes from a big drainage as does the Salmon, has a period of time during the summer when its temperature goes above the low 60s, then it is a good bet that steelhead are not there at that time. Otherwise, steelhead can be in a river at almost any time. However, there are peak months, and the only way to determine the best times is to talk to a guide, a newspaper outdoor writer in the area, a fisherman who knows the river or the local game warden. There are two rivers in British Columbia, the Babine and Kispiox, both excellent rivers and close to each other, with different peak times.

Other well-known steelhead rivers include the Skykomish, Snoqualmie, Humptulips, Bogachiel, Hoh, Queets and Quinault in Washington, and that is only a select few of the many steelhead rivers in that state. In Oregon there are the Rogue, the Umpquah and the Deschutes: again, a few of many—as in California, where

You don't have to be an athlete of Olympic caliber to land large steelhead on light tackle, but it helps.

the Klamath, the Eel, the Mad and the Salmon rivers are famous. Steelhead occur in rivers in only the northern half of California.

Most of our best rivers today are the shorter ones that come out of the coastal mountains and flow directly into the ocean. The reason for this is that such rivers have not been practical for the dam builders from the U.S. Army Corps of Engineers, the Bureau of Reclamation or the electric-power companies to bother with. The sad truth is that if a river is large enough to produce a big, dependable body of flowing water, these groups move in like vultures with bulldozers, destroying runs of millions of fish, both steelhead and salmon, by blocking them or by creating so many dams that the fish are killed going past them on their way either up or down, or by supersaturating the water with nitrogen so that the fish die from a condition much like the bends.

It is a sad comment, but the Salmon River in Idaho has suffered greatly from dams downstream on the Columbia River. The Idaho Power Company has blocked off the Snake River in Idaho with a series of dams for the almighty 110 volts AC and in doing so has killed off the last remaining runs of salmon and steelhead in southern Idaho. One run in the Snake River itself formerly went to within 60 miles of Boise. The other run was in the Weiser River, a fine little stream that produced thousands of steelhead and salmon. These streams today don't simply have fewer fish: they have *no* steelhead or salmon. And unless some solution to the menace of dams on the Columbia is found, eventually it may be that steelhead and salmon do not enter Idaho at all.

Similar examples are available in every state; but the dam builders still roll along. With each new dam they say that they will protect the fish runs, but they progressively and systematically kill them off—knowing full well, one begins to suspect, that when the fish are gone forever there will be no reason for fishermen to battle the construction of dams.

LAKE TROUT

BY TOM McNALLY

SALVELINUS NAMAYCUSH, the lake trout, is a product of clean, cold Northern waters. Generally speaking, the "laker" is found throughout the Canadian provinces, from the Atlantic to the Pacific, and in a few of the most northerly of the United States. Lake trout are called togue in Maine, where they are fairly common, and mackinaw in Northwestern states such as Montana and Washington. Over much of Canada they are referred to as gray trout.

Lake trout are reasonably plentiful in parts of Minnesota, Wisconsin and Michigan. Big Green Lake in south-central Wisconsin, only a couple of hundred miles from Chicago, is an extremely deep, cold lake with an excellent lake trout population, and it is fished avidly each spring and winter (through the ice) by followers of Namaycush.

The Great Lakes—mid-America's inland seas—also are notable for their lake trout fishing. Lake Superior, the coldest and probably cleanest of the Great Lakes, has always had good lake trout populations—large enough, in fact, to support not only a fine sport fishery but also commerical operations.

Within the last several years, the Lake Michigan lake trout population has made a remarkable comeback. Many years ago Lake

Michigan supported great numbers of lake trout, but they were decimated not only by parasitic, blood-sucking sea lampreys, but also by commerical netters who were foolishly permitted by authorities to overfish them. All that has changed, however, and as a result of effective lamprey controls, protection from overfishing and an abundant forage-fish supply, tens of thousands of lakers now cruise Lake Michigan.

The Michigan Department of Natural Resources should be credited with the initial attempts to bring back the Lake Michigan lake trout. About when Michigan introduced coho and chinook salmon to the Great Lakes, it banned commerical netting of trout in its portions of the Great Lakes and requested other conservation departments concerned to follow suit. Today, commercial netting and marketing of lake trout is forbidden by not only Michigan but also Indiana, Illinois and Wisconsin. Also, a sportfishing limit of five lake trout per day per angler has been imposed by the conservation department of each of those states except Wisconsin, where the limit is two fish.

With construction of the Saint Lawrence Seaway—the river, lock and canal system that joins the Great Lakes with the Atlantic—saltwater alewives entered the lakes and became a nearly inexhaustible, year-round food supply for lake trout and salmon. Alewives are particularly abundant in Lake Michigan, and as a result Lake Michigan's lakers have been showing phenomenal growth rates. Until recently, lake trout from Lake Michigan averaged about 2 to 3 pounds, with ones of 6 to 8 pounds considered good. By the early 1970s, however, lake trout of 6 to 10 pounds were commonplace, and ones from 15 to 20 pounds were being caught with regularity.

But the finest lake trout fishing remains in the wilderness waters of Canada.

Lake trout can and do thrive in some cold, shallow lakes and in certain rivers possessing the lakelike qualities required by lake trout, but they rarely do well in lakes not having depths of at least 100 feet. Lake trout need water with a high oxygen content, and therefore the larger, deeper lakes are most suitable. Wide and open lakes are frequently wind-thrashed and turbulent, and such heavy wave action aerates and agitates lake water—thus adding to and distributing oxygen. Very small and protected lakes, even though clean, deep and cold, seldom maintain respectable lake trout populations. Lakers cannot prosper where water temperature rises above 65 degrees, and they prefer a much lower temperature of about 45 degrees.

Lake trout are common to many lakes in Alaska, but Alaska as a rule does not provide trophy-size lake trout. Certainly the finest of North America's lake trout angling is to be found in selected lakes in Alberta, Ontario, Manitoba, Saskatchewan and the Northwest Territories. It is axiomatic that pure, hard-to-get-to wilderness lakes are where the trophy fish abound. It takes a long time to grow a lake trout of 40, 50 or more pounds, so one shouldn't anticipate mountable fish from waters that are seasonally pounded by hordes of anglers.

It is impossible in limited space to name all the Canadian lakes that offer extraordinary lake trout fishing, but among the best is Great Bear Lake, on the Arctic Circle in the Northwest Territories. This is a comparatively "new" lake to fishermen, but it has been opened up with the establishment of comfortable camps on its shores. As of this writing, there are four camps on Great Bear that provide five days' fishing; transportation to and from Winnipeg, Manitoba, and all other usual package items (guides, meals, etc.) for about $900 per person. Top fishing for Arctic grayling also is available at Great Bear, and fly-out trips to places like Tree River can be made for Arctic char.

Saskatchewan has numerous prime lake trout waters—and in fact, its Lake Athabasca once gave up a 102-pound laker, the largest known, though it was not caught on rod and reel. Lake Athabasca remains a superior lake trout angling spot.

The province's Black Lake, near the bush town of Stony Rapids, is another good lake and in my experience is ideal for the angler who prefers to cast for his trout rather than to troll deep down with wire or lead-core or heavily weighted line. Simply by casting out, allowing the lure (usually a lead-head jig) to sink 15 feet or so, I have taken lakers weighing 8 to 12 pounds on every other cast at Black Lake in late June and July.

Other famed laker spots in Saskatchewan are Wollaston, Cree, Reindeer and Lac La Ronge. All except La Ronge are fly-in lakes, and all have excellent northern pike, lake whitefish and grayling fishing in addition to the lake trout angling. I particularly enjoy

Giant lake trout like this 40-pounder are products of wilderness waters. This laker was taken at Black Lake in northern Saskatchewan. The specks in the photo are blackflies.

Wollaston Lake for the exceptional grayling fly fishing in the Cochrane River, which feeds it, and also for its fine shallow bays where the angler can easily boat a dozen or more northern pike of over 15 pounds in a single afternoon. You can drive to Lac La Ronge, put up in the town of La Ronge and either fish there or arrange for trips to distant points on the 450-square-mile lake.

Many of Ontario's lakes are more readily accessible than those of some of the other Canadian provinces; therefore Ontario waters are highly attractive to thousands of anglers—especially those coming from mid-American population centers such as Chicago, Detroit, Milwaukee, Minneapolis–Saint Paul and Des Moines. Numerous Ontario lakes, such as Rainy Lake at Fort Frances, which can be reached by auto, have been fished by both sport and commercial fishermen for years, and therefore provide only smallish lakers. Remote Lake Simcoe, in northern Ontario, is one of the province's best, having a heavy population of big lake trout.

The excellence of Manitoba's lake trout fishery closely approaches that of some lake angling in the Northwest Territories and Saskatchewan. Gods Lake, a wilderness fly-in spot, long has been known for its prime laker fishing, and even today it consistently gives up lake trout ranging from 30 to 50 pounds. There are at least two camps operating on Gods Lake, the oldest and probably best-known being Tom Ruminski's Gods Lake Lodge, which is ideally located on the lakeshore at the head of Gods River, famed for its large brook trout. Ruminski's camp is comfortable, has all the modern conveniences and can be reached by conventional planes as well as float planes, since in the mid-sixties Ruminski constructed a sizable landing strip.

An outcamp has been established by Ruminski a few hundred miles north of Gods Lake on the Wolverine River. The river drains a large lake, but while the lake has a good supply of trout, the interesting fishing is in the river. The river is broad, with a fairly good flow (there are even rapids in some areas) and a series of wide, shallow pools lakelike in character. The pools are stiff with trout of 10, 15 and 20 pounds, and there are 30-pounders, too. The pools generally range from 5 to 15 feet deep, with perhaps the deepest holes no more than 20 feet deep.

Because the trout in this section of the Wolverine are of such good average size, because there is current and because the water is shallow, I suspect there are few places where the fisherman can enjoy greater sport with lake trout. Anglers catch trout here by casting lures, rather than by trolling or bait fishing, and light spinning or bait-casting tackle—such as might be used in bass fishing—can be employed. This is also the place for the fisherman who wants a respectable laker on a fly rod. By drifting with the current and casting 6-inch-long yellow-red McNally Magnum streamer

This 15-pound laker was caught through the ice at Lake Simcoe, Ontario. (Canada Pictures)

flies, I caught dozens of Wolverine lake trout ranging from 6 to 28 pounds.

Ruminski's Wolverine camp is naturally somewhat primitive, without such luxuries as hot and cold running water, but it is a practical and very comfortable camp. Presumably it is being improved each year, but when I was there last accommodations consisted of a large general bunk house with canvas tenting for a roof and plywood sheeting for siding and floor. Beds and bedding were excellent, and the food couldn't have been better. Boats, motors and Cree guides also left little to be desired.

It should be pointed out, though, that a major drawback to fishing at such outcamps is the transportation and communications problem. Since the camp is reached only by bush floatplane, weather conditions dictate whether the camp is accessible or inaccessible. Communication with the outside world is via radio, and the amateur rigs have been known to fail on occasion. The point is that if bad weather should set in at these remote bush camps and someone in camp needs serious medical attention (for a heart attack, a broken leg, etc.), little can be done. North Country bush pilots fly by the seat of their pants, and while they are skilled airmen, they cannot and do not fly in inclement weather with bad visibility. Veteran bush pilots know that chances of survival are slim indeed if they should be forced down in the unbroken wilderness.

Now for something more about old Namaycush himself.

The laker is the largest of the trouts. Its coloration varies greatly, depending upon the area it's caught in and even the season. The majority of lake trout are a uniform dark gray, with irregular pale checking or spotting all over the body. The thin lateral sensory line is distinct, running from the topmost edge of the gill plate to the tail, which is deeply forked.

The flesh of lake trout may range from a soapy or creamy white to a bright orange-red. Many people consider lake trout something of a table delicacy, and as I indicated before, they are of commercial value. The smaller lakers, ranging from 3 to 6 pounds, are the best table fare—and at no time are they better-tasting than when quick-fried in deep fat over a wood fire on the rocky shore of a Northern lake. And no one can do this better than a Cree Indian guide.

The larger lake trout, 15 pounds or more, are usually steaked for cooking, or baked whole. Lakers of such size tend to be extremely oily, and are actually best if smoked. Smoked lake trout, properly done, pleases the palate of the most discriminating gourmet.

In most waters lake trout feed primarily on smaller fishes, especially smelt, chubs, ciscoes, lake whitefish, yellow perch, suckers and even grayling and smaller lake trout.

Most lake trout spawn in the fall in very deep water over rocky reefs or gravel bottoms. Though they often spawn at depths of 100 feet or more, in some suitable areas on the northern edges of their range they will spawn successfully in shoal waters. Naturally, spawning time varies according to locale: earlier in the fall in the Far Northern lakes, later in the winter in the southerly part of the lake trout's range. Generally speaking, lake trout spawn from the latter part of August to early January.

Because the lake trout is a trout, is a product of clean, cold water, readily strikes lures and is good to eat, it certainly rates as a most desirable game fish. But the lake trout is not one of the world's great game fishes. First off, it is most frequently caught only by very deep fishing, usually trolling, and such techniques do not afford maximum sport to the angler when a fish is hooked. Too, lake trout rarely jump when hooked. The typical scrap with a laker involves the strike, a short but fairly fast dead-away run, then a gradual twirling resistance as the fish is drawn close. Lake trout are notorious for rolling over and over, fouling the leader or line around the body as the fish gradually wears down. I have seen lake trout so rolled up in line that if the line were bandage, they would be wrapped like mummies.

None of which is to say that the lake trout is no fun to catch. It most assuredly is. When they can be taken by the casting of lures, even lead-head jigs fished very deep, lakers can provide sport. In some lakes lake trout will be in comparatively shallow water all of the open-water season and so can be fished for with light tackle and cast to, much as one might fish shoreline rocks, steep bluffs, peninsulas and shallow reefs for bass; and such fishing can be exciting, especially if the trout weigh 10 pounds or better.

Too, the angler seeking maximum sport with lakers can gear his tackle accordingly. In other words, if the trout are running smallish, 3 to 4 pounds or so, ultralight spinning tackle may be used—

Maximum sport can be had with even modest-size lake trout by the use of ultralight spinning tackle. Tom Mc-Nally hoists an 8-pounder from Eagle Lake, Ontario, that fell for a small jig fished with 4-pound-test line.

say a rod of 1½ ounces measuring 4½ feet long and line of 2-, 3-, or 4-pound test. Lake trout of any size will be a rodful on such equipment.

Even when deep trolling is required to take lake trout, and heavily weighted lines are necessary to get the lures down where the fish are, wise fishermen still can rig so that they get some action out of the fish they hook. First off, no extra-heavy, deep-sea tackle is necessary. Ordinary medium-light spinning or bait-casting bass tackle will do, and the line can be rigged with whatever lead weights are necessary—plus a sinker-release mechanism. When a fish strikes, the sinker release frees the lead weights and the fisherman then fights his hooked lake trout on a free line—thus getting maximum action from his fish.

Finally, great sport can be had with lake trout by fly fishing. Granted, reasonable opportunities to take lake trout on flies are not everyday occurrences, since the fish most often are at least 20 or 30 feet down; but at many lakes in the Far North lakers can readily be taken on flies. A lake trout of even modest size—say 6, 8 or 10 pounds—can provide a lot of action for the fly rodder.

There are, of course, many ways to fish for lake trout, and therefore the variety of tackle that can be used is considerable.

Probably the majority of lake trout caught are taken by deep trolling, no matter if the area fished is Great Bear Lake in the Northwest Territories or one of the Finger Lakes in New York State. Deep-trolling methods and tackle are fairly standardized, and in some places trout are being caught today just as they were seventy-five-years ago.

Stiff deep-sea rods, with big reels loaded with wire line and large spoons for lures, are typical lake trout tackle for the average angler in most parts of the United States and Canada. Even at famed Great Bear Lake, where the bulk of the trout are hooked at depths of 50 feet or less, most fishermen use heavy rigs. A very common outfit seen at Great Bear is a saltwater spinning rig—a stout spinning rod (surf type) 7½ to 9 feet long, a huge open-face spinning reel designed for surf casting and several hundred yards of monofilament line testing no less than 20 pounds. The popular lure is always a spoon, one as large as your hand, with treble hooks big enough to hold a 150-pound tarpon.

Some fishermen using wire line, which naturally takes the lure or bait deeper than conventional mono or braided line, use special reels designed for wire-line fishing. They are narrow-spool reels, but the diameter of the spool is great so that line can be reeled in quickly. The reels are designed with large-diameter spools so that the layers of wire line will not dig in and so that the line is spooled onto the reel in wide turns. Wire line that is tightly wound onto a small-diameter spool will kink and become unserviceable.

Lead-core lines also are used by some fishermen for their deep trolling, and as when wire line is employed, additional lead sinkers may or may not be used. Generally speaking, wire and lead-core lines are usually selected by fishermen striving to do away with lead sinkers. Lead is needed, of course, to get monofilament or braided lines down to any effective depth.

While the rod selected for deep trolling is chiefly a matter of preference insofar as action (stiffness), length, weight and type (whether deep-sea, heavy freshwater, boat or "bay" rod) are concerned, most fishermen who troll way down for lakers choose a stout glass rod about 5 feet in length. Usually it will have a strong handle, long enough to grip easily with two hands or to place solidly in a rod holder mounted on a boat's transom or gunwale.

If trolling is to be done with lines other than wire or lead-core, then large-capacity, multiplying reels with level-wind mechanisms are preferred. Light saltwater reels are excellent, since they normally are sturdy and have good line capacity. The reel for laker trolling should accommodate at least 250 yards of 15- or 20-pound-test line. It must be remembered that at times the angler may have to put a lure down to a depth of 300 feet and, with bowing of the line, it may be necessary to pay out 400 to 450 feet of line. Then, should a fish be hooked, it may run off another 100 or 200 feet of line before gradually succumbing to rod pressure. So a good store of line is frequently needed in deep trolling for Namaycush.

Monofilament, which is single-strand nylon line, is chosen over braided line by many veteran lake trout fishermen. They reason that mono takes on very little water and so usually spools onto a reel better than braided line. It also sinks more quickly than braided line. Other veteran fishermen select a braided line (of nylon, Dacron, etc.) because they do not want the stretch that often characterizes monofilament lines. Too much stretch, especially when yards and yards of line are out, makes hooking fish difficult.

The terminal rigging used in deep trolling for lake trout is as variable as the other aspects of laker trolling tackle. As a rule, a monofilament leader is desirable, its length and test depending upon conditions. When you're fishing for spooky trout in very clear water, or in areas hard fished, it is wise to use as long and fine a leader as practical. For most laker fishing a leader 6 feet long, testing 10 to 22 pounds, is adequate.

Leaders are usually tied with improved clinch knots to a three-way swivel, onto which are also tied the fishing line and a weaker line to which the sinker is secured. Having the sinker or sinkers tied to weak line will make it possible to break off the sinker, should it become fouled, without losing all of the terminal tackle.

The best sinkers for such trolling are bell types, or dipsey sinkers, if the angler intends to bump bottom. Dipsey sinkers do not readily foul on obstructions. Weights especially designed for trolling are the keel and drail sinkers, while some fishermen like clinch-on and diamond sinkers. Clinch-on sinkers are really a bad choice; they troll, or cut through the water, well but are pinched onto a line rather than tied, and so frequently loosen and are lost.

A barrel swivel, or a barrel swivel with snap, is desirable as a leader–lure connection. Just about any lure that is trolled will put

twist in the fishing line unless a swivel is employed. Swivels sometimes spook fish, however, so many anglers prefer to tie a single
barrel swivel into the leader about 2 or 3 feet up from the lure. So
located, a swivel will prevent line twist, yet will not likely be noticed by a striking fish.

Three-way barrel and barrel-snap swivels are available in different finishes—such as chrome, black or brass. Fishermen who
hope trout won't see their swivels generally choose black ones,
while other fishermen figure the flash from chrome or brass swivels
helps attract fish. I've gone both ways with good luck.

If you want to get maximum fight out of the fish you hook when
trolling deep with weights, use one of the many sinker-release
mechanisms on the market. A sinker release is a simple gadget
which, when fixed to the fishing line and the line leading to the
sinkers, releases the sinkers at the strike of a fish. The jolt caused
by a lake trout's hitting the lure or bait triggers the sinker-release
mechanism so that the sinker falls away, leaving the fish to fight
without the drag of a heavy weight. The result is much greater
sport with hooked fish.

I suppose keels and planers should be included in any discussion
of terminal rigging for deep lake trout trolling. Keels are metal or
plastic attachments, shaped much like the deep keel of a sailboat,
which are tied into the line not far from the lure to prevent twisting. Since the lake trout angler may troll for hours, frequently
circling, doubling back and crisscrossing previous tracks, a well-
designed keel in the rig can be well worthwhile.

Planers are unique little devices designed to get a lure or bait
down to the desired depth without the use of lead weights, or with
a minimum of lead weight. They're made of metal or plastic, and
while there are various designs, they are generally thin, rectangular units equipped with rings, snaps, etc., so they can be tied into
the fishing line or into a separate line used to take the fishing line
down. By virtue of their design and construction, planers dig deep
and dive when pulled through the water. They are effective and
are very popular among Great Lakes trout fishermen.

Downriggers are used also to get lures or baits down to about
any depth. In essence, a downrigger is a separate line—a strong
one—that is attached to a very heavy lead weight, such as a 10-,
20-, or 30-pound "cannonball"; an iron window sash or even a

coffee can filled with cement. A clothespin or a similar line release is attached to the downrigger line just above the weight, and the fishing line is secured in it. The downrigger takes the fishing line quickly down to the desired depth, and the line is payed out and trolled. When a fish strikes, the fishing line is automatically released from the downrigger and the fish is played on a free line. Downriggers have injected a great deal more sport into the game of deep trolling.

Other gadgets used by the deep-trolling laker fisherman are fish attractors such as "flashers" and "cowbells." The normal haunt of a lake trout and his friends is a vast one indeed, often including several dozen square miles of very deep water. At any moment Namaycush and buddies may be over here swimming at a depth of 30 feet, or way over there swimming at 100 feet; so it is not easy to locate lake trout. In addition, it's possible to troll a couple of lures or few pieces of bait close to the fish without attracting their attention. Fish attractors are used because they will often draw trout from great distances to look over a fisherman's offerings.

Cowbells are the oldest attractors used in lake trout trolling. A cowbell rig is simply a group of large spinners which are usually mounted several inches apart on a length of heavy wire. Normally the spinners are of different finishes and coloring, and big ones 2 to 3 inches long are preferred. There'll be barrel swivels and snaps at either end of the rig so that the cowbells can be tied into the fishing line several feet ahead of the lure or bait. Some fishermen drop cowbells down on separate lines.

Flashers are a comparatively new kind of fish attractor. They are rectangular pieces of metal or plastic, generally 6 or 10 inches long and 2 to 3 inches wide. They are very thin, mounted with swivels and can be used in the fishing line or on a separate line. Bright chrome flashers are most popular, but brass and bronze ones are available, as are some of plastic that have bright fluorescent red or yellow finishes.

Cowbells and flashers are trolled along with the lures or bait, and their sparkling, glistening light reflections can be spotted by trout in clear water at great distances. Trout are readily drawn to such attractors, and when close to them they spot the lures or baits and, frequently, strike and are hooked.

Since in most lake trout waters lakers feed primarily on smaller

fishes such as smelt and ciscoes, spoons are the most popular lures.
The size of spoon used depends chiefly on the average size of the
trout present, as well as on the sizes of the forage fishes available
to the trout. Small spoons, say 2 or 3 inches long, are about right
when the trout seldom exceed 3 pounds; ones 3 to 5 inches are better for trout in the 6-to-12-pound class; and when large trout are
expected, fish of 15 pounds or more, most anglers use spoons ranging in length from 6 to 9 inches.

What finish is best on spoons for lakers is problematical from
day to day. The smart angler will constantly alter his spoons as to
both size and finish until he finds the one(s) that takes fish. As a
rule, bright finishes are best: chrome, silver, brass, copper, etc.
Such spoons reflect the most light when fished at great depths or
in dingy or rain-clouded water.

*A 27-pound lake trout is gaffed at Saskatchewan's Wapata Lake. Notice
the large spoon, stout rod and saltwater reel used in deep trolling.
(Saskatchewan Government)*

Sometimes bright spoons are the best choice on dull days, and darker ones—even those finished in black—on bright, sunny days. Some of the colors that have been notable for taking lake trout over the years are orange, red-and-white, black-and-white, green, green-and-white, yellow and all of those colors with contrasting diamonds or circles of other colors.

Artificial plugs also can be trolled successfully for lake trout. Large plugs, either one-piece or jointed, are generally best, and any of the deep-running name plugs will take fish. As with spoons, though, the angler should keep switching plug types and finishes until he finds the one that takes the most fish. One of the really important factors in trolling for lakers with plugs is to use a plug that trolls well at various depths and that does not foul the line or its hooks every time the boat is turned tightly or the trolling speed is altered. Many plugs that are good fish getters when cast do not troll well.

Some lake trout fishermen troll with bait, and it is an oddity with lake trout that they will take cut bait as well as whole live or dead fish. Live smelt 6 to 8 inches long are an excellent bait, and dead ones of the same size are a good second choice. Also good are suckers, ciscoes, alewives, chubs, lake shiners and golden roach minnows.

There are countless methods of attaching minnows to hooks for lake trout trolling, but in general tandem hooks and wire minnow harnesses are utilized. If the minnow, alive or dead, is not carefully attached to the hooks, much fishing time will be wasted in replacing minnows that tear free during trolling.

One method that works well in trolling minnows for lake trout involves a long-shanked hook with a barbed pin for holding the minnow secure. The pin is inserted lengthwise through the minnow's body; it keeps the bait straight, firmly in position, and aids in preventing twisting.

Fishing with cut bait—which can be portions or halves of any of the baitfish mentioned—is sometimes done by trollers, but more frequently cut bait is used by still-fishermen or those who drift slowly in boats. The bait is fished at different depths and, of course, in different places until a laker bites. Drifting over deep reefs and bars, over sunken islands, in the vicinity of known springholes and off rocky peninsulas and bluffs is a good way to take trout on cut bait.

Ice fishermen after lake trout invariably use live bait, sinking smelt or other suitable minnows deep down in areas where they know from experience that lake trout winter. In some areas fishermen get more lake trout through winter's ice than they do throughout the open-water season.

Trolling for lake trout is, most of the time, a seek-and-hope-to-find affair. Three factors are important: trolling speed, depth and area fished.

Experienced anglers head for typical lake trout water—that is, water over deep reefs, rocky bars, submerged islands or rock piles and similar bottom formations. They begin trolling at moderate speed and check depths as the boat is guided over likely spots and from one promising area to another. Initial fishing may be at a depth of only 15 feet; then lures are consistently fished deeper and deeper, until, at some lakes, they may be fished 500 feet down. Of course, if it is known that lake trout at Big Flatbottom Lake are never hooked at depths less than 200 feet, then even the village idiot is going to start fishing his baits at a depth of at least 200 feet. Trolling speeds are altered continually too, since at any given time modest speed—or very slow or very fast speed—may take fish.

Trolling should be executed with some sort of pattern. Helter-skelter, aimless, nondirected trolling is illogical and a waste of time, with any catch coming chiefly as a result of luck. It's best to strike a straightaway trolling course, with a definite objective, or target area, in mind. One should project his thinking to the lake trout holding areas beneath the surface, deep down, and visualize the pattern of his fishing. A reverse course can be taken when the target area is reached, and that run should also be done on a straight line. If neither run produces fish, then a saw-toothed trolling pattern may be assumed, and finally long, curving, S-shaped patterns may be run over the area. During all trolling runs different depths are tried, as well as various lures. If no fish are taken from a specific area by these tactics, then another area should be fished.

"Wind trolling" often is a good way to take lake trout. It involves motoring upwind to the far end of a lake, if it is a small one, then drifting back with the wind while trolling baits or lures. The skiff is turned broadside to the wind when the downlake drift is started, and all persons aboard sit toward the downwind side of the boat. This will raise the upwind side enough for the wind to shove under the boat and push it steadily down the lake. Rods are held over the high side of the skiff, lures released and allowed to reach fishing depth; then reels are thrown into gear and trolling begun. Generally this is a slow trolling system, but it can be particularly effective on some lakes because it allows lures to reach maximum depths and to be fished slowly and tantalizingly. This same system can be used to very good effect in the fishing of lead-head jigs, with the angler yanking his rod in a uniform cadence, giving his jig vigorous action as it hops over the bottom.

Jigging, incidentally, is a productive system for taking lake trout. It involves the use of lead-head jigs, those weighted lures which have been used in fresh- and saltwater fishing for years but which are considered new to laker fishing. A jig is a single-hook, lead-bodied lure with a skirt or tail of a material such as bucktail (dyed), saddle hackle, impala, marabou or strands of nylon. A jig's lead head can be any of several shapes, ranging all the way from ball-shaped to flat or coin-shaped. Some jigs are equipped with a spinner blade or two.

All jigs have one thing in common: they cast like bullets and sink like lead—which is what they are. The jig's ability to get down deep in a hurry is the feature that makes it so popular with so many lake trout fishermen.

Deep jigging can be done with spinning or bait-casting tackle. Anglers cast out the jig, allow it to sink to or near bottom by paying out line and then fish it tantalizingly over the bottom. A "pumping" routine is most commonly used in bottom bouncing with jigs. That is, the rod is twitched sharply upward to make the jig hop off the bottom a foot or so; slack line is quickly respooled; then the rod is twitched or yanked again so that the jig hops again. When this is repeated to a cadence, the result is that the jig hippity-hops along, fishing in a very lifelike manner at precisely the depth the angler chooses. Few techniques involving repetitious casting are more potent on lake trout.

I have enjoyed very good lake trout fishing at numerous lakes by casting lead-head jigs shoreward along granite bluffs, over shallow reefs, etc. Lake trout will frequently be found in such areas at depths of 15 feet or less in the northern lakes, and a jig cast from a slowly moving boat will go down to the fish quickly and, when pumped along properly, entice hard strikes. I particularly enjoy fishing ⅝-ounce yellow marabou jigs that way on bass-weight bait-casting tackle for lakers of 6 pounds or better.

Modern electronic fish finders are a real boon to the lake trout fisherman. First off, most electronic fishing aids reveal water depth, which is of major importance to the lake trout angler. Some also show the kind of bottom present—whether it is mud, gravel, weeds or rocks. And still others, the better ones, will reveal the location of any fish present, showing the precise depth and, with some margin for error, even the quantity and sizes of the fish.

Such fish locators are invaluable to the serious lake trout angler, since they can reveal whether or not he is working over productive or at least promising lake trout water—rock, sand or gravel bottom as opposed to mud, weeds, etc.—to say nothing of their ability to actually pinpoint the locations of fish.

It must be realized, though, that finding fish and catching them are two different things. It's quite possible to locate, via an electronic fishing aid, a fine pod of lake trout and then be unable to entice them to strike. At least the angler would know, however, that he was fishing over fish and not over empty water.

There is no disputing the practical value of electronic fish finders, including special electronic depth meters and temperature gauges. There are battery-powered items on the market today that instantly give the depth of water and the temperatures from the surface all the way to the bottom. The well-equipped lake trout hunter will have not only a quality fish locator but also a temperature gauge and, if his locator does not reveal specific depths, a depth meter as well.

In spring and sometimes again in early fall, lake trout will be found at or near the surface in many lakes, even in the southern extremity of the fish's range. And at many Far North lakes, trout can be taken close to the surface throughout the open-water season. For example, Nokomis Lake, northeast of Cranberry Portage, Manitoba, will produce lake trout in shallows of 15 feet or less all summer long. I have fished Nokomis several times—usually with Willard McPhadrain, a former Cranberry Portage camp operator—and each visit we had fast fishing for lakers by casting with light tackle along the jagged rock banks and points. Nokomis, however, has mostly small trout, on the average well under 8 pounds.

When lakers are within 15 feet of the surface, they are setups

Rocky shores are good places to look for lake trout when the water temperature is cold. This one was caught on light bait-cast gear. (Erwin Bauer)

for the angler who wants to spin for them, or to use bait-casting tackle. And they can also be taken at this depth by fly fishing if the fly rodder uses a sinking line or a weighted fly and gives the fly time to sink.

I have been fortunate to enjoy many days of lake trout fishing in many areas where all we had to do was paddle slowly along rocky shores and cast spoons, plugs or jigs on spinning or bait-casting outfits to take laker after laker. At times such fishing is just like working a shallow lakeshore for largemouth bass.

The tackle used for this fishing is not unlike bass tackle, either, with the ideal spinning outfit being a rod of 6½ or 7 feet, medium action, mounted with a medium-size freshwater open-face spinning reel. A line testing 8 or 10 pounds is about right. The bait-casting outfit also should be medium, with the rod 5 to 6 feet long, carrying a quality level-wind reel with good drag, and line testing from 10 to 15 pounds. I prefer nylon monofilament line to braided line because for me it casts better—much smoother going through the guides, with less friction—and it is certainly less visible in the water than are most braided lines.

Good lures for this type of lake trout fishing are wobbling spoons, sinking plugs, spinners, spinner/feathers or spinner/bucktail combinations and lead-head jigs. Such lures should be retrieved rather slowly, although change-of-pace retrieves with quick jerks and stops sometimes trigger hesitant trout to strike.

The most pleasant days I have had in pursuit of old Namaycush have been those trips on which I was able to take trout either on ultralight spinning tackle or on fly tackle. Many fishermen, unfortunately, never even consider trying for lake trout with flies—which is pathetic considering that a lake trout likes nothing better than a big, lively streamer fly and that such great sport can be had fly fishing for lakers.

Appropriate fly tackle for lakers is a bit on the heavy side. Ideal for the purpose is a bass-bugging outfit or a light saltwater fly outfit such as you would use for bonefishing. The rod should be 8½ to 9½ feet long; I usually use a hollow glass rod 9 feet long weighing 5 ounces. It has a fast tip action but a slow, powerful butt, so that short casts can be made with ease yet long casts can be made very quickly with a minimum of false casts.

A quality fly reel should be used in fly fishing for lake trout because one never knows when a 20-pounder may hit. The reel should be single-action type, with a strong, dependable drag. At least 50 yards of 15- to 18-pound-test backing line should be on the reel behind the fly line, which should be three-diameter, or triple-taper type, of a size to match the rod. For the rods mentioned earlier this line would be at least a GBF or WF-8 line, or a GAF (WF-9) line.

Author Tom McNally collars a small lake trout hooked on a 3-inch-long streamer fly. Trout hit flies readily when in the shallows.

The leader for lake trout naturally depends upon overall fishing conditions—clarity of the water, time of day, wariness of the trout, size of fish, etc.—but generally a leader 9 to 12 feet long and tapered to a tippet of 6-, 8- or 10-pound test will do.

The most productive flies are streamers—which is not to say that lake trout cannot be taken on wet flies, nymphs and even dry flies. I have caught a zillion lake trout in shallow water fishing Phillip's Bead-Head, Multi-Wing streamers and fairly ordinary streamers with saddle-hackle wings, measuring about 3 inches long. I have caught much larger trout, though not as many, on two streamers of my own design. One is the McNally Magnum; the other, the McNally Smelt. The Magnum is red-yellow, ranges in length from 5 to 7 inches and is made of superlong, flowing saddle hackles with chenille for a body. The Smelt is more complicated—tied of tinsel, polar bear hair (when available), grizzly hackles, bucktail and other goodies like peacock herl and guinea fowl cheeking. Anyway, both flies have exceptional action in the water and have been proved as lake trout takers. I'm sure, though, that any good streamer of a decent size, say at least 3 inches in length, when properly fished around lake trout is going to catch lake trout. Hook sizes for laker streamers should be 1/0, 2/0 and 3/0, the last-mentioned being plenty big enough to handle any lake trout most fishermen will ever encounter—which means a laker of 60 pounds or more.

If you are going to be into very large trout, then stout leaders may be called for—not because lakers are such terrific battlers, but because they tend to roll up in leaders and line, and fine leader tippets cannot take that kind of abuse.

A halting, darting, jumping action should be imparted to the streamer after you cast it to where you hope Namaycush awaits. Strip the fly along through the water in foot-long hauls, pausing only momentarily to let the fly settle—its wings fluttering lifelike in the water—and to give any trailing lake trout a chance to home in on the fly, decide it is too good to resist and then swat it mightily.

Excepting those rare instances when lake trout can be taken on dry flies—such as at Great Bear Lake in the wee hours after midnight—streamer fishing for lakers is the pinnacle of the sport. I hope that you experience it.

LARGEMOUTH BASS

BY HOMER CIRCLE

HEAD AND FINS above all other sport fishes in America stands the largemouth bass. So rugged is this rascal that he is found in all states but Alaska. And to me he is so engaging and challenging that I have pursued him over four continents and for over forty-six years.

He's a tough antagonist. Would you believe that the entire first year I fished for bass I got my eye wiped? That's right. Not one bass. And, Lord, how I tried. I was a real competitor, age 12 at the time. Why, those bass had my dobber so low it wouldn't even make a shadow.

Maybe that's why I stayed with it. I found other sports fairly easy to learn. But that bass defied, outwitted, frustrated, befouled and eluded me to the point at which I—not he—was the one who got hooked!

And looking back, what wonderful memories those nearly five decades hold! In the hope that my own observations, notes, tricks, tactics and techniques may help to start you on the same enjoyable chase, I offer you the following.

First, let's take a close look at our quarry. It helps to know a few things about the world of the largemouth and some of the significant items that will give you a feel for his personality.

The largemouth bass is the heavyweight of the black bass family and is due most of the credit for the fighting image of its clan. It has a number of attributes that make it a great game fish.

It has impact on the strike; leaping and tail-walking energy to burn; stamina for strong runs and bulldog tussling; sufficient cunning to lose you if you fumble, even momentarily; comparative abundance—and above-average flavor when properly kept and cooked.

The quickest and most certain way to identify a largemouth bass, from a wee one to a whopper, is to close the mouth and observe the jaw joint, or maxillary. If it ends at a point well behind the rear margin of the eye, it's a largemouth.

The dorsal fin is another indicator. It will be deeply notched, with no membrane between the spiny and soft dorsal segments. Coloration varies, even among bass in the same lake, so that that is a poor method of identification.

Originally, the largemouth bass thrived from the Mississippi River to the Atlantic Coast—essentially, the eastern half of the United States. But today, thanks to the amazing ability of this fish to adapt itself to marginal environments, it is found throughout the United States and southern Canada, as well as in numerous foreign countries.

The world record for this fish stands where it has since 1932 when George Perry hit the jackpot with his 22¼-pounder from Montgomery Lake, Georgia. If this record is broken, I believe the largemouth bass that does it will come from Georgia, Florida or Southern California.

The largemouth is a solitary fish by nature. It will take over a stump, pocket in the weeds or lily pads or other guardable area and run off any other fish that approach. That's why it is fairly easy to locate one around cover such as bushes, logs, ledges, roots, lily pads, dark pockets, rock piles, sunken islands (reefs) and fallen timber.

The largemouth is motivated by water temperatures. When it reaches upwards of 55 degrees in the spring, the largemouth yields to the spawning urge. It appears to be most active, and is most readily caught, when the temperature is in the 60-to-70-degree range. When the water temperature soars into the 80s, you'll find it difficult to locate largemouths—unless it be during the cooler hours of night.

The largemouth is a steady feeder and about as omnivorous as they come. The list of creatures that have been taken from stomachs of its species would fill a page. Included in the list are birds, mice, cigarette filters, baby muskrats, bottle caps, various other metallic objects and sticks. Its normal diet will be covered later in this chapter.

Such a voracious feeding habit often makes the largemouth easy to catch—but not always. To be a consistent catcher one has to go often, learn the whereabouts of largemouths in his area and keep returning to those spots which are currently paying off.

Be prepared to get your eye wiped about half the time, with few or no bass despite your best efforts. But there will be those minutes, sometimes hours, when these fish turn it on and give you some of the most memorable sprees a man could hope for. Persistence is the keynote. Without it, don't expect to achieve much of a reputation as a largemouth bass expert.

Look for the explosive largemouth among submerged brush and in weed beds. (Kentucky Department of Fish and Wildlife Resources)

In lakes, the largemouth will be found along the shorelines most of the year. Where you catch one good bass, remember the exact spot and return: another bass will take over the vacated hangout, and the more of such places you know, the better will be your score.

As you move along a shoreline, look for overhanging branches, stumps, fallen trees, rocky shores or points of land that run into deep water, overhanging cliffs, midlake islands, deep holes, undercut banks, wrecked boats, etc. Get the idea? Anything that offers a hiding place is where you'll find Mr. Bass.

And here are the reasons: it offers the bass protection from his enemies; it provides him concealment from which he can spurt to seize and devour smaller fish and it is a resting place, a haven.

In streams, look essentially for the same types of cover as mentioned for lakes—plus these: where the current flows into deeper water; where sand or gravel bars have been built up midstream; at the heads and tails of riffles; below dams; along abutments; below overhanging banks—in fact, anywhere you deduce a bass could hide, fish there.

The normal diet of a largemouth is made up of smaller fish, frogs, worms, snakes, insects, crustacesans, leeches, crawfish, tadpoles, salamanders and its own young.

Like all the basses, the largemouth requires no specialized type of fishing tackle. Even a cut willow pole with a piece of store string and a hook baited with a chunk of bologna can be classed as productive bass tackle.

The important thing is to be able to present a lure to the bass in a manner that will induce it to strike. So let's talk about lures and the types required to reach the various depths and varieties of cover where bass are found.

Surface lures float, can't be made to sink on the retrieve and are designed to make some sort of surface commotion or noise. The best times to use these are early and late in the day, or whenever the water is calm.

There are many ways to manipulate surface lures; each specialist has his own pet methods to make his lures dance, jiggle, jump, twitch, etc. But here are some proved methods for using basic types.

A lure with one or two spinners should be twitched with short jerks of the rod tip to make the spinner, or spinners, give off a minimal splutter and flash. If you could work it in a foot-square area for half an hour, this would be ideal—so move it as little as possible; the idea is to entice the bass, not spook it.

Surface lures with a cupped head should be worked with quick, sharp jerks of the rod tip. This makes them *pop, chug, bloomp* or make the other odd noises certain fishermen impart to them.

Some experts prefer to keep their lure coming at a steady pace, *bloomp*ing it all the way to the boat. Others prefer a stop-and-go tactic, allowing the lure to pause for a few seconds or for several minutes, believing this is more attractive to the larger bass.

Animating of surface lures that have no features for making noises—usually slim torpedo-shaped creations—requires a greater degree of skill. A darting, dipping, dancing action is effective for taking wary bass with this type when the noisier models won't do it—especially in clear water.

I find that a little lead wire or split shot added to the shank of the rear hook of a surface lure can have two benefits. One, it imparts a different balance and action to give some lures more pizazz. And two, it lowers the tail end of the lure and makes it a deadlier hooker.

Floating-diving lures float because of their buoyancy but dive when retrieved, thanks to a lip that causes them to plane downward. Also, the lures' resistance to the water sets up an oscillation which causes them to wiggle.

You can use these as surface lures by making them dive with a sweep of the rod tip, then allowing them to float back to the surface. Also, just twitching them to make surface turbulence, suggesting an injured creature, is effective.

But the primary way to fish a floating-diving lure is to cast it near bass cover and then reel it fast enough to make it dive and wiggle. As it goes swimming past the bass's lair, it offers an attraction that's difficult for the fish to resist.

This type of lure also makes an ideal trolling lure because when it snags on the bottom, or in weeds, it will usually float free of the obstruction if you give it slack line.

Sinking lures cover a wide variety of lures such as weighted plastic plugs, spoons, jigs, metal spinners and wobblers. These types are valuable for probing the deeper waters where other models, such as floating or floating-diving, won't operate.

For lures that are designed to be fished on the bottom to do their job effectively, each has to be fairly weedless or it will continually be snagging.

But remember this: a perfectly weedless lure hasn't been designed that doesn't also miss fish. So plan to get hung on bottom cover on a certain percentage of your casts. This is an acceptable aspect of bottom fishing. If you aren't getting hung, then you aren't fishing where the fish are.

Bottom lures come in a wide variety of models, shapes, sizes and functions, but the preferred types are weedless spoons and jigs that have wire or plastic weedguards, pork chunks on weedless hooks and plastic worms in assorted riggings.

Unquestionably, more bass are caught by fishermen using bait-casting and spin-casting outfits than are taken on other rigs. So let's go into these first. They're closely related.

A spin-casting reel has an enclosed spool and is used on an offset-handle casting rod. A thumbing lever or button holds and releases the line for casting. The line is monofilament, with a smooth surface, nearly invisible to fish.

The beauty of such an outfit is the ease with which it can be operated. Beginners can become proficient enough to catch fish with no more than a thirty-minute practice session in the backyard.

In my opinion, spin casting has created more fishermen than any other method. And the reason is simple. Spin casting makes the act of fishing so easy that anyone can do it, provided he or she has a thumb to press the release lever.

My recommendations for an all-around spin-casting outfit would be: rod, 6 or 6½ feet, standard action; reel, any recognized name brand, properly filled with 12-pound monofilament line. Properly filled means to within ⅛ inch of the spool's edge.

Bait casting duplicates the function of spin casting, because virtually the same lures can be used. But it gives a finer degree of control for casting of lures into difficult places, and you'll need considerably more skill to become proficient at it.

I prefer a bait-casting outfit for my primary fishing needs because it can do more of the things my wide-ranging fishing requires. But my backup outfit is a spin-casting rig, and I use it primarily for casting lighter lures, in the ⅛-ounce-and-under category.

My recommendations for bait-casting outfits are:

Bait-casting tackle, favored by many experts, winched these hefty, largemouths from a Tennessee Valley Authority reservoir. (Tennessee Valley Authority)

(1) For surface lures and trolling, 5- or 5½-foot rod with muscle from butt to tip; reel, either the standard level-wind variety or the more efficient type with the slip-clutch drag system and the more sophisticated centrifugal or fluid brake drag. The line should be no less than 12-pound-, preferably 15-pound-, test monofilament— if your reel will handle it.

(2) For all-around casting, meaning lures in the ¼-ounce-and-up range, I recommend a 6- or 6½-foot rod with a graduated action from butt to tip. Steer clear of rods with a butt like a poker and a tip like a juicy noodle; these feel nice but perform poorly.

(3) Where extra leverage is required, such as in distance casting and working of bottoming lures, I recommend a 7-foot rod with a grip 3 inches longer than normal. This rod has the power to pound out long casts with heavier-than-usual lures, has the sweep to set the hook on deep-feeding fish and is ideal for trolling for larger fish, both fresh- and saltwater.

Spinning is another popular method of fishing for bass. A spinning reel is an open-face reel with a stationary spool that hangs below the rod. The line spins off the spool during the cast. This system provides an effortless, simple way to propel a lure.

For spinning I recommend a 6½- or 7-foot rod with a gutsy but gradual action, bending from butt to tip in a graceful curve. Again, no noodly tip. The reel should be the best you can afford and have a smooth drag with plenty of latitude for adjusting the tension. A drag that adjusts too quickly is apt to freeze up on you during a long run by a fast fish.

The line should be at least 8-, preferably 12-pound, test, and should fill the spool to within ⅛ inch of the lip. For extremely light lures it is necessary to use 4- to 6-pound-test line, but don't use these fragile tests around snaggy cover or you're asking for lost fish.

Fly fishing for bass is great sport, especially with bass bugs or poppers early and late in the day. For beginners, I recommend an 8½- or 9-foot rod with a gradual bend from butt to tip.

The fly reel should be one that won't get you in trouble, so make it single-action, of the best quality you can afford. The line should be an L6F, which means a level, mediumweight, floating line. And make the leader 5 feet long, level, 10-pound test.

This is a good starter outfit, one that will do an all-around job of fly fishing for bass. For lures I recommend that you start modestly with an assortment of hair bugs, poppers, streamers and wet and dry flies, tied on strong 1/0 or 2/0 hooks. Colors should be varied also, and be sure you have yellow, white, black and brown among your basics.

Spinning tackle, deadly in the daytime, can be a potent producer after sunset as well.

*The moment when a largemouth erupts under one of these fly-rod lures
is one of the most exciting in freshwater fishing. (The Orvis Company)*

And while we're on lures, let's wind up this discussion of tackle by going into spinning, spin-casting and casting lures. They're essentially the same except for a variance in sizes.

First off, buy a tackle box large enough to allow for an expanding collection of lures. This expansion is just as certain to happen as rain in April—but make it happen logically: don't buy several dozen bass lures just because you want to fill up tackle-box slots.

Buy a dozen lures, such as three each surface, floating-diving, sinking and bottoming types. And assort your colors to include white, yellow, black and natural scale. In plastic worms, be sure to include whatever colors happen to be hot in your area, such as purple and blue.

Then, don't buy more lures unless you have a reason. Reasons might be: you see another fisherman catch a batch of bass on a "Super Popper"; or a smaller lure than you have is doing business while your larger one isn't; or you don't have the right color in a certain lure. These are legitimate reasons, of course. Also, don't ignore hunches to buy certain lures when they appear capable of doing certain jobs your present lures won't do; these pay off too.

Above all, pay attention to the advice of good fishermen in your area and see for yourself which lures are the ones the bass prefer. These will change with the season, so keep on top of the situation by asking questions of those bringing in the bass.

Now, a word about terminal tackle.

The question often posed by even experienced bass fishermen is: do you tie your line directly to the lure or use a snap? Well, here's the way I look at it.

I know that a line tied directly to the lure has these disadvantages: (1) it can adversely affect the action of some lures; (2) it will weaken from the continued shock of casting.

Also, I know from experience that: (1) a snap will allow each lure to have maximum freedom to swim, wiggle, pop, *bloomp* or splutter the way it was designed to; and (2) a snap when properly tied is stronger than line alone as a connector to a lure.

So I use a snap, always. Why not a snap swivel? Because unless a lure tends to twist on the retrieve, a swivel is not needed. Why give the fish any more to look at than necessary? However, when I do feel the need for a swivel, I prefer the ball-bearing type because it never binds, always spins. Costs more, yes, but worth it.

Realizing I'm sticking my neck out, because fishing hot spots can change like women's hemlines, here are the places I recommend as above average, year after year, for producing limit catches of largemouth bass. There are three that stand out.

Texas' Sam Rayburn Lake, enriched by the Angelina River, and growing since 1963 in bass production, should be best for lunkers from November through May.

Greers Ferry Dam, in Arkansas, was filled in 1962 and hasn't slowed down one year since. So there's no reason to believe it will do anything but yield more lunker bass.

Florida has many big bass lakes, and they can be hot or cool, depending upon weather fronts and temperature drops. But my pick to repeat each year is Lake Kissimmee, which can be hotter than a potbellied stove during the period from January through April.

For information on these lakes, write: Parks and Wildlife Department, John H. Reagan Building, Austin, Texas 78701; Game and Fish Commission, Game and Fish Commission Building, Little Rock, Arkansas 72201; Division of Game and Fresh Water Fish, 620 South Meridian, Tallahassee, Florida 32304.

It isn't much of a problem to catch the smaller bass. If you'll move quietly along a shoreline endowed with the previously described types of cover and cast lures that range from surface to bottom, you will catch fish.

The challenge comes in catching larger bass—those of braggin' proportions. These make the hair rise, the pulse pound and the memories. So let's go for the trophy fish. Here are techniques that will produce them.

First off, don't fall into the trap that too many veteran bass fishermen succumb to—fishing with only two or three lures in which they have the most confidence. It's human for them to do so because these lures have caught the most fish for them. But that does not mean these pets will catch the most, or the biggest, every trip. Here's a method that will help you give a bass what it wants, not what you guess it wants.

Before you start fishing, select a dozen different lures; assort both colors and depths of water they will cover, in addition to a range of sizes.

Most expert fisherman keep two, even three, outfits set up, ready for use. They often have a surface lure on one, a floating-diving on another and a bottoming lure on the third. It's much simpler to change outfits than to rig up with a new lure, so you will tend to employ a greater selection of lures when you fish this way. And you'll probably catch more fish because of it.

Don't run for an hour to get to a supersecluded spot; this wastes valuable fishing time. Some of the biggest bass are caught close to docking areas.

If the water is calm, start fishing with a surface lure. Give it twenty-five-casts, no more. Change to a floating-diving model . . . then a sinker . . . and then a bottoming type. If you catch no fish, start reducing the size of lures in these types, and vary the colors as well. This way you are giving the bass a virtual smorgasbord of lures, and you will usually find one or more that they prefer. Stay with the producers, but not overly long. Give them twenty-five-casts, then change.

Next to lure selection and a time limit on usage, the most important item is a pattern for fishing. Bass are where you find them, and a pattern for fishing will assure you of fishing lures to almost every possible place a bass should be.

Most of the time the fish are against the shore, so that's where you should start. Initially, if you are fishing from a boat (we'll cover wading farther on), try casting directly into shore from about 50 feet out.

And don't fall for the theory that long casts cover more water. They do yardagewise, but they don't cover the productive water like shorter, more accurate casts. Fifty-foot casts directly at the shore are long for me. Mine normally average in the 20-to-30-foot range, because when bass are against the shore, the strikes usually come in the first few feet of lure movement.

If the straight-in casts don't do it, then position your boat about 20 feet from shore and make 50-foot casts ahead of the boat and angling toward the shore. This, normally, is my favored pattern.

The next maneuver is to anchor your boat against the shore and fish the open water in a semicircular sweep, using bottoming lures. Crawl these up the bottom, inch by inch, until they lie just under your boat. Obviously, this tactic calls for weedless lures such as jigs, plastic worms and spoons. It is especially deadly for fishing a rocky point that juts into a lake or stream. Bass come to such protuberances to find the small fish they feed on.

When you have exhausted your shore-fishing tactics, you can assume the bass are "out there." This calls for deep-water fishing with heavier lures that get down to 20- or 30-foot depths fast—meaning those that weigh ½ ounce or more—or deep-water trolling.

Of the two, I prefer deep-water trolling. And I start with the smallest, liveliest lures I have—those that have concentrated weight, like the fast wigglers with no lips but lots of vibratory motion. These should be fished at various depths from a few feet to 30 or 40 feet.

If my normal, slow trolling speed doesn't produce, I try it abnormally fast. This can be amazingly productive at times.

And if all the aforementioned tactics go for naught, then here is a trick that all live-bait bass fishermen either know or should know:

Take a small green frog and insert a 5/0 weedless hook upward through both of its jaws. Add just enough sinker to sink the critter. Start just at the break where deep water meets shallow and drift with the wind, either along the break or out into midlake. Keep the frog bouncing, just off the bottom. When you feel a pickup, don't set the hook. Yield slack line and let the bass munch on the frog. Then, when you can't stand it another second, *set the hook!* And hang on like the expert you are!

Now, to the wading fisherman. As you walk, cast along the shoreline ahead of you in a fan-shaped pattern, using the same lure-change method described earlier. The quietest possible approach is called for, because bass lying close in can detect stumbling feet at a surprising distance. This is especially true when you're wading a stream, because the current carries vibrations better than still water.

Especially fish the fast runs in a stream, both head (the upper) and tail (the lower) stretches. And always fish the holes from the shallow side—because the current is carrying food into the deeper side, where bass normally feed.

Until the plastic worm made its debut in the early 1950s, beginning fishermen had only an outside chance to catch a big bass. The main reason was that big bass lie in deep cover—which spells trouble unless you are rigged to fish it. Few beginners knew how.

Well, the plastic worm arrived and soon became the great equalizer. It is the near-perfect lure for coming through all types of snaggy bottom cover and does not require any special skill to use.

A beginner with a weedless plastic worm and a normal amount of patience can catch the biggest bass in the lake his first trip out—if he happens to let his cast settle in front of Mr. Big.

To make certain you understand the fundamentals of plastic-worm fishing, let's go through it step by step.

First, you look for typical bass cover like brush, weeds, a fallen tree or other cover near deepening water. Cast your worm close to the cover and let it fall until it touches bottom. You can tell because your line will suddenly go slack.

Sometimes the bass will inhale the worm on the way down. Other times he will pluck it off the bottom. Then again, he'll nail it the instant you lift it off the bottom. Your eyes must constantly be riveted on your line at the point where it enters the water.

Many times your eyes will tell you the bass took your worm, because you see the line make a sudden kick or jump too minute to feel. So alertness is a big part of bass fishing with a worm.

If you don't get a pickup on your initial cast, reel the slack out of your line while lowering your rod tip and pointing it toward the worm. Next, raise your rod tip sharply to cause the worm to jump off the bottom; then drop the tip to give the worm slack so it can plunge suddenly back to the bottom. It is the jumping, falling motion of the worm that grabs the attention of the bass.

Fly rodders set themselves up for a double bonanza—scrappy panfish and bull-strong bass. (North Carolina Department of Conservation and Development; Joel Arrington)

It's important to fish the worm slowly, repeating this process until you feel that electrifying tug as a bass inhales your worm or until you see your line make that telltale kick. When either occurs, lean toward the bass, point your rod tip toward it and quickly reel all slack out of your line.

Set the hook *instantly!* Set it hard, with the entire sweep of your rod and all the muscle you can muster. Try to break your line. (You can't, of course, but this gives you an idea of how vigorously you must set that hook.)

And here's why. The bass usually has the entire worm balled inside its mouth. Before you can dig the hook into the fish's hard mouth membrane, you have to drive it through that balled worm. And you won't do it with a gentle touch.

Now, you're going to hear a lot of static about counting to 10 before you set the hook, or letting the bass run the second time. Don't you buy it! I know, because I've watched bass underwater to see precisely how they take a worm.

A bass doesn't grab a worm by the tail, as you will hear. Nor does he always hit the head to kill it. Nor does he bite it, in any sense of the word. A bass swims up to a worm, opens his mouth and flares his gills in a delicately timed maneuver. This causes the water to rush into his mouth and out through his gills, creating a suction in front of the open mouth. And the worm flows smoothly into the bass's mouth.

By the time you are aware of any movement on the part of the bass, the worm is inside him. And every second you delay in setting the hook diminishes your chances to hook that fish. The time to set the hook is *now!*

Well, that's the way I fish a plastic worm, and I hope it works as well for you as it does for me. I know of no deadlier way to fish for big bass. Master it and you will be a master fisherman.

Now it's time for a few words on what to do after you set the hook—because now is when tactical errors can cost you the biggest fish of your life.

When you feel the bass struggling, keep your rod tip high, your rod butt at right angles to the fish and your line tight. If you feel the fish run into cover, keep pressure on him; usually he will work his way back out of the cover.

Once you get him headed toward you, reel rapidly enough to

keep a taut line and, as you play the fish to tire it, take a quick look around. Look for any object around which that bass could ensnarl your line—like the outboard prop, an oar, your electric motor, a stringer, etc. Either get these out of the water or pressure the bass away from them.

Should the bass power his way under your boat, yield him line until you can sweep your rod tip around either end of the boat and regain a direct pull.

If he is so big he rams for bottom cover and wraps the line around a snag, don't hit the panic button. Maintain a tight line for a while to see if the bass will untangle itself. If it won't, try strumming on the line as if it were a giant fiddle string. This can annoy a bass into dashing out of cover. If it comes to a standoff, and it's worth it to you, just shuck your clothes and dive down to where you can work the fish loose.

When you have a big bass on, play it cautiously until it tires enough to be led. Then you can land it a number of ways: with a large dip net; by gripping its lower jaw and lifting it aboard; by grasping it firmly over the back of the head so that your thumb and fingers exert pressure on both gills. Or you can use the "belly lift" method of landing advocated by Glenn Lau, who has used it to catch tons of Lake Erie bass.

Lead the bass alongside your boat and gently slide your hand rearward on its body, holding it just the way you hold a banana. Exert a slight pressure just ahead of the anus with your middle finger and slowly lift the bass out of the water. It will lie quietly because its own weight is pressing its organs against the central nervous system, causing near paralysis. This is a handy tactic when a bass has a hook exposed in its jaws and you stand a chance of becoming impaled if it flops as you reach for a jawbone grip.

Today's deluxe bass boats are equipped to do an all-out job of bass fishing. Often powered by engines of up to 135 horsepower, these sleek, roomy 16-foot boats can cover a lot of water in a day's effort.

Once a modern bass fisherman arrives at his destination, he flips on his electronic depth reader and constantly watches it as a bow-mounted electric motor moves him about with cat quietness.

Scanning the bottom with his depth reader, he can pinpoint shoals, reefs, old creekbeds, brush, wrecks, bridges and other structures not visible from abovewater. These are congregating spots for bass that no one but another depth-finder owner will know about. (An invaluable tool for use with the depth reader is a hydrographic map showing the contour of any lake bottom that has been charted by the Corps of Engineers. With this you can trace the course of old, submerged roads, riverbeds, gulleys, etc.)

Aerated live wells on board keep fish fresh and lively, while ample storage compartments contain refreshments, extra fishing tackle, rain gear and emergency equipment. In short, today's bass boat is designed for maximum bass-catching efficiency.

Well, let's wind up this bass talk with an observation about bass fishermen.

To me they're a dedicated, hardheaded, long-suffering, hairy-chested bunch of characters who wouldn't travel 1 mile to catch trout if bass could be had 100 miles away.

The action comes fast and heavy when the pros tackle the big bass at the country's popular bass tournaments. (Kentucky Department of Fish and Wildlife Resources)

In the Northwest, where the trout, steelhead and salmon are royalty, the bass is a commoner, a rough fish, an outcast—except to bass fishermen who wage a steady fight for their sport. When the fish-and-game departments poison out lakes to remove the bass and plant trout for the majority who prefer them, they're surprised when bass again appear after a year or two. But not the bass fishermen, who sneak them back into these lakes to keep alive their favorite sport.

A largemouth bass is a roughhousing fish that is totally unpredictable. When you think you have mastered a surefire system for taking it, it wipes your eye and brings you back to reality. No one *ever* becomes the complete master of the bass.

And I don't think true bass fishermen would have it any other way. That's the essence of bass fishing. Long may it endure—together with the grand fishermen who pursue it!

SMALLMOUTH BASS

BY JEROME B. ROBINSON

THE SMALLMOUTH black bass is a fish that stirs more controversy than any other freshwater gamester in the piscatorial parade. His legions of followers pronounce him "pound for pound the gamest fish that swims," quoting a line first written by Dr. James A. Henshall in his *Book of the Black Bass* and repeated so often that the words now serve as a banner under which all smallmouth fishermen go forth.

As fully as he is revered by bass fishermen, the smallmouth is hated by many members of the trout and landlocked salmon fishing fraternity. They rightfully convict the smallmouth as a major predator upon young trout and salmon in the streams and lakes the species inhabit together and rue the day that sportsmen and fish-and-game commissions began stocking bass in waters in which the salmonids had reigned ancestrally.

Some of the best smallmouth fishing in the United States occurs in Maine, New Hampshire and Vermont—states whose fishing addicts damn the bass and spend all their time chasing trout and salmon. Bass fishing is considered less sport than shooting rats at the dump.

When the northern New Englander does fish for bass, it is not for his own pleasure but "jest because the boy thought it might be fun," and he doesn't give two hoots for the string of smallmouths he brings home, even though he admits "they do taste good"—and they surely gave him more action than the little brook trout he loves so dearly.

Oh, sure, there are some bass fishermen in these states. If you inquired, somebody would know that Lake Winnepesaukee and Lake Wentworth in New Hampshire offer pretty good bass fishin', and in Vermont somebody would undoubtedly steer you to the Connecticut River or Lake Champlain. Mainers would point you to Grand Lake or the Belgrades. But you'd have a hard time finding anyone who would take your bass-fishing enthusiasm seriously.

I'll guarantee nobody will tell you the truth—for the truth is that in Vermont and New Hampshire the bass fishing beats hell out of the trout and salmon fishing. There is more good bass water and there are more large naturally produced smallmouth bass in Vermont and New Hampshire than there are trout or salmon.

In every other region of the country, the smallmouth is approached with respect; he is sought after with more dollars' worth of equipment than any other freshwater game fish in states where he is recognized as the great, scrappy sport fish that he really is.

One thing about the smallmouth: he never gives up. Smallmouths generally go into the air on the first prick of the hook, and their runs, jumps and bulldogging underwater tactics must be dealt with slowly and without too much pressure. A smallmouth is still fighting when you have him flopping in the boat.

Originally, smallmouth bass were native from the Saint Lawrence drainage basin and the Great Lakes down into the Ohio and upper Mississippi River drainage systems. But as their popularity as game fish grew in the early 1800s, it was predictable the smallmouth's avid supporters would transport the fish into new waters.

In the latter half of the 19th century, the range of the smallmouth bass spread with the growth of the railroads. Tanks of young bass fingerlings were hauled south and west as the rails pushed toward new systems of lakes and rivers. Trains brought the new fish into the Middle Atlantic States and to the Southeast largemouth bass country. Smallmouths suddenly burgeoned throughout the Midwest and down into the Southwestern cattle country, where they propagated in stock ponds and irrigation canals.

This *"gamest fish that swims"* is well known for its high-flying acrobatics. (Illinois Department of Conservation)

Today the smallmouth reproduces naturally in every state except Alaska. In Hawaii, smallmouths are considered a great new game fish. European fishermen began importing smallmouth fry before the turn of the century. Southern Canada and northern Mexico have fine smallmouth fishing. Only in Florida have smallmouths failed to flourish.

In his native range and in the new waters to which he has been introduced, the smallmouth is a fish of cleaner, clearer waters than his largemouth cousin, who seeks weedy cover and murky water and avoids current when possible.

The smallmouth thrives in the clear waters of mountain lakes and sand-bottomed reservoirs. Rocky bottom suits him best, and he achieves good size in the deep pools and backwaters of rivers and streams that are native trout waters. Large river systems are ideal waters for smallmouths; you'll find them where the current quickens over rapid stretches and in the eddies just outside the main flow of the stream.

Smallmouth black bass is an odd name for a fish that, in the first place, is a member of the sunfish family. Furthermore, the smallmouth is never black; he comes in many shades of bronzed brown or green, depending on the color of the water and the bottom. Even the "smallmouth" designation is questionable, since his mouth is usually one of the largest in the waters he inhabits.

In many waters smallmouth and largemouth black bass are found together and appear quite alike, since they are similar in shape and both quickly take on the color of their surroundings.

Large river systems are ideal smallmouth waters. This happy angler caught her fish in the Saint Lawrence River. (New York State Department of Commerce)

The vertical bars of darker scales which mark the smallmouth are not always distinct.

The two basses may be easily distinguished from each other, however, by the structure of their jaws. The upper jawbone of the smallmouth never extends beyond the back of the fish's eye. Conversely, the largemouth's upper jawbone always extends considerably past the back of its eye.

There are other differences, too. The largemouth has larger scales. If you care to count them, you will find that largemouths in Northern states have 58 to 66 along the line from gill cover to tail, whereas the smaller-scaled smallmouth has 68 to 80 scales along the same line. Also, note the dorsal fin. Both largemouths and smallmouths have a double fin in which the forward section has spiny rays and the rear section is soft-rayed. In the case of the smallmouth, the forward and rear sections of the fin are divided by a shallow notch. The largemouth has such a deep notch between the fin sections that they appear to be two separate fins.

The smallmouth is a more slender fish and has a wider tail.

But perhaps the biggest difference between the two species of bass is in the way you fish for them. Largemouths like big baits and noisy lures; smallmouths want smaller baits and scare easily from noise of any kind.

To really catch smallmouths, you have to use a quiet approach. If you fish big-water lakes or large rivers from a motorboat, it's a good idea to have an electric motor mounted on the bow. Use your outboard to get near the fishing places, but then sneak in quietly under silent electric power when you are maneuvering into casting range.

A number of smallmouth fishermen go so far as to carpet the bottom of their bass boats. That sounds extreme, but it helps. The scrape of a tackle box on metal or the clang of a dropped oar is all it takes to drive a smallmouth right out of casting range.

The silent approach continues into the way you fish for smallmouths. Forget the splashy surface lures. They are great for largemouth bass, but a smallmouth doesn't like commotion. He wants a quiet, lifelike presentation.

For instance, if you are popping for smallmouths with a fly rod, you will catch more fish if you swim the popper rather than actually popping it. One of the best smallmouth fishermen I know uses poppers exclusively early in the season from dawn until the sun hits the water with direct overhead rays. He claims that yellow is the fish's favorite color.

Drifting in a quiet boat, he makes short, quiet casts into bassy-looking spots—close to protective boulders, stumps and underwater logs. If bass are on their nests, he casts as close to the nest as possible.

Smallmouth fishermen after maximum sport often pursue their quarry with fly tackle.

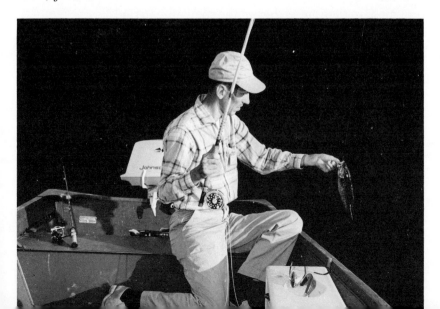

But once the popper hits the water, he just lets it float there.

He waits about half a minute. If nothing hits the bug, he gives it just enough twitch to move the bug without popping it and then begins slowly swimming the popper back toward the boat. He retrieves it about 10 feet, lets it sit another half minute—then picks up the popper and casts to a new location.

His method is based on two facts of smallmouth fishing. Smallmouths don't like noise, number one. And, two, if a smallmouth is going to hit, he comes fast either when the lure first hits the water or within the first few feet of the retrieve. There's no need to fish a popper all the way back to the boat.

The habits of smallmouths vary according to the latitude at which you find them and the amount of fishing pressure and other disturbance they must put up with.

In the clear lakes and rivers of the Northeast, smallmouths are found in the shallows during May and June, when they are nesting, and in the morning and evening of hot summer days, when they venture along the shoreline hunting food. During the rest of the year, the Northern smallmouths stay in the deeper water, where midday summer temperatures are cooler. Given a choice, they stay where the water is near 65 degrees during the heat of summer.

In warmer areas of the country, the typical smallmouth becomes a night feeder during the warmest part of the year. On lakes where there is much water-skiing traffic, smallmouths are quickly put off their feed and tend to sulk all day in deep water and feed along the shoreline only at night.

Smallmouths are notorious for their eagerness to hit lures that pass close to their nests during the spawning period.

The male smallmouth builds the nest by thrashing out a pocket of gravel and sand usually in water from 2 to 10 feet deep. He then lures a female to the nest, often driving off other male fish that attempt to attract her away. Courtship is a brief affair in which the male makes dashes at the female, causing her to retreat toward his nest. The female then lays her adhesive eggs in occasional spurts, and the male fertilizes them as they fall into the nest and adhere to the stones.

Nature has an interesting way of ensuring that spawning bass will reproduce in large numbers. The female produces 2,000 to

7,000 eggs per pound of body weight, but these eggs are ready to be spawned at different periods.

Thus, when the female spawns in the nest of one male bass, she passes only half or a third of her total egg supply. Once the spawning ritual is completed, she leaves the nest in the care of the male and swims away ready to spawn one or two more times with other male bass that have nests prepared to her liking.

The male is also polygamous and usually lures two or three different females to spawn in his nest. Depending on water temperature, the eggs hatch within two to ten days. During the period of incubation and for several weeks after the eggs hatch, the male is zealously protective. He guards the nest interminably, leaving it to feed only during hours of darkness. Any intruder, be it a predator fish *or a fisherman's lure,* is walloped by the grouchy male bass. In most smallmouth waters, the greatest dent fishermen put in the bass population is made at this time, and the protective males make up the majority of fish caught.

The males stay on the nests for nearly a month, until the tiny fry absorb the yolk sac that nourishes them during infancy and lift from the nest to begin feeding on plankton and other microorganisms. At this time the male's protective attitude is overcome by a cannibalistic instinct, and perhaps motivated by the near starvation of the past month, he drives into the school of his tiny children and gobbles up as many as he can before they disperse and hide in thick cover.

Only where the floor is covered with branches and submerged brush are smallmouth bass nests nearly impossible for fishermen to reach with lures. If the nest is at the bottom of a submerged tree, branches guard it from approach by artificials. That anglers make sincere attempts to probe the nesting areas is clear by the number of bass lures visible beneath the water surface, caught in the branches of the protective overhanging trees in newly impounded bass waters where land has been flooded and underwater brush remains as cover for the fish.

Cannibalism of the young by the male bass is also reduced by the protection of the branches that overhang the nests. When the fry lift off the nests and rise toward the surface, they automatically enter the thick protective cover of the flooded tree branches, where it is harder for their paternal parent to launch his attack against them. In such areas, where fewer fish are killed by anglers during the nesting period and far fewer bass fry are eaten by their fathers, the result is often a smallmouth bass population so dense that the food supply is exhausted and the lake fills with stunted bass that never grow to decent size. For this reason, most states permit fishing during the bass nesting period and have found that except where fishing pressure is overwhelming, a balanced population of large bass and small is the result.

When the male smallmouth is on the nest, he strikes anything that he thinks threatens him. This means that if your casting is accurate, almost any lifelike lure that you bring across the nest will produce a strike. The fish is not hitting out of hunger—in fact, he doesn't eat during the nesting period; he is hitting to kill the intruder. Your strike must be quick and hard.

Early in the morning, fly-rod poppers and dark bucktail flies are deadly on nesting bass in shallow water. Later in the day, when the sun is overhead, deep-running lures in lifelike minnow shapes are killers. And at any time of day, black plastic worms can be used to drive a sulky bass to desperation.

If you cast a plastic worm close to a bass nest and leave it lying still on the bottom, the bass will circle it and eventually rush in, pick the thing up and run off—carrying the worm away from his nest. He's not interested in eating it, merely in removing the pest. Hit him quick, when he starts to run.

In July and August, smallmouths get finicky. They gather now in the deeper pools of the rivers and congregate in schools in deep lakes. The fisherman who knows where a rocky reef humps up to within 20 feet of the surface of a deep bass lake has the secret.

Deep-running minnow-shaped lures work well early in the morning and in the evening on the big lakes, but during the day hellgrammites, crayfish, live shiners or night crawlers are prescribed—and you've got to know where the bass holes are.

Generally, boat channels, offshore reefs in 20 feet or so of water, buoys and other submerged objects that offer cover will be where you find the smallmouths.

In rivers, too, the smallmouths retire to deep, cool pools or lie in the shadow of large rocks or submerged logs. If the fishing pressure or boating activity is not too disturbing, you can catch summertime smallmouths right through the middle of the day. The secret is to use fine, almost invisible line, no weight, and to cast precisely with either tiny lures or live bait.

Smallmouths are put off by commotion at any time of year, but they are particularly finicky in midsummer. Even deep-running minnow-shaped lures sometimes scare summer bass, apparently because of the heavy splash they make when they hit the water. To catch August smallmouths consistently you must be careful, accurate and quiet.

For the most fun as well as the most delicate presentation, the new ultralight spinning rods and reels are ideal. These outfits are designed to handle lures weighing as little as an eighth of an ounce, and when equipped with a spoolful of 4-pound-test monofilament, they can be used to cast the tiny lures nearly as far as you can cast heavier lures and stronger lines.

Though at first you feel that you are casting with a broom straw, you soon find that the little ultralight outfits give you pinpoint accuracy. A quick flip of the rod sends the lure as far as a heavy overhand cast. The lure lands on the water without commotion, and the nearly invisible 4-pound-test line alights without causing so much as a flicker of disturbed surface.

I have found that, in New England anyway, the lures that seem to take bass consistently are the artificial-minnow types. They look real to the fish, cast lightly and can be thrown good distances with an outfit carrying 4-pound-test line.

The greatest combination of all, however, is an ultralight rod and reel, 4-pound-test line and a live hellgrammite. I haven't met a smallmouth yet that could resist a live 3- or 4-inch hellgrammite. A light spinning outfit is perfect for casting this killer bait without benefit of additional weight.

There's some technique to this kind of fishing that is important to know. For one thing, smallmouth bass don't wolf down a live hellgrammite. They come over and have a long look. Then they pick up the gruesome-looking bait in their lips and carry it away hanging out of the front of their mouths like an old cigar stub. After a 10- or 12-foot run, the bass may drop the bait and pick it up again before he decides to swallow it.

Strike too soon and you just yank the bait out of his lips.

You must let him make his run, keeping your bail open and let-

The hellgrammite, hooked through its collar as shown, is the author's favorite smallmouth bait. (Milt Rosko)

ting the coils of light line spill out of the reel. When he stops, you close the reel and wait for him to move off and tighten the line. When it's good and tight, you hit him. Hit him two or three times in succession, for the noodly little ultralight rods don't have much backbone and you have to sort of hammer the hook home in that tough bass jaw.

Bass have sharp, rough teeth, and 4-pound-test line doesn't stand much wear, so it's a good idea to tie a foot-long shock tippet of 9-pound-test mono between the lure and the end of the 4-pound line. (Four-pound and 9-pound line will hold firmly together with the standard barrel knot.)

When you hook a good bass on an ultralight outfit, one rule is paramount: *When he pulls, you don't. When he doesn't, you do. Reel in when you can.*

You must keep your drag set very lightly. When a bass makes a run on 4-pound-test line, you want to give him plenty of freedom. Keep the line tight, but keep the pressure off. It's delicate fishing, but that's the challenge.

The drag setting on your reel is critical when you are light-lining for bass, and for that reason it is recommended that you avoid the cheap discount-house reels. They store the line properly and wind it in without problems, but unless the reel has a good, solid drag setting, you are going to break off a big bass.

It may take a long time to bring in a bass over 2 pounds on a light outfit. When the fish wants to run, you've got to let him go.

Don't reel while he is taking line out, for that will put a permanent twist in your line.

When you have a good fish hooked, you should put the click on so that the reel handle does not wind backward when the fish is taking out line. With the click on, you just hold the rod firmly, keeping the tip high so that the rod takes the full strain of the fish's fight, and keep your hand on the reel handle. The minute the fish stops taking line out, you begin pumping and reeling back line as you can.

The most crucial time comes when the fish is near the boat. Since the rod is fully bent, you have little leverage if the fish decides to go under the boat or head for the anchor line. You must realize this and take ample precautions.

If you are in a boat, get the anchor up. If you're wading a river, get into the shallows where there is nothing to snag the line during those last crucial moments.

Biological surveys have shown the following pattern of typical smallmouth movement in lakes with average boating activity and fishing pressure. In April and May the smallmouths move in large schools along shore, primarily in 10 to 15 feet of water, feeding on

Many professional smallmouth guides choose crayfish as their standard bait. (Milt Rosko)

small sunfish, forage fish such as alewives or shiners, crayfish in rocky areas and large larvae such as hellgrammites in flowing water.

In June the big fish will be in the nesting areas, usually where the bottom is sandy or gravelly with rocks and boulders interspersed. Smallmouths prefer not to nest on muddy bottom if given the choice.

Late in June and through July and August the large lake small-mouths will be found in about 20 feet of water feeding close to the bottom during daylight hours and prowling the shoreline at night. Poppers and surface lures work well at night, and deep-running lures and live bait are in order during daytime.

During late August and September there is a steady movement of bass from the open water to the shoreline late in the afternoon. Popping bugs work well at that time of year, when grasshoppers and bumblebees are most prevalent.

Some of the best shoreline fishing of the entire year can occur in the late autumn—October into November. But then, in most places, the fishermen's fancy turns to hunting and the fishing pressure slacks way off. At that time the big bass lose their wariness of lures, for the simple reason that they see fewer of them. The fishing is tops, and few fishermen compete for the high harvest that is to be had.

Large rivers like the Saint Lawrence, Ohio, Delaware, Hudson, Connecticut, Potomac and Tennessee, many of which rise in forested hill country and run clean over intervals of rocky rapid stretches, are ideal smallmouth rivers; and the streams that flow into the big rivers usually afford good smallmouth fishing in their lower stretches.

River bass spawn in backwaters and calm stretches outside the heavy current. In midsummer, these big river bass head for deep runs and pools below the rapids or migrate upstream into the feeder rivers and brooks, which normally run a few degrees cooler. Waters around the mouths of these incoming feeders are hot spots for bass early in the morning and just before dark in the midsummer months.

Smallmouths are great movers. Tagged fish have been found to travel as much as 20 miles in big rivers, though most are likely to settle down and feed within the confines of a home pool or run once they have found a satisfactory hangout.

In lakes, bass move in small schools when they are in deep water feeding along reefs and rock piles. For this reason, you should fish known bass hangouts for 20 minutes to half an hour even if nothing is biting. The school bass move along in a slow feeding pattern, and you have to stay put long enough for the fish to work back into the area where you are casting.

When a smallmouth reaches trophy size, however, he is less likely to travel far from his permanent haunts. Smallmouths of 3 and 4 pounds and more can usually be found close to the same spot day in and day out.

The shadowy dark spots between large underwater boulders are favorite hangouts of the bigger bass, as are the dark spots in the shade of piers, submerged logs and the deeper pools and hollows below dams in flowing bass waters.

Biologists report that smallmouth bass rely on small fish for the greatest part of their diet. Small sunfish, perch, all types of shiners and minnows, smelt and smaller members of the trout and salmon

Trophy-size smallmouths can usually be found close to the same spot day after day. (Illinois Department of Conservation)

species are preyed upon by smallmouths. Crayfish, frogs and insect larvae are the other primary foods.

In the choice of a bass lure, therefore, chances are best that a good replica of a small fish will take the most bass. If I had to fish with only one lure, I'd choose one of the balsa smelt-shaped lures such as the Rebel or Rapala which closely resemble a live fish in shape, color and action.

In summer I'd fish the deep-running models; in the spring and fall, when smallmouths are feeding close to shore or are nesting in shallow water, a floating model that runs 2 feet or so below the surface would be my first choice.

Smallmouth bass feed most actively in water temperatures between 60 and 70 degrees in most parts of their range. This means that during the summer, smallmouths will be found feeding in the thermocline, that middle level of moderately warm water.

Lake water is divided into three basic levels according to water temperature. The lowest level is cool and dark and harbors little life, since it contains less oxygen. The top level is bright and too hot for most game fish during sunlight hours during the summer.

The middle level is where you find the fish. You may find this thermocline within a few feet of the surface or down as much as 25 feet—depending on the weather, the amount of wind and the depth of the lake. Fishermen who use thermometers to check the water temperatures at different levels know how deep to troll, cast or hang a bait for greatest success.

Ordinarily, smallmouths will be found near the top of the thermocline during the heat of the day. At dawn and dusk they work toward shore to feed, moving at a level near the top of the thermocline until the lake bottom planes up to meet that level; here they do their most active feeding.

Once you have determined the depth where the thermocline meets the bottom, trolling with a minnow-shaped lure at 3 or 4 miles per hour or casting with either bait or lures should be concentrated along that line. Fish close to the bottom.

Crayfish, live minnows, small frogs and night crawlers are all good smallmouth baits, but the best bait of all, as I said before, is a live hellgrammite. And for some reason known only to the bass, hellgrammites work best when the sun is on the water.

Smallmouths do not grow as big as largemouth bass. A smallmouth over 4 pounds is a big one anywhere, and 6- to 8-pounders are uncommon enough to be considered true trophies. Smallmouths over 8 pounds are extremely rare. The record smallmouth is a whopping 11-pound-15-ounce fish 27 inches long that was caught by D. L. Hayes on July 9, 1955, at Dale Hollow Lake, on the Tennessee–Kentucky border. The Canadian smallmouth record is held by a 9-pound-2-ounce fish caught at McCaulay Lake, Ontario, in 1951.

Just as he is a delight to fish for and a challenge to catch, the smallmouth bass is at the top of the list as table fare. The firm, white, flaky flesh of a clear-water smallmouth smells faintly like celery when it is first filleted, and it has a delicate flavor.

If you want a real treat, take along a skillet, some butter and a small bag of pancake flour next time you go smallmouth fishing. Powdered with pancake flour, salted and peppered lightly and fried in butter over a hardwood blaze along the shoreline, smallmouth fillets are at their very finest.

The smallmouth is a handsome fish, streamlined and colorful. Fish of 1½ to 2 pounds are trim and fight with speed and raucous acrobatics. As they grow, they start to put on bulk and their backs become more humped, their bellies more rounded. But they never get sluggish. Even the big bass put on an aerial show that never ceases to startle and excite a fisherman. The bass jumps with his mouth open and his head shaking like a terrier's. Given any slack, he will throw the lure right back at the boat.

You can't call a smallmouth yours until he's on the stringer. But when you've got him, if he's over 3 pounds you will admire him for what he put you through.

No question about it: every smallmouth you catch does his best to uphold his oft-repeated reputation—"pound for pound, the gamest fish that swims."

ATLANTIC SALMON

BY LEE WULFF

WHY WILL an individual angler pay as much as $5,000 per week for the privilege of fishing for Atlantic salmon, when far lesser sums will bring him many more pounds of other game fish? The answer is complicated by the many exciting facets of salmon angling which make fishing for the Atlantic salmon more valuable to those who can afford to choose their quarry.

The Atlantic salmon is anadromous—a fish that spends part of its life in fresh water and part in the sea. Trout, striped bass, white perch, catfish, eels and many other fish are anadromous too, but with the salmon there's a difference: the others need and take food for their sustenance in fresh water; the salmon rarely, if ever, takes food in the streams, and he needs none. In tempting the Atlantic salmon to take a fly, the angler is reaching for the fish's mind instead of his stomach. As one salmon angler puts it, "It's the difference between chess and checkers." The "thing" in an Atlantic salmon's mind that causes him to take a fly is still a mystery.

At one time the theory was advanced that although the salmon did not feed in the general sense, he did need vitamins and therefore he would take an occasional insect into his mouth, squeeze it between his jaws and extract the vitamin-bearing juices. Then he

184

would spit out the carcass. This was to explain both his taking of the flies and the complete absence of any sort of food in his stomach when captured.

The flaw in this theory lies in the comparative indifference of big salmon to flies. If salmon need vitamins for survival in fresh water on their spawning runs, then big salmon would need more vitamins than small ones and would, therefore, be forced to rise more frequently and take many more natural insects than the smaller fish. Instead, the reverse is true. Small salmon rise *much more freely* than the large ones do.

Sometimes salmon in the Canadian streams are seen to rise and take down a natural insect. In Europe, where fishing with bait is legal, Atlantic salmon are frequently caught on sea shrimp and on worms, both of which they take down as if to swallow them. Why, then, do we never find the remains of food in their stomachs? Is it because the sea shrimp are never found in the freshwater rivers and worms almost never—at least, where a salmon could reach them? Or because they immediately spit out anything they take?

To try to understand the paradox of a nonfeeding fish that will take a fly or lure or a very occasional insect, we have to reach back to his background and his special needs. The average Atlantic salmon spends three or four years in the stream before making his first journey to the sea. If he comes back as a small salmon, or "grilse," of just over one year's sea feeding, three-fourths of his life will have been spent as a small, under-6-inch fish called a "parr" in the stream where, in competition with the trout and the other parr, he raced to reach each bit of food first. Anything bite-size, moving or falling into the water, he engulfed in his jaws without thought and spat out later if it turned out to be a flower petal, a seed or something else that was inedible.

It could well be that a salmon, returning to his early river environment, has a conditioned reflex to revert to the voracious feeding habit he had as a fingerling. It follows, logically, that such an instinctive reaction would remain much stronger in a fish that has been away from the stream for only one year than it would in a larger fish that has been away from the stream for two or three years in his sea feeding. In fact, the salmon's tendency to rise to a fly seems to come out at about the inverse of the square of the time spent in the sea. In other words, the one-sea-year fish rise most freely. The two-sea-year fish rise about one-fourth as frequently and the three-sea-year fish with about one-ninth the grilse's readiness, exploding the vitamin-juice theory!

A further factor to be considered is the mood of the salmon himself. When he returns to the river from the sea, he has grown from 6 inches in length and a couple of ounces in weight to 2 feet and about 5 pounds in a single year, to 12 pounds on the average in two years and to almost 30 in three—a fantastic rate of growth for a 4-year-old fingerling. The returning salmon has stored up, within his sleek, silvery body, enough energy to carry him through the long, arduous trip to the spawning grounds, the rigors of courtship and spawning, a winter under the ice and then, hopefully, a rough return through flood-swollen spring rivers to the sea, an odyssey of almost a year. And he is able to do this without any feeding to renew his strength. He's supercharged with energy in comparison with the average game fish that renews its lesser store of strength from day to day or week to week. He's like a top athlete primed for the event of a lifetime—but to an even greater degree.

The Atlantic salmon often finds himself back in his native river months in advance of spawning time. He has time to spare, but instinctively he knows his store of energy is not limitless. He must conserve it against the rough water and the falls that lie ahead, as well as for encounters with predator eels and otters and fish hawks. He chooses his lies with care, seeking places where he can rest with little exertion, yet where he can have the soothing flow of the current moving over his restless body. He waits, tense, like a bridegroom outside a locked bride-to-be's door—waiting . . . and waiting. Periodically, to reassure himself of his strength and vitality, he'll leap or swirl—or, as a man might do, take a swat at a buzzing fly. He takes the fly partly, one guesses, out of annoyance and partly, perhaps, to reassure himself that his reflexes are still good and that his superb strength and speed are still with him.

Most salmon, it seems, rise out of a combination of instinct, conditioned reflex and annoyance. They're most likely to move toward the fly the first time it comes over them. As the second and third and subsequent casts pass over them, their tendency to rise dissipates, except in the rare few fish that will, eventually, be goaded by continued casting into rising to the fly.

The word "fly" is used here because fishing with an artificial fly

In Quebec, a high percentage of the population fly-fishes for Atlantic salmon. Here's why. (Film Office of Quebec)

in the accustomed method of fly casting with fly-casting tackle is the only angling method permitted by law on Canadian and American salmon waters.

The most plausible explanation of why returning Atlantic salmon do not feed in fresh water—in contrast with the trout and other anadromous fish of the area, which do—is that if these fierce, swift fish that grow so rapidly and feed so savagely in the sea were to continue this rapacious feeding once they entered their native streams, they'd soon clear the stream of all other fish life, including their own line of succession, and still be hungry. It is reasonable for Nature to nauseate them as a hangover does a man on a "morning after." In such strange but simple ways does Nature take care of her own, patterning each form of life individually and not, as man so often thinks she should, in a pattern after his own thoughts and actions.

The salmon's strange cycle makes him a very special fish. He's confined to a river with only a few pools suitable for his resting spots when the rivers are low. The angler knows where he must lie (he's so big that in most rivers he's easily spotted) and can reach him hour after hour with his flies. He cannot escape the angler's wiles; his only survival lies in refusing his offerings. In my experience in opening up wild rivers to fishing, I've found that although salmon endure fly fishing and continue to thrive in spite of it, the trout (which are feeding fish) that share the rivers with them fall prey to hunger and take the flies so much more readily that after a few years the trout are practically eliminated from the section of the river where serious salmon fishing goes on.

A brief review of the salmon's cycle will give a greater understanding of this remarkable fish. Salmon normally spawn in November, and the fertilized eggs come to life in midwinter as alevins, tiny fish with a great, full stomach bigger than they are that is made up of the greater part of the egg, still remaining. For months their sustenance will come from this egg sac, so that they can strengthen their muscles inside the spawning bed out of sight of potential predators. They can wriggle and show life in the small spaces where the water flows through the gravel in which they were spawned. Slowly they develop their muscles and by spring, when the supply of the minuscule living things upon which they can feed is the greatest, they leave the gravel beds and become free-swimming fish—miniature salmon, hungry and able to fend for themselves, but prey, too, to a host of predators. At this stage they become "parr" and are shaped like salmon, but have barred and mottled coloring with prominent red spots.

For the next two, three, four, five or possibly more years, these parr will live in the stream and feed ravenously. Though they'll grow far more slowly than the trout that are their stream companions, they will build up within their small, fantastically strong bodies the capability of rapid growth once a suitable food supply is available. Their feats of speed and strength are magnificent for their size. They can leap more than a dozen times their length up into the air. They will tackle other fish almost as big as they are and are often caught on flies bigger and heavier than they are themselves.

In the spring, just before the big runoff comes, some of the parr will ripen for the next stage. Their coats will change from their mottled, barred and red-spotted coloring to one of silver sides and bellies and dark, blue-green backs. They will look like miniature sea salmon, but with rounded tails and softer fins. They will have been coated by Nature with the protective coloring of all the free-swimming ocean fish and be readied for the new saltwater world they are about to enter. From above, a predatory bird will see them as dark and as blue as the sea around them. They will be as silver as the mirrored undersurface of the waves when an ocean predator looks up at them from below. Along with the spent salmon that have been fortunate enough to winter under the ice, these parr with silvery coats, now called "smolts," will sweep downstream in spring in the floodwaters to the sea.

The change from within that causes a parr to become a smolt may come in his second year or it may not come until his sixth. The time will depend upon his heredity, his rate of growth and other factors. Normally the most precocious and fastest-growing of the parr will become smolt soonest, will stay longest in the sea and will, in the end, return as the largest salmon.

Once at sea this baby salmon shows a mysterious and amazing ability to navigate. As a 6-inch fish, with no previous sea experience, he embarks unerringly on a course that will bring him, perhaps a thousand miles later, to the great Northern sea feeding area where the rest of the salmon from the rivers of the North Atlantic —with their unique ability to be fierce and active in cold, cold water—will have a great Arctic shrimp ground almost entirely to themselves. There in the Northern seas, he will fill out his sea time, whether it be one year, two years, three or, in very rare instances, four.

When the salmon ripens for change again, this time for spawning, he will make the long return journey to his native stream and ascend it to the area of his birth to find a mate and spawn, setting up a new cycle of life. A female salmon of 10 pounds will lay about ten thousand eggs. If two of each female's fertilized eggs develop to maturity and provide two salmon on the spawning beds to replace their parents, the population will be maintained in balance. If more than two come back, the population will increase, or the increased competition on the spawning bed will, as Darwin determined, tend to produce a stronger, more efficient strain. With our present long-continuing decline in North American rivers, fewer than the small replacement percentage have been making it back to the spawning beds.

With the variance of years spent in the river as well as in the sea, a complete catastrophe in either fresh- or saltwater environment for a single year could not completely eliminate the salmon stocks.

The salmon's great growth comes from his years at sea, and the individuals that stay out the longest before returning to spawn grow largest; a salmon's weight is not necessarily related to his age. A 6-year-old fish may weigh as little as 2 ounces or as much as 30 pounds, depending upon how he's spent his years. If he still has not ripened from parr to smolt, he'll still be a stream fingerling. If he stays in the stream five years and then goes to the sea for one year's feeding before returning to spawn, he'll weigh from 3 to 5 pounds. If he goes to sea at 4 years of age and stays out for two years, he'll return weighing as much as 30 pounds. In each case he is 6 years old!

During a heavy salmon run, there are fish enough for every rod in rivers like New Brunswick's Miramichi. (Canadian Government Travel Bureau)

Once a salmon returns to the river to spawn, it is axiomatic that if he survives and returns to the sea to recuperate, he'll return to spawn again the following year. Unlike the Pacific salmon (no relation), which disintegrates chemically upon its return to fresh water, Atlantic salmon have been known to spawn as many as four times.

Grilse, the name given to salmon that spend only one year feeding in the sea, are more like human dwarfs than teen-agers. They are usually just as old as the much larger, fully matured and square-tailed two- or three-year sea-feeding fish, but are slimmer and much smaller, with thinner tail stems and forked tails. Like human dwarfs, who can mate with normal humans and produce offspring who themselves are normal but carry the dwarfing tendency, grilse carry the hereditary tendency for a short sea stay and an early return. They usually stay at least as long in the stream and eat just as much as any other parr of the stream's supply of food, but they bring back a much smaller return in poundage from the ocean and are, therefore, a less efficient form of salmon for either sport or food.

The salmon's life history can be read on his scales. The scales grow in rings at a rate of about twenty-five rings a year, varying slightly with individual fish. When the rings are close together they make a dark band, indicating a period of slow growth (winter). When they are spread apart, with greater space between each ring and the next, they indicate a rapid growing period (summer). By winters and summers the years of a salmon's life can be counted both as a parr and as a sea fish.

Although they do not die automatically at spawning, relatively few Atlantic salmon survive to spawn a second time. Varying from river to river, the percentage of fish surviving for a second spawn may be over 20 percent in rare cases; in many rivers less than 5 percent of the salmon entering in each spawning run will have spawned before.

When a salmon comes in to spawn, his body is firm and well rounded. During the period he stays in fresh water and doesn't feed, he loses about half his weight, absorbing his fat and body strength in order to survive the long fast. By the time he returns weakly to the sea in the spring runoff, he's as thin as a rail. His skin has shrunk to fit his body, which is as long as it ever was, but much

Joan Salvato Wulff, the author's wife and a champion fly caster, lands a champion fish with a light rod. (Jack Samson)

smaller in girth. His scales, shrinking in proportion, stay just as long as they were but they shrink on the sides with his shrinking girth, the edges being absorbed to help him survive. The scales on a spawned-out salmon will, therefore, have open ends at top and bottom of the outside rings of his most recent growth.

When he returns to the sea and starts to grow again, he grows in all directions, particularly in girth, and a new series of rings builds around each old scale and around the raw ends of his "spawning mark." His scales will thus show a mark of new ring ends for each spawning, just as they show light and dark periods for each year of his life.

Tackle for Atlantic salmon has been growing lighter with the years. In the 1930s a 12½-foot rod was a very light one, and 19- and 20-footers were still in common use. Now a rod of more than 9½ feet is unusual on this continent, and some anglers fish with rods of only 6 feet weighing well under 2 ounces. Because the lighter rods can be balanced with lines of smaller diameter, modern reels are smaller and lighter too. The weight of the whole outfit has come down markedly. The trend to lighter tackle has led to smaller flies, finer leaders and, I believe, superior skill in the playing of these difficult fish.

This swing to very light tackle was sparked by a few of us on the Canadian rivers. Its movement to the Old World was slow. I can remember meeting an angler in 1962 on a beat I'd rented on

the Aberdeenshire Dee in Scotland who professed to be fishing for
trout. His most convincing argument came when he shook his rod
vigorously and said, "See! This is a trout rod, and it's only eleven
feet and very light. Eight ounces."

I smiled and shook mine, saying, "Yes! And this is my *salmon*
rod and it's six feet long and weighs an ounce and three-quarters."
He just shook his head, thinking I was crazy, and walked away.

We, on this side of the Atlantic, pioneered both light rods and
the releasing of salmon after their capture. In the beginning, I can
remember putting salmon into slack-water puddles and bringing
the guides back the following day to see them alive and watch
them swim off when I put them back in the river's main flow. Having seen badly seal-mauled salmon continuing determinedly on
their way up to spawn, I was sure mere "playing" wouldn't deter so
game a fish, so near the ultimate goal of all his endeavors, from
carrying on. The guides, in particular, didn't want to believe a
salmon could survive the playing ordeal and go on. They wanted
to take them to the camp or to their homes to eat. My own guides,
at the camp I ran, didn't take to the releasing of fish until I bought
commercially caught salmon from the nearby nets and brought
them to the camp to give them to take home. I bade them release
any fish we caught ourselves that we didn't need for our table. I
take pride in having been in the vanguard of these movements, for
I believe they have increased both the pleasure to be found in
angling and the number of fish we still have to fish for.

A special note of importance: anglers, like the management
agencies, should keep the runt fish, if they plan to keep any, and
release the bigger ones they catch in order to improve the spawning stock. I know of one major club on a great river where, re-
grettably, the anglers release their lesser fish and keep the biggest
in order to bring up the "average" weight of the catches they
record. Since most of them have inherited some money or at least
a good start in life, they *must* believe in heredity; how can they
help realizing that as they bring up the "average" weight of their
catches in this fashion, they are also bringing down the average
size of the fish that get through to spawn and dwarfing the runs of
the future?

An interesting comment can be made on the practice of releasing salmon to fight again or to go on and spawn. Some biologists in

studies (studies that were not, I believe, made on Atlantic salmon, though they tend to include this fish in their thinking) claim to have found that so large and so game a fish played out enough to be captured creates, through his exhaustion, certain toxic substances in his body which will cause his death in a short time *even if he's released*. They should have been at my salmon camp in the early days.

I'm sure a salmon *can* be "played" to death; but a capable angler doesn't have to fight his fish that long or that hard to capture him. At the Portland Creek camp in the early days in Newfoundland, before we had any refrigeration, I caught hundreds of salmon, played them until I could pick them up by the tail and carried them, sometimes a hundred yards or more, to a pool in the feeder brook at the camp. There they rested till we needed them for food. A newcomer to the camp would go to the brook, stand on the bridge and look down at them in amazement—before rushing to his cabin to rig tackle and get out on the stream. Some of those salmon even rose to a fly in that confined brook pool after a few days in captivity. Ninety-eight out of every hundred survived for five days or more until we were ready to eat or smoke them. I kept a few of the biggest ones, as a live display, for more than two weeks.

I *know* salmon can survive being played, unless the angler is callous or very inept and plays the fish to utter exhaustion or damages it on the rocks of the shore, on the bottom of the canoe or even by hard handling and banging in the net. I would rather put back ten salmon, even if I knew *half* of them wouldn't make it, than kill them *all*. Better five live, swimming and, hopefully, spawning salmon—or even *one live one*—than ten dead ones, killed to provide food we can readily obtain from another source of supply, because a biologist is "afraid" they might die.

How does an angler go about catching a salmon? Normally he starts with a wet fly and makes his cast, quartering downstream, across the pool. In the beginning, unless tutored by a very wise guide who knows where every salmon lies at the prevailing height of water, he will want to cover the pool completely, and the wet fly will give him the greatest and most uniform coverage. He casts his fly at a 45-degree angle with the flow and lets it swing with the current till it straightens out below him. Then he retrieves, moves

forward a step and makes a similar cast. His fly will then follow a
similar course just a bit farther downstream and so, by steadily
moving through the pool, he will cover it completely.

The wet fly, because it moves in relation to the flow, appears to
be alive. Its very motion gives it the semblance of life; to a salmon
it appears as a living insect, fish or crustacean. A dry fly normally
drifts freely with the current. It has no movement of its own, and
if it appears to a salmon to be an insect, that is because of its "look"
rather than its movement. A dry fly, therefore, must be a more convincing imitation of an insect than a wet fly has to be.

A dry fly, too, travels more slowly and over a shorter course on
each cast. Consequently, it covers far less water than a wet fly in
the same period of time. The dry fly is most effective when the
water is low and the fish are concentrated in the well-known pools;
least effective when the water is high and the fish are more widely
scattered throughout the expanded river.

A third method, the "hitched" fly, brings the conventional wet
fly to the surface, making a V-shaped wake, and for some reason is
often more attractive to the salmon than the same fly underwater.
The trick is to make two half hitches behind the head of the fly
after it has been tied to the leader. If the current is running from
the angler's left to his right as he faces it to cast, the hitches should
lie on the right-hand side of the fly's head. If it runs from right to
left, the hitches should be on the fly's left-hand side. This will
cause the fly to ride, or "skim," with the point downstream, facing
the fish as it approaches him.

When a salmon takes a skimming fly, as when he takes a dry fly,
he must come to the surface to get it and the surface rise, the sudden appearance of so big a fish for so small a fly, lends greater excitement to these two methods of fishing.

For the hitched fly to skim, it must travel at a certain speed. If
it travels too swiftly, it will bobble on the surface and throw spray.
If it travels too slowly, it will sink and twist or spin underwater.
Neither action seems to attract salmon. It is the fly traveling the
surface at the normal skimming speed that is most attractive.

To make the fly's speed stay "right," the angler must occasionally speed it up by drawing in line through the guides or lifting his
rod. Similarly, when the flow is swift, he must slow the fly's speed
by lowering his rod or letting line slide out through the guides on

the retrieve. It is quite interesting that this "right" skimming speed is close to the same speed that will draw most strikes when the fly is fished in a conventional underwater retrieve. When an angler has become practiced with the skimming fly, which he can see, it is easy for him to fish his underwater fly just as skillfully at the same speed, even though he cannot see it. A light-colored, visible fly line helps a great deal here, as the line indicates where the fly will follow.

Salmon that have recently come into the rivers from the sea tend to rise most readily and will accept brighter-colored, flashier flies. As their time in the rivers lengthens, they come to prefer the drab patterns of mottled gray and brown and black. Perhaps as the stream life becomes familiar to them again, they will be moved only by truer imitations of the insects they see around them like the alderflies, stone flies, mayflies, etc., rather than the colorful creations dreamed up by the fly tiers that match even better than reality the salmon's remembrance of his river's insects while he traveled the far-off sea.

Salmon change their positions not only with the rising or falling of the river but also with the falling of darkness and the coming of daylight. During the darkness a salmon need not fear attack from the birds of the air, but he must still worry about danger from swimming predators such as the otters and seals. Perhaps this is why he'll leave deep water and move to the shallow bars or edges where he can be approached from deeper water only on one side and through water shallow enough to make a predator's approach more apparent on the other. Fish for him close in in the early morning, in ankle- to knee-deep water where you'd normally wade to cast to his usual daytime positions.

Presenting a fly to a salmon in such a manner that he'll be triggered to rise to it is difficult to learn. On many salmon rivers, one rise a day is all an angler can expect. Out of thousands of casts, only one will draw a rise. After days of fishing, an angler may know only that a dozen casts, perhaps casts that differed widely one from another, drew rises. He will try to find, in those dozen casts, a common denominator—a combination of the fly's speed and angle with the current and its relation to the salmon in his particular lie.

A great many anglers like to have their fly swim directly across

The author is shown fishing in Newfoundland, where guides are required for nonresidents on many Atlantic salmon waters. (Newfoundland Department of Tourism)

the stream as much as possible. To accomplish this they hold their rod upstream at the start of the cast to keep the fly from heading downstream as it moves into the swifter water. Then, to keep it from heading upstream at too sharp an angle, they move their rod downstream and toward the shore side from which they are fishing. Or they mend their casts with a partial upstream roll cast. This does make a fly more visible to the fish as they lie facing upstream, and it may make it a little easier for a fish to catch and take the fly squarely.

Whether to hold the rod steady and let the fly sweep smoothly across the current on its travels or to twitch the rod to impart an uneven motion to the fly has worried a good many anglers. Salmon can be caught by both methods. One angler who constantly works his rod and whose fly is swimming in a pulsating manner will swear by it and will catch many salmon. At the same time, from the same river, another angler who simply casts his line and holds his rod steady or moves it in slow, easy sweeps to correct the fly's movement will do just as well. Whether or not to work the rod on the retrieve seems a matter of personal satisfaction for the angler more than an increase of effectiveness with the salmon. In fishing a number of pools in a day, I've alternated in fishing each new pool, first with a pulsating fly and then with a smooth swing, and found no noticeable variation in drawing rises or hooking fish.

Truly, to learn how to present a fly well to a salmon, an angler must have long salmon-fishing experience and, in a sense, he must have learned to think as a salmon would about what will tease or disturb him into rising. He may find that not only do the salmon's preferences for fly patterns change with each year and each different run of salmon, but the habits of taking a fly differ from river to river and from fast water to slow.

Going back into memory, I can think of many instances in which an unusual cast or fly activity was the key to getting a rise. I remember well a particularly big salmon lying in a clear 3-foot-deep run in a Labrador river that I worked over with both wet and dry flies for several hours. I'd try a series of wets, rest the fish and then try a series of dry flies. He seemed to move once or twice in reaction to a fly, and then I'd try a number of similar flies, larger or smaller, and return always to the fly that had sparked the interest. There were few salmon in the river, and this big fish seemed worth a lot of fishing time. I was drifting a No. 4 White Wulff over him from below and to his right when I finally decided to call it quits and go back to camp for lunch. As a final gesture, I made a long cast above him to allow a maximum float for the fly in approaching him. Sometimes, I think, when you've been pounding a dry fly over a salmon's head for a number of casts, a long, slow approach builds up tension that will draw a rise. This time, when the fly reached the fish, instead of letting it float on over him to be picked up well behind his tail, I gave a twitch of the rod and sank the fly just as it came over his nose. I pulled just enough to take the fly under, not enough to move it more than an inch or two out of its normal drift. With speed that was so fast the eye could hardly follow, that salmon twisted around and took the fly squarely, going away, downstream.

Another unusual retrieve calls for very high speed. A good many anglers have found, after fishing a pool in the manner that normally produces salmon for them, that by stripping in line on the retrieve and making the fly move through the water as swiftly as possible, they'll draw rises from fish that have ignored all their other efforts.

It remains a source of wonder for most of us that a salmon can move so swiftly and so accurately in the swirling currents of the rivers. Standing at the tailrace of a deep pool where the water sped out so swiftly that a fly touching it was whisked downstream in a fraction of a second, I doubted if any salmon would hold in that swift flow because of the energy it would require to hold in the 7- or 8-mile-an-hour current. But, failing to draw any rises in the slower flow farther up in the pool, I finally let my dry fly drop into the tailrace. To my surprise, a salmon took it almost as soon as it touched the water and before the current could have carried it a foot. I'm still amazed that a salmon could find a resting place in an eddy under so swift a flow, could see the fly land through 2 or 3 feet of foam and bubble-flecked water and, finally, could break up through that racing flow with such accuracy that he got the fly. It is this same fantastic speed of movement that continues to amaze salmon fishermen. Very often an angler who is intently watching salmon lying, perfectly visible, in a still deep flow will not even realize the fish has moved from his steady lie until the fly is sucked in and the rod is bending.

Where do the salmon lie? Knowledgeable trout fishermen are often baffled by salmon. They recognize that salmon pools and trout pools are very much alike, and they find themselves fishing with their "trout" tackle, even their trout flies, for this much heavier, faster fish. So they tend to fish as they would for trout— and they are in for surprises. Sometimes salmon lie where the trout do, but more often than not they lie in places trout would rarely choose.

The trout, a feeding fish, has three factors to consider in choosing his lies. He must worry about his safety, his comfort, but above all, his food supply. A salmon need have concern for only two— comfort and safety. So he lies where he has access to water deep enough for safety. He seeks comfort where he'll have the soothing effect of a gentle flow of water by his body. He generally chooses an eddy, where a rock or an uneven stream bed creates turbulence where he can rest without spending any more than necessary of his precious store of energy.

Often, beginning anglers wade to their knees where salmon

were lying before they waded out and frightened them. They stand where the fish were and cast to where they are not, but where trout might be.

An experienced salmon angler, knowing what a salmon needs for safety and comfort, can fish any stream well; not as well, however, as an angler who has seen the river in high water and low and has seen the salmon change their lies as the waters have dropped or risen. It is a benefit to know the skeleton of a river—the bare bones of drought, which it fills out in flood time.

If an angler were to come upon a poolful of fish that had never encountered man before, he could, with a suitable bait of worms, minnows or insects, catch practically all of them—unless they were Atlantic salmon. Then he'd have to fish in a certain manner, with a lure or fly of a certain size, and present it in a certain way or he'd not catch even one. Atlantic salmon have an instinctive, built-in resistance to being caught by anglers.

What triggers a salmon to rise is still a mystery. Why, if an angler fishes over a group of salmon in a pool with the same fly for three hours, one particular salmon will decide to take the last cast he is going to make is anyone's guess. Why did he wait so long? Why did that particular salmon rise and none of the others? A salmon angler finds himself fishing for an "ideal" salmon. He doesn't fish for all the salmon in the pool as much as for a particular fish that he can reach with his message. Much as he'd like to take every salmon in the pool, it is rarely that more than one salmon in three can be caught.

A long time ago the canny Scottish fly tiers decided that turn-down-eye hooks should be used for trout flies and that turn-up-eye hooks should be reserved for Atlantic salmon flies and that the flies would be very fancy and very expensive. These standard salmon-fly patterns were works of art. Bodies used several different silks, wools, tinsels and feathers. Wings were "married" by the working together of feather fibers of different colors from different birds. The search for suitable feathers was worldwide, and the results were magnificent.

A perfectly tied, true-to-pattern Jock Scott, Silver Doctor, Silver Wilkinson or Dusty Miller is something to treasure, for today's fly tiers rarely take the time or have the skill to duplicate these famous patterns. Instead, most modern fly tiers cut corners and simulate the old patterns, often using hair instead of feathers and eliminating many of the fancy furbelows the highly developed patterns called for.

It is no secret that the simpler patterns and some of the newer, simpler flies developed on this side of the Atlantic take fish just as well. In fact, anglers have found, sometimes to their surprise, that trout flies with *turned-down eyes* are extremely effective for salmon, especially in low water. The moral is to give the salmon the flies they like best and, if you have some of the beautiful old patterns that you think are irreplaceable, save them for a panel on the wall or a very special occasion when you think a reluctant salmon that's refused everything else you've offered might be charmed by the precise skill of a master fly tier and by feathers from India and Africa—of which, of course, he could have no knowledge or appreciation. Most salmon anglers have added faith in a fly that has already taken one salmon. They have greatest faith in a fly that has taken many and is a somewhat beat-up travesty of its original sleek self. Some anglers tie their flies that way.

With the coming of low water, anglers go to smaller flies than previously and find that they catch more fish under difficult summer conditions.

Low-water flies are tied on lighter hooks of finer wire. These hooks have a larger bite for the same weight—and by tying flies two sizes smaller on this type of hook, the angler can tempt a salmon with a fly of small bulk but greater holding power than flies on the standard hooks offer. Thus a No. 6 low-water fly is about the same size as a No. 8 in bulk, but holds a fish better. Low-water flies, in addition to being lighter for the same hook size, are simplified in design. Their effectiveness helped open up the field of salmon flies to many of the simpler modern variations.

Dry flies vary from high-riding, fluffy bivisibles through the hair wings and hair-bodied flies to the very sparsely dressed spiders and skaters. Dry flies are a relatively recent development in salmon angling. We've had wet flies for hundreds of years, but the dry fly came into use in the 1920s, and only in very recent years has it reached wide popularity. Consequently, dry-fly patterns do not have the variety or give as complete a coverage of the fishing possibilities as wet flies do. Dry flies offer great opportunities for the development of new and effective patterns—a challenge many salmon-fishing fly tiers are now taking up.

What size fly should one use? In high and cold water, large wet flies are in order. They are easier to see and, being on heavier hooks, they tend to sink a little lower in the faster, deeper waters of high runoff. Fish of the first run, fresh from the sea coming into the tail end of the spring high water are willing to take not only bigger but brighter flies than they will once they become accustomed to the stream and the water drops to summer level. As the days pass, they seem to accept their fasting more completely. After a month or more in the river, when they've taken on a dull stream-protective coloration, they'll spurn flies entirely except for special occasions like a sudden rise of water or the start of a major rain.

Dry flies are rarely effective in cold, high water. Their time comes in mid- and late season or in unusual early-season low water. The size of the dry fly doesn't parallel that of the wet flies. Large dry flies are effective in low water and late season at a time when only the smallest of wet flies will attract the salmon. More salmon are caught on flies in the No. 4 to 8 range than are taken on all other sizes. An angler should have a few as large as 3/0 and a few as small as 12 or 14 to have good coverage.

Suggested fly patterns:

Wet flies:	conventional	Jock Scott, Black Dose, Silver Gray, Silver Doctor, Wilkinson, Dusty Miller, Blue Charm, Night Hawk, Mar Lodge
	recent	Haggis, Hairy Mary, Green Butt, Whiskers, Muddler Minnow, Lady Joan
Dry flies:		Bivisibles, skaters, Surface Stonefly, Adams, Rat-Faced MacDougall, White Wulff, Grey Wulff, Royal Wulff

Salmon, as they move up through the river to their particular spawning ground, are affected greatly by the height and quality of the water. They like it high enough so they can travel the shallower stretches of the river; they like it fresh, renewed by rain.

Salmon tend to travel the rivers at night or in dull periods more than they do in full sunlight. The rate of travel up a river will vary greatly with individual runs of fish. They have the capability

Here are a few of the most famous of the salmon flies—several of which sport double hooks and all of which sport fancy plumage. The Gray Wulff and Royal Wulff, top center, and the White Wulff, bottom right, were created by the author. (The Orvis Company)

of traveling many miles a day, if they wish, and often the first fish to be caught are taken well up near a river's head. Some fish speed right through, while others dawdle along and move a little farther upstream on each small rise of water. Most salmon, with weeks or months to travel the river, seem to prefer to move upstream a few miles at a time.

There are many "rules" of salmon fishing—some of which an angler can understand and some that baffle him. It is relatively easy to catch salmon just as the water starts to rise with a major rain. It is almost impossible to catch them after that first flurry is over and the river has come up a few inches. The salmon will usually take no notice of flies again until the spate has reached its height and the river is dropping—a period that may take days.

There's a saying that salmon will not take a fly when the air is colder than the water. Why this should be true of a fish that doesn't have to expose more than the tip of his nose (if he needs to expose anything) to the chill air to take a fly is beyond me. But, by and large, I've found it's true.

Salmon do not take a fly well in pools just under falls. This is said to be because they're preoccupied with the problem of leaping the falls. This intentness on their immediate problem overcomes the normal restlessness that makes them take a fly. This rule too seems to hold.

Salmon are leaping fish, yet anglers are always trying to figure out why they leap. Some attribute their leaps to the settling of the maturing eggs or milt within their bodies. Others say it is to shake off parasites that they may feel, or think they feel, clinging to their bodies. I think they jump because it is part of their nature. All young animals, in their play, do the things that build up the muscles they'll need for their basic activities of maturity.

Salmon on their spawning runs must travel rough water and leap the falls. If they came to these barriers without prior leaping practice, they might well fail to make them. So they leap—in the sea, in the pools and runs and over the falls when they meet them.

A salmon may leap a falls with a straight drop of as much as 12 feet, but most salmon find a passage up through the turbulent water where their speed is greater than the flow they face. This is demonstrated often by the fish one sees leaping up into the falling water and then swimming up over the lip of the falls, overcoming the slower flow with a burst of speed.

Most salmon are lost to anglers either at the rise or at the net, and practically always because the angler held too hard. If an angler sees the rise or feels the pressure of a fish taking his sunken fly, his tendency is to set the hook and, if he's used to trout or smaller fish, to hold him or turn him in his direction.

Under such hard pressure, a salmon *moves*, and *fast*. If an angler isn't ready to release his pressure as swiftly as a salmon can move, he'll reel back an empty leader. Even a 30-pound-test leader will be snapped by a 5-pound salmon if he's solidly held.

During the playing of a salmon, slack line is not the bugaboo most anglers hold it to be. The fly is small and light, and unless its hold has been worn by long playing, slack line will not cause it to come free.

The angler's pressure on a salmon should be light—an effort by the angler to make the fish spend his store of strength in leaps and runs—rather than heavy, as if to move him by force from far away to close by. Only when a salmon is close and tired does a fisherman feel free to put his tackle to a severe test.

Here, Wulff carefully applies the brakes to a running salmon. (New-foundland Department of Tourism)

The best anglers sense when a salmon can be led, when he can be frightened into a long run or a series of leaps and when he can be conned into turning into the current to rest instead of continuing downstream and out of the pool.

A change of the angle of pressure as well as the amount is important, both in wearing fish out and in guiding them into safer playing water. A hooked fish, as he tires and finds that sheer speed and leaps will not free him, tends to turn his body against the flow and put as much pressure as he can upon the thing that is trying to draw him to a given spot in a given direction. If the fisherman changes the angle of the pull, the fish must change his angle with the current. By forcing the fish to change to a narrow angle and then swinging the rod downstream, the angler makes his pull very much more effective. By turning a tired fish slightly on a slow, steady run, the angler can lead the fish into a curve that will head him right back toward the fisherman as the strength of his surge diminishes. An angler should use all the "angles" his rod will permit.

And when a fish is tired, the angler should make his play by a judgment of the fish's power, rather than the angler's wish to force him in. Even though tired, a salmon is too heavy to hold when it wants to move.

A salmon angler's reel should hold from 150 to 250 yards of backing behind his casting line. There's no substitute for a lengthy line with a wild, sea-trained fish in a large or difficult river. And anglers who have always played fish on relatively short lines will be amazed at how far a fish may go and still be saved. The secret in saving fish that have run far off is to play them gently. The drag of the line in the water creates its own pull on the end of the line that is near the fish, and the last thing the angler wants to do is add tension to that already heavy drag. Instead, his solution is to change his position, moving toward the line's pull. If the line sweeps downstream in a great belly, the fisherman *must* go downstream to try to get the line straighter—to take out the belly and eliminate the belly's heavy pressure on the fish. If he can do that, he can, with much less pressure, shorten his line as he works back upstream toward the fish.

Usually a salmon with a long line out is a little tired from his run and will rest awhile. An angler, following his line slowly and clearing it of the rocks around which it may be caught, will find, more often than not, that his salmon is still on when he gets close to him. Too many anglers give up when a salmon is far off and try to hold him or to bring him back by pressure. This won't work very often, and any movement of the line that the fish can feel, even though the line may be around a rock or snag that inhibits free movement in either direction, will cause him to move again—and that's the last thing an angler wants when a fish is far away and the line semisnagged.

Fish react to changing pressures and as an angler plays an individual salmon he can learn whether a gentle pressure will turn him better than a harsh one or a sudden pressure better than a gradual one. A good angler can make a salmon move where he wants him to much of the time. An excellent example of the effect of pressure is that a salmon can be "walked" upstream against a current, by an angler moving slowly and steadily without any reeling or change in pressure, more easily than he can be brought upstream by reeling or pulling in of line through the guides. The movement of the line in relation to the rod by these latter methods seems to generate vibrations that upset the salmon. When a salmon hangs on the lip of the pool above a stretch of rough and roaring water, the angler's best hope is to walk him up into the quieter, deeper part of the pool and hope to be able to hold him there either by changing angles or by tackle power.

An easy leading of the fish to the net or beach will often accomplish the desired end faster than pure pressure. Remembering that he must play the fish till the final moment, an angler should always be prepared to let a tired salmon have his last run or leap and then another surge or two or three even after he has come within inches of the beach or the landing instrument. Far too many fish are lost because the fisherman held too hard at the net instead of letting the play continue for just a minute longer.

Then, when the salmon is finally conquered, an angler should show him the respect he deserves. In death he should have the same honor one gives him when he lives and swims free in the rivers as a great angling challenge. He should be handled carefully, out of respect for his fight (and for all the money and effort it cost the angler to catch him), and not treated as if he were not worth keeping clean or were not good to look at. It has always bothered me to see a guide, whose very wages depend upon the respect his employer has for this fine fish, throw one on the bottom of the canoe as if it were a sack of cement or tear out its gills and split its fins by careless handling, turning it from a thing of great beauty into a dirty, bloody mess.

Although many salmon anglers use guides because of their knowledge of the fish and let them help in landing the fish, it is possible for the largest salmon to be caught by an unaided individual angler. In this way a salmon probably offers the greatest challenge a fisherman can find in all of angling.

During the spawning time, salmon must work into shallow water so that the fertilized eggs will lie in the best riffles. At times such as this, they are in great danger. Bears, fish hawks, eagles and otters can prey on them. Eels too have been known to kill salmon, reaching their gills and hanging on when a fish is too tired to shake them free. But of all the predators, man is the fiercest and most deadly. Hopefully, man is at last turning a corner as far as the salmon are concerned and is willing to control his predation for the good of the species and the sport.

He is magnificent, this Atlantic salmon: game beyond the capabilities of most game fishes of similar weight; discriminating in the size and pattern of the flies to which he'll rise; a lover of clear streams and sweeping water. He's the game fish that takes the smallest lure for his size and requires, therefore, the smallest hook.

It may not be, as with most fish, the leader or line that is the weak link in the tackle chain, but the hook. Taking a 27-pound salmon on a single-hooked No. 16 fly represents an angling challenge that may not be equaled by any other.

How does this special fish fare in this modern world and what is his future?

If we look back to the 1850s, we can picture the citizens along the Connecticut River meeting and raising money to build a power dam. Electricity! It was a magic word. Without it a man must continue to fumble in the dark for a whale-oil lamp and a sulfurous match to light a dim glow poor indeed for reading or working. With it, he could enter his house on a dark night, press a switch and have light of a brilliance previously undreamed of. Little wonder the dams went through, with only a few soon-stifled voices asking what would happen to the salmon.

The dams came; the salmon died—not only in the Connecticut, but in the Merrimack, the Kennebec, the Penobscot and all the major rivers of New England. Canada, less industrialized, was able to keep her salmon, but, mainly through lack of adequate protection and the greed of her commercial fishermen, they were brought gradually to a very low ebb.

To favor a few of the major commercial netters who preferred to take the big, more valuable salmon, the government passed laws that set up a minimum mesh size—a size that permitted the salmon of 5 pounds and under to pass through and reach the rivers to spawn, while capturing and killing the larger fish.

If a biologist were given the problem of *reducing* the size of any species, he would kill off his best stock and breed his runts. This is what the Canadian government forced all of its commercial salmon fishermen to do—with the result that the average size of salmon in the runs plummeted. The biologists, apparently fearful of their jobs, kept quiet. Not one in authority raised his voice in dissent over this wasteful policy. As a result, with the run changing from almost exclusively big salmon to dwarfish grilse in most rivers, the return in pounds of salmon for a given amount of river food dropped alarmingly.

Then, in 1964, the hitherto unknown feeding grounds of the salmon off western Greenland was discovered, and a high-seas fishery, with drift nets many miles in length, came into being.

With salmon already on a decline, the sudden taking of a quantity on the high seas as great as that taken in all of Canada proved disastrous.

The United States, under pressure spearheaded by the Committee on the Atlantic Salmon Emergency (CASE), passed a law authorizing an official government boycott of fishery products from any nation operating in contrary fashion to conservation policy on the high seas.

The Danes, the holdout nation for high-seas fishing for salmon, finally agreed to phasing out their fishing. It is to be phased out very slowly, but it was a victory for the conservation movement. Canada, realizing the extreme gravity of its salmon situation, banned all commercial fishing in two of its provinces and in its offshore waters. Strong actions at last, which should start the salmon back on its road to recovery. Hopefully, these regulations may become permanent.

Iceland, of all the salmon-producing countries of the North Atlantic, shines as a bright example of good salmon management. Thirty years ago, Iceland's fishing was little heard of, as the country was considered bleak and the salmon were generally smaller than those in the more southerly areas. Little by little, the "better" rivers of the other nations saw their salmon fishing deteriorate until Iceland's fishing, which maintained its early level, became the best in the world.

Iceland was able to maintain and even improve its salmon-fishing quality. Early in its history, the owners of the farms through which the salmon rivers flowed established their rights to the salmon, and sea netting of the fish was eliminated. Some netting was done in the tidal waters of the rivers, but now even this has been almost entirely eliminated, making the salmon, in effect, a game fish.

The sea feeding grounds of the Icelandic salmon have not been found and subjected to a devastating fishery. Iceland has used preferred genetic strains to supplement its stream stocks, even to using fly-caught fish to strip for eggs and milt for hatcheries.

Making the salmon a game fish is a natural development, as anglers have always been ready to pay a higher price for the fish than the commercial market could bring. Commericial nets have been bought out at a price that has pleased those who were netting, and the improvement in fishing has made the return from angling greater and pleased the anglers, too.

America's foolish judgment that all fishing is equally valuable, that for a single license all rivers, regardless of quality, are open to an angler, has never been considered in Iceland or the European nations. The fee for fishing there depends on the quality of the angling, just as the price of a car or a rod depends upon its quality.

Icelandic rivers are divided into "beats," and on the better rivers each "beat" is expected to produce between 1,200 and 1,500 salmon per season. The fees for fishing vary with the accommodations and the size of the fish.

In America, if one river is better than the rest, a newspaper or magazine article will tell all the anglers about it, and they will swarm upon it and beat it down until it is no better than average. We in America have our "democracy" of fishing; in Iceland and Europe, wise practices have saved the quality. Our only hope—if salmon are returned to our major New England rivers—is to do with salmon as Colorado does with its bighorn sheep—limit the taking to maintain the quality and the species.

The answer to salmon conservation lies, I believe, in making the Atlantic salmon a game fish. Those who have been earning their living by netting salmon can be made happy with money the sportsmen will gladly pay for the better fishing they'll gain. Somehow this pattern can be worked into our American democratic system.

The prices for Icelandic fishing have been skyrocketing. I believe that to make the situation fair, the Icelandic government will soon pass a regulation holding for Icelandic fishermen, at a reasonable price, a large percentage of the fishing.

The balance will be open to nonresidents at whatever price they will pay. At present, the better fishing is going for $1,500 to $1,800 per week per angler. Within a few years, it will probably double. Overpriced, you say! Nothing is overpriced when there is a waiting list to buy it. Angling has a value we Americans have been slow to recognize. We no longer have the best fishing in the world, and many Americans now go abroad to find it.

A great hope for the future is the farming of salmon for food. In Iceland there is a "farm" where salmon are raised to smolt, released to find the sea-feeding area, captured on their return and sold, just as range cattle are raised, rounded up, slaughtered and sold. In Norway, there's a successful farm where salmon are raised to maturity, controlled in both fresh and salt water by careful hatchery methods and feeding.

Society will be served best both in sport and economically if the salmon rivers produce salmon for sport alone and the "farms" produce them for the market. This, I believe, is the hope of the future.

PACIFIC SALMON

BY LARRY GREEN

THE MOST crucial period in the life of a Pacific salmon begins after the fish has reached maturity. Overcome by an uncontrollable urge to spawn, the adult salmon abandons its carefree life in the open waters of the Pacific Ocean in exchange for a more serious undertaking and an inevitable rendezvous with death.

As an egg or sperm sac begins to develop within the salmon, a modification of its life-style is set into motion. Primed now with a new sense of determination, the fish begins a migration away from its ocean feeding grounds—feeding grounds so abundantly rich with small fish, pelagic larvae and other marine life forms that they have provided the salmon the rapid growth and stored fat needed for its long journey to the spawning grounds.

The spawning migration, begun at sea, is first directed toward the shoreline of the Pacific Coast, where numerous rivers and smaller streams flow into the surf. Following the coastline, each salmon carefully seeks out the sweet taste of river water through some marvelous sensory mechanism which remains undescribed in books of anadromous ichthyology. The taste or scent which each adult salmon seeks is not that of just any river; it is that of the same river in which that particular salmon was spawned.

Once the correct water is identified, the adult salmon enters the river willingly, though perhaps knowing it will never again return to the sea. All salmon, with only one exception, die after spawning. The Atlantic salmon (*Salmo salar*) does return to the sea again after completion of spawning.

Once the salmon has entered the river, it must undergo a difficult period of acclimating itself from salt to fresh water. This is the period when the salmon takes on a new wardrobe. Its brightly scaled torso, which readily lost fluids in the salty waters of the sea, now begins to retain much of the natural body fluids. Darkening of the scales occurs as well as some disfiguration of the otherwise streamlined body shape. The freshwater migration has begun.

Adorned in their death masks, the hook-jawed males and plump-bellied females ripe with spawn begin their grueling ascent to the higher reaches of the same river in which they once frolicked as fingerling salmon in quiet pools and oxygen-rich riffles.

The salmon's journey upriver becomes more and more difficult as wide, easily navigable channels turn into narrow, turbulent creekbeds. The salmon's race is now against time as well as distance as an irreversible biological deterioration begins to drain energy and life from their bodies. It is this deterioration, closely comparable to multiple sclerosis in humans, that means ultimate death to the salmon that survive the hazards of the spawning run.

Once the spawning grounds are reached and its genetic instinct has assured each salmon that it is indeed within a close proximity of its place of birth, spawning begins. Males and females join in frantic attempts to rid themselves of eggs and sperm in the fine gravel of the streambed. Completion of spawning is closely followed by the death of both parent fish.

Within sixty to ninety days, the fertilized eggs begin to hatch, and out of the deaths of two adult salmon emerge potential thousands of fish which, if they survive, will in time follow the migratory paths of their parents downriver, out to sea and back again— one generation following another as has been the case for years beyond number.

There are five species of Pacific salmon that make up the fishery of the Pacific Coast. These five are the chinook, or king, salmon (*Oncorhynchus tshawytscha*); the coho, or silver, salmon (*Oncorhynchus kisutch*); the pink, or humpback, salmon (*Oncorhynchus gorbuscha*); the sockeye, or red, salmon (*Oncorhynchus nerka*) and the chum, or dog, salmon (*Oncorhynchus keta*). Though all five species contribute to the commercial salmon fishery, only three species, the chinook, coho and pink salmon, are considered to be of primary importance to the sport fishery. Both the chum and sockeye salmon are sought primarily for their food value by commercial interests.

The chinook is the largest of the three species sought for sport. One chinook caught commercially in Alaska weighed 126 pounds; however, the largest caught on sport-fishing tackle was a 92-pound monster taken from the Skeena River in British Columbia. Generally, male chinooks mature at 2 to 5 years of age, whereas the females mature at 4 to 5 years of age. Mature males 2 years old are nicknamed jack salmon, and they too provide great sport.

The coho salmon looks very similar in coloring and body shape to the chinook, with only two noticeable differences. For one, the coho's upper jaw tends to be more hooked than the chinook's prior to spawning. Also, the bottom of the coho's jaw around the gum line at the base of the teeth is white, while the chinook's is black.

Cohos do not reach the weight that chinooks do, although a record coho of 31 pounds was taken by a sport fisherman at Cowichan Bay, Vancouver Island, British Columbia. Cohos usually reach maturity at 3 years of age, with the exception of sexually precocious 2-year-old jacks.

The pink salmon is the smallest of the three species, reaching a maximum weight of about 15 pounds. Though the pink ranges primarily in the more northern streams above the Puget Sound, Washington, area, it does make up a substantial part of the northern sport fishery.

The pink salmon is seldom found south of the Puget Sound area, as its spawning grounds are located in British Columbian and Alaskan waters. The pink, however, is considered a sport fish in all waters north of Puget Sound. The only two species of Pacific salmon that range the Pacific Coast from central California to the Alaskan peninsula are the chinook and coho salmon.

Though all three sport fishes—chinook, coho and pink—are commonly sought by saltwater fishermen trolling spoons and baits on the open sea, Pacific salmon are most vulnerable to waiting anglers who greet them as they enter the rivers to spawn. Light-tackle pur-

This 21-pound-1-ounce coho taken by Frank Allen in California's Paper Mill Creek is a giant of its species.

suit of these handsomest of all Pacific game fishes in an environment uniquely different from that of the open sea is considered the ultimate sport by its devotees.

An observant salmon angler knows that there are actually three very different fishable habitats within most large river systems, each of which has a direct influence on migratory Pacific salmon. These three habitats are: the *mouth of the river,* where fresh, sweet water suddenly meets and mixes with the high-salinity waters of the Pacific Ocean; the *tidal water,* which, depending on the influx of the ocean's tides, often creates large brackish-water (half salt, half fresh) lagoons that may extend more than 2 miles upriver from the mouth; the *upper river,* which includes all the river from the protected spawning grounds downriver to tidewater.

Successful fishing for migratory salmon in each of these different habitats requires fishing skills that are as varied as they are unique. To best acquaint himself with all these habitats, the river salmon angler must explore the full potential of each.

Fishing the River Mouths

There is one term unique to the river salmon fisherman's vocabulary. It describes a fishing technique practiced at the mouth of most of the larger migratory rivers when the salmon first arrive. That term is "hog-line fishing."

When word gets out that salmon have begun to enter a particular river, anglers with small outboard-powered skiffs line up just inside the mouth of the river, forming a hog line. They anchor their skiffs with the bows pointed upstream and the transoms pointed toward the open ocean.

When a good run of salmon is in progress on a large river such as California's Klamath, Oregon's Rogue or Washington's Columbia, as many as 50 to 100 skiffs may anchor themselves oarlock to oarlock in a hog line stretching clear across the mouth of the river.

Hog lines do create some animosity among other river salmon anglers, particularly the trollers and shore casters fishing farther upstream. Protesting anglers claim that hog lines often become overcrowded and that the mess of anchor lines and fishing lines is so closely woven across the river's mouth that it actually spooks the salmon or hinders them from penetrating to the higher stretches of the river. On numerous salmon rivers along the Pacific Coast, hog-line enthusiasts actually string cables across the river between buoys so that they can tie up their skiffs rather than attempt to anchor them in the river's strong current.

Hog-line fishing is highly competitive. In most cases there is little room to breathe, let alone fish. What fishing is attempted must be done directly off the stern of the boat. The line must run straight out behind the skiff to avoid tangles with those of other fishermen.

The standard method of fishing for salmon in a hog line is with baits or, occasionally, spin-type lures. Enough weight is applied to the line to carry it to the bottom. Often as much as a pound of lead is needed to touch bottom in a strong current. Attached either directly to or just above the sinker is a 7- to 9-foot leader with a bait hook carefully threaded with a whole anchovy or a herring fillet. The weight of the sinker keeps the bait near the bottom, where it moves briskly from side to side under the prodding of the current.

Lures are used in the same manner. They are snapped on the end of the leader with the aid of a free-turning swivel, preferably of the ball-bearing type. The lures, be they spinners, wobblers or spoons, turn and flutter rapidly in the current. A salmon, moving into the river from the ocean, spots one and attacks it savagely. Once the hook is set into a striking salmon, the angler must quickly retrieve his anchor—or release his bow line, if he's tied to the cable —and allow the current to carry him downstream and away from the other boat anglers in the hog line.

If, before the angler can free his boat, the salmon decides to make a sudden run across the current rather than with or against it, the result is usually a complete jumble of lines, anchor ropes and disgruntled fishermen.

The angler must always start his engine before freeing his anchor or bow line, so that he can gain control of his boat before the current sweeps him out to sea. Once free of the hog line, he must motor his boat toward the riverbank and out of the current, provided his salmon is willing to cooperate.

If, for any reason, his motor should fail, the situation could become critical. On calm days with no surf, the current will simply carry the angler, fish and all, out to sea. But if the surf is running rough at the river's mouth, a boat with a stalled engine could be sucked under the breaking surf and smashed to pieces. So many drownings have occurred over the years as a result of hog-line fishing that at many river mouths the U.S. Coast Guard stations fast boats on ready alert, during the salmon season, for the sole purpose of rescuing hog-line fishermen.

Despite the risks involved and the growing animosity toward hog liners by anglers who claim it is an unsporting way to fish for salmon, hog lining seems to be expanding in popularity with each new season.

For one thing, there is something to be said for the success of this method, even though the question of what is sport fishing may hang in the balance. Hog-line fishing in a river mouth is very productive of fresh-run salmon. Hog liners are virtually guaranteed a fresh, healthy fish, be it a chinook, a coho or a pink salmon. All fresh-run salmon are as bright as shiny new silver coins when they first enter a river from the sea. Catching migratory salmon at the mouth of a river also assures the angler that his salmon will be full of fight.

Anglers who are discouraged by hog lines often seek their fishing pleasures on the smaller rivers along the Pacific Coast where hog lines are seldom tolerated. Occasionally on smaller rivers, one or two anglers will anchor near the mouth in search of a salmon; however, the majority of the salmon fishing at the mouths of these smaller streams is done by wading or shore casting. Bait drifting with a glob of fresh salmon roe, rigged anchovies or cut baits is a standard practice among the shore casters. The baits are cast out and across the current with just enough weight to keep them moving along the bottom.

Lure fishermen use wobbling lures, spinners or spoons, which they also cast across the current, retrieving them slowly to keep the lures active.

Occasionally, brave fly fishermen will wade the edges of a river

The mouth of Oregon's Rogue River is treacherous but rewarding. Note the Coast Guard boat standing by.

The pink shrimp fly is an excellent pattern when fished in river mouths or tidewater for Pacific salmon.

where it pours into the sea. Often the difficulty here is keeping one's back cast out of the sand dunes and piles of driftwood. Lead-core or high-density, fast-sinking lines are used when the tide is out and the river's current is swift. On slack tides, floating or slow-sinking lines are often used. Pink shrimp flies or other brightly colored fly patterns often result in the successful landing of large fresh-run chinook or coho salmon.

Though some might argue the point, I do not believe one can set his watch to the time periods in which the salmon decide to enter the river from the sea. I'm inclined to believe that whenever there is a sufficient flow of water to keep the mouth of the river open, the salmon will move into and out of the river on several occasions before the decision is made to begin their freshwater migration to the spawning grounds.

Perhaps the salmon are frustrated, confused and torn by two forces—a strong urge to spawn and a hesitation to leave an environment that has comfortably hosted them through most of their maturing lives. But the spawning urge always wins out.

At the mouths of many of the salmon-producing streams along the West Coast, rock seawalls or jetties assist the salmon as well as the fishermen. The arms of a seawall escort a river out into the deeper parts of the ocean, keeping the mouth free of sandbars that could threaten closure of its entrance to the sea. Wherever jetties escort a flow of fresh water into the surf, you'll find anglers walking them in pursuit of salmon. Casting wobbling-type lures or drifting cut and rigged baits with the moving tide is an acceptable method of fishing for salmon from a jetty.

One of the most popular methods of taking salmon at or near the mouth of a river is a technique known as "mooching." Mooching is a term used for fishing a cut bait (usually a 4- to 8-inch piece of herring) by bouncing it along the bottom with the flow of the current or by trolling slowly if the current is slack while the tide is at its ebb. Moochers use hooks that range from 1/0 to 4/0 in size on a leader that keeps them 7 to 8 feet away from a 1- to 5-ounce banana-type sinker. The longer leader allows the salmon to pick up, mouth and swallow the offering before feeling any tension induced by the weight.

Mooching is one of the most highly successful methods of taking chinook, coho and pink salmon at river mouths or areas of the open ocean adjacent to the river mouths in the more northern waters of the Pacific Coast.

Fishing the mouth of any river in pursuit of migratory salmon is a challenging experience because so many varying factors are involved. The changing of such elements as tides, temperatures, salinity factors and sedimentation all contribute to the unpredictable nature of salmon fishing.

Fishing the Salmon in Tidewater

Once a salmon has overcome its strong bond with the sea and enters the river determined to fulfill its spawning obligation, it moves quickly upstream away from the strong currents at the mouth of the river. Here, schools of adult salmon linger in quiet stretches of tidewater, completing their acclimation to the new environment. Time must be allowed to pass as the salmon's gills undergo the physiological modifications necessary to adapt to drastic changes in a body of water where the salinity factor is continually altered by the action of the tides.

That which is considered tidewater within a river is all of the lower portions of the river that are affected by tidal action, from the mouth upstream to the farthest point to which the river backs up at high tide. If the river drops greatly in elevation just before entering the sea, the tidewater portion will be slight or nil. But if the topography of the river channel is like that of most of the larger rivers of the Pacific Coast—flat and low in elevation—then chances are the tidewater will reach for miles upstream from the mouth.

At extreme low tide some rivers may appear to be relatively narrow, yet the same rivers at extreme high tide might change drastically in appearance as large, flat lagoons form and marshlands are flooded.

It is within these tidewater portions of the lower river that the majority of migrating salmon are taken by anglers. Here the fish begin to assemble in large schools as they prepare for their ascent to the upper stretches of the river. The tidewaters are brackish, with salinity factors that can vary from 10 percent to 60 percent salt water, depending on the fluctuating tides. When pursuing the salmon in tidewater, anglers find a variety of fishing situations, such as currents that run in either direction, or lengthy stretches of slack water.

When thousands of salmon gather in tidewater, they often roll or porpoise on the surface. This is the sort of visual stimulation that attracts anglers.

Many explanations are given for why salmon roll in fresh water when they are not known to do so in salt water. Some biologists say it is a way of relieving the itch of dying sea lice that scamper over their bodies in search of saltier water. Others say it is merely an expression of contentment, similar to that of a colt kicking up its heels out of sheer joy. Whatever the reason, when a beautiful salmon rips open the surface of the water, exposing its broad silver sides, it's bound to have a profound effect on pursuing anglers.

Areas that host the salmon during their acclimation period are known as holding pools. If a riverbed does not change drastically from one year to another, you will find that the salmon tend to use the same holding pools year after year. These are usually tidewaters where the currents are mild. Some holding areas might consist of very deep pools, while others might be very shallow. The salmon may even move about the lower portions of a river with the tides. This may have something to do with changing salinity factors.

Whereas both the pink and the chinook are caught mainly by fishing on or near the bottom in tidewaters, the coho is not, being a congenital surface feeder. Whether you're trolling a rigged bait, casting a lure or retrieving a fly, you should remember to work your offering just under the surface if you wish to entice a coho into a strike.

One of the most widely accepted methods of fishing all salmon in the tidal portions of a river is by trolling from a small skiff. A great variety of attractors are used, including rigged baits (with or without flashers), wobbling lures, spoons and flies. Spinners, either single- or double-bladed, seem to work very well on salmon lying in tidewater. It is a good idea to work over schooled fish that are showing on the surface, as long as you're careful not to run a powerboat directly over them.

If the angler is totally unfamiliar with a stretch of tidewater in his pursuit of fresh-run salmon, the best way to locate good holding areas, other than following local anglers, is to scan the river with binoculars from a high vantage point. Watch for rolling or breaking fish. Salmon acting this way are generally resting in their holding areas. This brings up a controversy about fishing for rolling salmon in tidewater.

Some expert salmon anglers claim that if a salmon rolls or porpoises on the surface, it's a good indication it is *not* in a feeding mood. They claim that the best time to fish over schooled salmon in tidewater is when the fish are erupting violently on the surface, causing sizable splashes.

When the salmon is resting in tidewater, acclimating itself to the transition from salt to fresh water, its disposition can best be defined as moody, or sulky. Don't be surprised if on occasion you encounter large schools of migrating salmon tightly stacked and visible in clear pools, only to discover that the fish will not show the slightest response to any offering you toss at them. Nothing, but nothing, is more stubborn than a salmon off the bite. Countless hours have been spent by frustrated anglers working over big, tempting salmon at rest in quiet pools in the lower portions of a river.

When this situation is encountered, it is best to select a more appropriate time of day. Generally, salmon are most cooperative when they are restless or on the move. In addition, salmon in tidewater seem generally to be stirred at two periods in the day: very early morning and late afternoon—usually a couple of hours prior to sunset. Salmon also become active during periods of heavy rainfall, though I have found no one with an explanation for why this is true. An obvious guess is that the salmon instinctively know the rains signify periods of high water and greater opportunities to advance upriver.

At some point during the salmon's stay in tidewater, its gullet, or throat, tightens and it ceases feeding entirely, surviving on stored body fats. At this stage of the game, lures, spoons, rigged bait and spinners do little more than occasionally irk the fish into a strike.

This is the period, however, when fly fishermen dominate the tidewater. Salmon seem to be much more inclined to accept small flies than other, larger offerings once they have been in tidewater for a substantial period of time.

Fly rodders who know the tidewater holding areas work over resting salmon with a variety of weighted flies. In the case of chinook and pink salmon, the artificial flies producing the best results seem to be those sporting colorful materials of fluorescent reds, yellows and oranges with some silver ribbing trim. Also pink shrimp flies or bright green Woolly Worm–type patterns are excellent for tidewater salmon. The flies are usually tied on nickel-plated hooks sized No. 2 or 4. The flies are fished near the bottom and retrieved slowly in front of a salmon's nose, hopefully inducing a strike. If and when the strike does come, it may be only a slight nudge or bump, though the fish may be a salmon exceeding 50 pounds.

Coho (or silver) salmon are enthusiastic takers of artificial flies in tidewater. But the flies should be fished just beneath the surface for best results. A good coho pattern in tidewater is an extremely colorful pattern, usually sporting some splashes of purple, lavender, red and orange and also with some silver ribbing trim on the body. The fly should *not* be weighted and should be fished with a floating or extremely slow-sinking line. A fast, jerky retrieve usually induces more coho strikes than a slow retrieve. A coho bent on

Roe, lead weight and conventional bait-casting tackle are the primary choice for river salmon fishing.

engulfing an artificial fly usually hits the offering very hard. Once the hook is set, this salmon will outjump its cousins the chinook and pink 10 to 1.

There are other rather unusual baits—like live crayfish or the meat from the tail of a crayfish, as well as ghost shrimp and sand crabs—that have also been acclaimed as tidewater salmon secrets. All have some credibility, but fished properly, artificial flies, single-bladed spinners and properly rigged anchovies are all hard to beat as consistent producers.

Fishing salmon in tidewater, be it in small, narrow lagoons or huge, open bays, is a challenge that is always supreme. Time is a limiting factor, for once acclimated to fresh water the salmon will be eager to move upriver toward the spawning grounds. Once the migration upstream has begun, the adult salmon will not return again to tidewater.

The condition of the water usually determines when the salmon move on to the upper stretches of the river. If there is an ample flow of river water, they acclimate quickly and move upriver almost immediately. But if drought or low-water conditions prevail upstream, the salmon may choose to hold in tidewater—often for weeks. Then, when the rains finally come and the river swells with fresh, murky rainwater, the salmon's instincts, urge them toward the spawning grounds.

Fishing the Salmon in the Upper River

If a migratory salmon survives the rigors of its journey to its final spawning place, it is assured protection from anglers by state fish-and-game laws. The higher reaches of all prime spawning grounds on the majority of the salmon streams in the Western United States and Canada are preserved as sanctuaries where the salmon conducts its spawning unmolested by man. Protected spawning areas are clearly posted, though the public is often welcome to come and observe this most interesting sight.

The length of a salmon's journey from tidewater upstream to the boundaries of its spawning ground depends on the course of the river. Two extreme examples of how this distance can vary are found in California and Idaho.

There is a small stream, appropriately named Salmon Creek, located near Bodega Bay, California. The point considered the salmon spawning area is less than half a mile upriver from the mouth. Fishing is legal only from the Highway 1 bridge to the mouth (approximately 300 yards). Despite its size, the creek hosts an annual run of coho salmon upwards of 10 pounds. Most of the river is considered tidewater.

Compare the spawning grounds found near Lewiston, Idaho. Salmon, as well as steelhead, first enter the Columbia River at its mouth on the Oregon–Washington border. In order to reach their spawning grounds in the Snake River near Lewiston, these migrating fish must travel more than 1,600 river miles. Yet, ironic as it may seem, some of the salmon and steelhead that reach the upper Snake are as prime in color and shape as the salmon that traveled only a few hundred yards up the lagoon of California's Salmon Creek.

The biological deterioration of the salmon's flesh is so timed that it corresponds perfectly with the period needed for each fish to reach its own spawning area. This is but another of the many mysteries of these anadromous fish.

Anglers who pursue the Pacific salmon in the upper reaches of a migratory river, from tidewater to the spawning grounds, might do best to think of the salmon as an overgrown trout and fish for him accordingly. Though this statement is an oversimplification, anglers *can* benefit by applying a little trout-fishing technology. This is especially true in rivers and streams small enough to fish without the aid of a boat. In such waters, too, the salmon will occupy the same oxygen-rich riffles, quiet pools and swift runs as do stream trout.

But there is one important difference between the trout and the salmon. Whereas the trout strike because they are hungry and on the feed, the migrating salmon do not. Though there has been no way found to prove it, it is believed that the salmon strike because of an irritable, protective and aggressive nature brought on by their spawning urge. One basis for this belief lies in the fact that river salmon are known to strike more readily at brightly colored flashing-type artificials than those which more closely resemble natural foods.

Though it is generally accepted that salmon migrating upriver to spawn do not eat, as is indicated by the absence of any food in their stomachs and the presence of constricted muscles in their throats, there is evidence that the fish are possessed of a rather strong attraction to the scent of food, if not food itself.

A good example of this can be witnessed each fall on California's largest salmon-hosting river, the Sacramento. It is in the central Sacramento, between Knights Landing and Anderson, that hundreds of anglers gather to fish for chinook and coho salmon with some rather unorthodox techniques.

Ensconced in powerboats, they troll against the current, drift or anchor while fishing special deep-running lures that offer good side-to-side action. Lures most commonly used are the Hot Shot, Flatfish, Fishback, Rebel and a few others with similar action. They are fished with a combination of lead weights which keep them on or close to the bottom.

The lures by themselves often account for good catches. However, the most successful of these fishermen attach strips of cut bait—usually sardine, herring, anchovy or other highly scented baits—to the backs of the artificial lures with the aid of rubber bands. The results are amazing, and the anglers who fish this way claim the scent from the cut bait is the key factor in producing strikes. In addition, bank fishermen along the Sacramento River also take a fair share of migratory salmon (primarily chinook) by still-fishing deep holes and swift runs with whole or cut baits. And these techniques are being used more and more on other Western rivers with equally spectacular results.

On the other hand, if one were to run a census on salmon caught in the upper stretches of all the major salmon rivers in the Pacific Northwest, it would probably be found that the majority of salmon caught between tidewater and the spawning areas are taken on artificial lures rather than bait. Wobblers, single-bladed spinners, spoons and some plugs are all effective on salmon in these waters. Artificial lures plated with a nickel (chrome) finish seem to be more effective in the lower tidal areas than farther upstream. Artificials that produce the most strikes upriver are plated in either brass or copper.

Fly fishing for salmon in the upper rivers is a most challenging and productive method. Each fall, chinook salmon in the 50-to-60-pound class fall victim to well-placed weighted flies. Two rivers along the Pacific Coast—Oregon's Chetco and California's Smith—are especially noted for producing the huge chinooks. These are

Frank Bertainia winched this 47-pound monster, a chinook, from California's Smith River.

the favorites of fly-rod purists who hunt the sea-run giants in the hope of establishing a new world record.

Both the Chetco and the Smith are endowed with very deep up-river pools. Here, in depths that often exceed 40 feet, monster kings fin against the current as they prepare for their final ascents.

Specially prepared fly line must be used to get an artificial fly down to these fish. Cut into 30-foot sections, nylon-wrapped lead-core lines make ideal sinking lines for penetrating the great depths. A lead-core section is tied in front of monofilament backing line. To the front end of the lead-core is tied the leader.

West Coast anglers call this "shooting-head line." It can be cast for great distances and sinks rapidly to place a brightly colored artificial fly at the nose of a resting salmon.

Though some lead-core fly fishing is done both at the mouth and in the tidewater portions of the Chetco and Smith rivers, it is in the deep pools of the upper river that lead-core-line fly fishermen are most successful. Using this specialized line along with colorful salmon flies tied on stout No. 2 or 4 hooks, the purists who fish these waters each fall account for numerous chinooks in the 50-pound class. Tying into a fresh-run king of this size with a fly rod and 10-pound-test leader is an event that is seldom forgotten. Even the most skilled anglers must often battle the stubborn, powerful kings for hours before the fish will concede.

The Chetco and the Smith are by no means the only Western rivers where huge chinooks are caught during the fall migrations, but they are the two best known to fly rodders out for trophies.

Compared with other types of Pacific game fish, the anadromous fishes are relatively short-lived. Five years is about maximum for a chinook, and its size at the end of that five-year span, be it 20 pounds or 100 pounds, is dependent on its environment and genetic background.

Attempts have been made on the Pacific Coast to breed a super-race of chinook salmon. These fish are produced by eggs and sperm taken from only the largest and heartiest of chinooks. They are reared in hatcheries and released in prime spawning waters, to which they will someday return to reproduce new generations of superchinooks. The results of these experiments have been extremely gratifying, with a return of 3- to 5-year fish that weigh in excess of 50 pounds and are the handsomest of their species.

Fish on! Fly-rod anglers often have to battle huge chinook salmon for hours before the fish finally concede.

As we have seen, the Pacific salmon's struggle for survival is strewn with many pitfalls, of which a relatively minor one is pursuing anglers. Only a small percentage of a salmon spawn survives long enough to absorb their egg sacs and become free-swimming fry. Then, the fingerlings that live must make their way toward the sea. Along the way, many become food for natural predators such as birds, raccoons, otters and predatory fish. Power dams stop some and slow the rest, and polluted waters take their toll. For those salmon that do reach the Pacific, another struggle begins.

Though food in the sea is rich and abundant, the young salmon learn quickly that they are as much prey as predator, for the sea is often cruel and unforgiving. The salmon must be on constant guard for large predatory fish. The nets of Japanese, Russian and American commercial fishermen seek them out as well.

Then, their sojourn in the sea completed, the survivors home in on their parent rivers. At the mouths of those rivers swift-swimming sea lions gather for a feast.

The moment the salmon enter the river, they are marked for certain death, and yet another struggle begins. That struggle is a race

MUSKELLUNGE, NORTHERN PIKE, PICKEREL, WALLEYE

BY DOUG KNIGHT

The Muskellunge

The largest member of the pike family (Esocidae), the muskellunge (*Esox masquinongy*), is a champion fighter among freshwater game fishes. The muskie is widely admired for its explosive ferocity when hooked, its great powers of endurance and its furious runs for liberty. Powerful and voracious, muskellunge can grow as huge as 8 feet in length and 100 pounds in weight, according to Jordan and Evermann in *American Food and Game Fishes*. The current world record is a 69-pound-15-ounce lunker taken on the New York side of the Saint Lawrence River on September 22, 1957. Yet interestingly enough, the Michigan state records published in 1972 show a 110-pound, 88-inch-long monster muskie taken on hook and line in 1919 on Intermediate Lake in Antrim County, Michigan. Perhaps the reason this fish doesn't show in the world records is that the fisherman is listed as "unknown."

To any angler who has had the thrill of seeing the huge, foreboding frame of a 35-pound northern pike break water close to his boat, the idea of a muskellunge 8 feet long pulling up alongside is enough to boggle the mind—if not also capsize the boat!

Few fishermen have ever seen a muskellunge. Fewer yet have ever had one on the end of their lines. There have been various esti-

This giant muskellunge, taken in Intermediate Lake, Antrim County, Michigan, in 1919, weighed 110 pounds and was 7 feet 4 inches long!

mates on how many casts it takes to hook a muskie—anywhere from 1,000 to 5,000. Many an outdoorsman who has called himself a "muskie fisherman" has gone a full season without even a sure muskie strike to show for his long and lonely hours of work.

Why, then, the great interest among anglers in a fish so tough to take?

For one thing, he's a trophy in almost any size because he's so seldom caught. For another, he's the finest eating of the pike family, rated by some similar in flavor to the salmon. But, most important, because of his size and ferocity the muskie is widely considered the king of freshwater game fishes. No other freshwater fish can match his spectacular rushes or his slashing, surging strike at the lure. Only the salmon can leap more spectacularly or the bass more often. But neither can match the awesome sight of its 30 pounds of malevolent sinew exploding from the water close to the boat. No other fish inspires such trepidation when finally brought up alongside, its razor-sharp fangs glistening in the dimming light of dusk. Any muskie from 10 pounds up loose in a boat is a definite hazard until subdued with a billy club or a length of lead pipe.

The Indians had a name for the muskie—the "ugly pike." They wanted nothing to do with this sinister freshwater barracuda. The Ojibway dialect for ugly is *mas,* and the word for fish is *kinononge.* It is easy to construct a possible origin for the name muskellunge from such a genesis. The muskie has many names—more than fifty at last count—including maskinonge, the official designation in Canada. Other names includes musky, muskalonge, tiger muskellunge, leopard muskellunge, northern muskellunge, Mississippi muskellunge, barred muskellunge, spotted muskellunge, great muskellunge, great pike, blue pike and jack pike.

In appearance, the muskie is quite similar to the barracuda, with an elongated body and a large head shaped like a duck's bill. The dorsal and anal fins are set well back on the body. The cheeks of a muskie are scaled only on the upper half, whereas the northern pike has fully scaled cheeks. Another way to distinguish between a northern and a muskie is to count the sensory pores under their lower jaws. More than five pores on each side indicate a muskellunge; five or fewer and it's usually a northern.

The coloration of a muskie varies from green, or green with a brown tinge, to grayish. Sometimes plain-sided, the muskie is also found barred and dark-spotted, differing from the adult northern pike, which usually has light-colored, beanlike spots on the sides.

There is some controversy between experts over the subspecies of muskellunge. The first two identified here are generally accepted. The third is not yet widely recognized as a true subspecies.

The northern muskellunge (*Esox masquinongy immaculatus*), also called the Mississippi muskellunge, is found mainly in Minnesota, Wisconsin, western Michigan and Canadian waters tributary to Hudson Bay. Coloration of this fish varies considerably, but is usually of a bluish-gray cast with an olive tinge. Dots on the sides give the effect of faint bands. This fish is also called the tiger muskellunge. A Royal Ontario Museum of Zoology study in 1945 identified a new variety of muskellunge on Vermilion Lake in Ontario. It called this new variety the "true tiger" muskellunge and believes it is a cross between the muskie and the pike. This fish has a stouter body, longer and deeper head and longer fins.

A number of Ontario lakes are well populated with big muskies. Fishermen find them an exciting challenge on mediumweight tackle. (Ontario Ministry of Industry & Tourism)

The Chautauqua muskellunge (*Esox masquinongy ohioensis*), also called the barred muskellunge and Ohio muskellunge, is found principally in Lake Chautauqua and southward through the Ohio River drainage. This subspecies has a bronze-colored back, with tones of silvery bronze along the side, marked with a series of dark spots that give the illusion of bars when viewed at a distance.

A third subspecies is identified in some references as the Great Lakes muskellunge (*Esox masquinongy masquinongy*) and is unique to the Great Lakes basin.

Muskie territory extends eastward from Minnesota to Quebec, bounded on the south by the southern borders of Minnesota, Wisconsin and Michigan. The line then extends up the western borders of New York State and the Saint Lawrence River. Although these are the principal ranges of the muskie, the fish are also found as far south as West Virginia, Kentucky and the Tennessee River.

Top waters are Lake of the Woods, Little Vermilion and Eagle Lake in northwestern Ontario; the Saint Lawrence River, Chautauqua Lake and Black Lake in New York; Lake Court Oreilles, the Flambeau Flowage and the Chippewa Flowage in Wisconsin; Leech Lake, Big Mantrap, Lake Belle Taine and Winnibigoshish in Minnesota; in Michigan, the Saint Clair River and Grand

Traverse Bay on Lake Michigan; Pigeon Lake, Thousand Islands and the Nicolet River area in Quebec.

Muskellunge spawn later than northern pike, generally in May in Minnesota and Wisconsin. The eggs are usually deposited in tributary streams and on lake bottoms rather than in the weedy areas frequented by pike. The male and female muskies make no attempt at constructing a nest. Muskies' eggs are about ⅛ inch in diameter and average about 50,000 to 60,000 to the quart. A 30-to-40-pound fish can produce up to 250,000 eggs—5 quarts! The eggs are semibuoyant and nonadhesive. Pike and muskies have been reported spawning together, the milt of one fertilizing the eggs of the other. Hybrids showing intermediate characteristics are not uncommon. Optimum temperatures for spawning are 48 to 56 degrees, but muskies have been known to spawn in temperatures as high as 60 degrees. Spawning usually occurs at night.

At first, the muskellunge fry feed on water fleas, but they soon graduate to the fry of suckers, minnows and other game fishes. By the time they are 2 inches long, muskie fingerlings are dining on lake shiners, dace, fathead minnows, small bass, sunfish and perch fingerlings. In sixty days, a young muskie is anywhere from 1¾ to 6 inches long, depending on forage available. To make 6 inches, the fingerling muskie consumes from 500 to 600 forage fish. With a ravenous appetite of this sort, it is not surprising that a muskellunge might eventually reach 100 pounds. The muskie is one of the fastest-growing of the freshwater fishes. Greatest growth occurs in early summer, late summer and early fall, when the temperatures are optimum and the most food is available. Needless to say, these are good times to fish for muskies.

It takes about 6 pounds of forage fish to grow 1 pound of muskellunge. A tagged muskie in Dale Hollow Lake in Tennessee grew from 2.5 pounds to 7.3 pounds in just eleven months. That indicates plenty of available feed. Biologists who have tagged and later recaptured Saint Lawrence muskies in the 20-pound class have found they gained an average of 6 pounds a year. Considering this an average growth factor for mature fish, it is not hard to imagine how large a 20-year-old muskie might grow.

Muskies netted and checked in other waters have not shown such spectacular growth as their Saint Lawrence brethren. A combined study showed the following averages:

Age (years)	Length (inches)	Weight (pounds)
1	7	.5
2	12½	1.5
3	17½	3.8
4	22	5.5
5	26	7.1
6	29	10.0
7	34	13.0
8	39½	15.5
9	42½	18.0
10	44	21.4
11	45	24.0
12	46½	27.2
13	48	30.1
14	49½	33.0
15	50½	36.3
16	52	39.2
17	52½	41.9
18	53½	44.7
19	54½	47.6
20	55½	50.8

Examination of both scales and vertebral rings is used to determine the age of a muskie. A number of interesting facts important to anyone aiming at taking record fish were developed in the growth studies. Researchers learned that the rate of muskie growth improved the farther east they extended their studies. Muskies in eastern Ontario's Lake Nipissing area grew faster than muskies in the Lake of the Woods, Ontario, area. And Quebec muskies had the edge on their Ontario relatives.

Researchers also learned that rapid growth in the early years can be maintained only as long as forage fish are available. Muskie growth slowed greatly on two of the Wisconsin lakes studied as soon as muskie predation had cleaned out most of the 2-year and older yellow perch. Lack of food fish has also slowed the growth of muskies in a number of Ontario lakes.

Only in the Saint Lawrence River, where the supply of forage fish is almost limitless, are the growth statistics impressive. Several Saint Lawrence muskies in the 20-pound class were tagged a few years back and released. When they were recaptured, they were found to have gained an average of 6 pounds a year! Checking back to the chart of typical muskie growth, we can see that a 20-

pound-class fish on an average can be expected to gain about 3½ pounds a year. The Saint Lawrence fish gained almost twice that. No wonder then that so many huge fish have been coming out of the Saint Lawrence in recent years. Evidence shows that female muskies usually grow faster than males, especially after the fifth or sixth year. Females also live longer than males. The oldest muskie ever recorded weighed 69.7 pounds and was determined by its vertebral rings to be 30 years old.

When fishing for muskellunge, remember that there is no tougher North American freshwater game fish, and make sure your tackle is equal to the task. For a fish that takes upwards of 5,000 casts to bring to the net, you don't want any equipment break-down to cost you a trophy—not after all that work. You can go for muskies with spinning, bait-casting, fly and trolling gear.

If you've never caught a muskie, I'd recommend you start with trolling gear. From my experience and from the records, more big muskies are taken by trolling than in any other way. For one rea-son, the muskie is generally a loner, rarely traveling in schools (al-though it has been reliably reported that muskellunge do loosely school up on the Saint Lawrence). Until you know your water inti-mately and are positive you know the location of the "muskie holes," you figure to waste an awful lot of time beating on empty water with casting gear in hopes of hanging that one lone lunker lurking somewhere along a quarter mile of shoreline.

My favorite muskie trolling stick is a 5-foot Heddon stainless-steel-wire–wrapped Pal "sturdy-action" rod. The reel is an Ocean City 994 with star drag and interchangeable spools. On one spool I keep 50-pound-test lead-core color-coded line. On the other is braided minimum-stretch 50-pound Dacron. For leaders I get the best 36-inch 50-pound-test wire I can buy, or braided wire. On the terminal end, a Sampo ball-bearing swivel and snap.

Next—and most important, since we have to entice a strike be-fore we can test our tackle—comes the lure. Although plenty of big fish have been caught on flies and tiny lures, I have personally caught my largest fish on lunker-size lures. My choices of muskie lures include the largest Dardevles, Magnum Rapalas, Pikie Min-nows, Flatfishes and Red Eye Wobbler spoons. For some reason, almost every muskie fisherman I've ever heard of (except one) ad-vises the fast retrieve. I'm not against fast retrieves; but I'm more

Muskellunge do take streamer flies and smaller lures; however, as these oversize muskie takers show, the author subscribes to the philosophy that big lures take big fish.

in favor of using constantly changing speeds. I never stick to one technique. If it isn't producing, I change.

Big fish are habitually interested in conserving energy. The easier the meal the better. A big, slow-moving wobbling spoon or a lazily fluttering Flatfish looks like a free and easy meal to those big muskies and pike. They just swim up behind it, inhale and clamp down. Time and again, my biggest fish have been taken this way—the spoon or plug deep down in their gullet, hooked for keeps. If you play your fish carefully with that 36-inch leader extending well past those razor-edged teeth, you may have a tough fight on your hands, but you will also have yourself a big muskellunge.

Records indicate that 90 percent of all muskies caught are taken by trolling, and 90 percent of these are taken by deep-running lures in water 15 to 20 feet deep. Fast trolling causes most spoons to plane—to rise toward the surface, thus defeating your purpose. A slow trolling speed, plus lead-core line, gives me the control I need to get my lure down to where I want it—down with the lunker fish.

An important tool for the modern fisherman is the electronic sonar depth finder/fish locator. When I'm fishing new waters where I have no idea of the underwater contours—ridges, points of land, deep holes and falloffs—the depth finder is an invaluable tool for trolling. By watching the depth readings I can maintain my trolling path over the water depth I want to work. With color-coded lead-core line, if I want to be down 20 feet, I can let out two "colors"—meaning 20 yards out and 20 feet down. If the finder reads 20 feet and I occasionally feel my big spoon spank bottom, I know my lure's traveling at the correct depth and speed.

A bonus with the depth finder is the intermediate echoes you receive indicating "fish below." As you become adept at reading the meter, you can even develop a feel for whether you're passing over a big fish or a small one.

If you bring along lake or river survey maps, as I often do, and mark the approximate locations of those big-fish echoes, you soon develop a feeling for the hangouts of the big ones. When you're seeking big muskellunge, this learning process is invaluable. There's no reason to waste time on unproductive waters. The good spots soon show up as clusters of Xs on your map.

A great many people wonder why muskies are such difficult fish to take. They sulk for days; suddenly go on a feeding rampage; then, just as suddenly, subside again. I don't believe the answer is too complex.

I've had several opportunities to observe northern pike feeding, and when food is abundant, a pike will gorge himself until the tail of the last unfortunate is sticking out of his mouth. The stuffed northern will still hit other food fish, but not to eat, since he no longer has any room to swallow. He will continue to strike, apparently, for the joy of killing. Then, as the killing urge drains away, the pike sinks to a water level where the temperature suits him and lies there, somnolent, until the food digests. Until it does, and the pike is hungry again, any forage fish that swims within range is safe. With a 2-pound pike, this can be three days.

For a 30-pound muskie, the nonfeeding, food-digesting period should be at least three days, and could be much longer. If after three or four days a fat 15-pound lake trout should cruise slowly by and disturb his rest, the muskie might refill himself immediately and go back to his resting state. Even after three days, until disturbed by some intruder in his environment—a boat, another fish or an attractive lure—the fish will lie there, often deep in a weed bed. If the weather turns bad and the barometric pressure changes, the fish returns to aggressive awareness quickly. This is why foul weather and a good chop on the water often bring good pike and muskie fishing. Since muskies do much of their hunting in weed beds, your fishing should be predominantly close to or in these waters.

Of concern to all serious fishermen, regardless of what fish they are after, is water temperature. By late June, most lakes in the Northern states and Canada have begun to stratify. In thermal stratification, which takes place in the summer, the deep water is much colder than the surface waters. The layer in between is known as the thermocline. This is a layer in which the temperature rapidly changes from warm to very cold. The thermocline can be anywhere from 1 to 20 feet or more in thickness and usually harbors numbers of game fish in summertime.

As the waters warm up, the foraging game fish flee the shallows and head for deeper waters, seeking out the temperatures that suit their particular metabolism. Muskellunge prefer water temperatures in the 60-to-70-degree range. The only way to find the depth at which that temperature range is located is with a thermometer. The only professional way to match temperature with depth is by using one of the several good electronic water-temperature meters that use thermistors to give a direct reading on a dial. One can be bought for under $35 from companies like Lowrance Electronics and Vexilar Engineering. The weighted temperature head is lowered until the dial reads 70 degrees. Note the depth markings on the waterproof cable, lower away until a 60-degree reading is registered, then note that depth too. The fish should be cruising between the two depths.

The biggest muskies will probably be hanging near the deepest 60-degree line, *close to the bottom.* If you know 60 degrees is 20 feet down, use your depth finder to locate where the bottom rises or lowers to 20 feet and that's the contour you should be fishing. Find where the weed beds run out into or near the deepest 60-degree waters and fish their edges. Once your trolling tactics have produced results, and you know which weed beds the muskies prowl, it's time to consider other tackle—bait-casting or spinning gear.

For bait casting, I use a Heddon sturdy-action 6-foot rod with stainless-steel-wrapped guides, 12-pound-test monofilament line and an 18-inch braided steel leader. The reel is a Heddon Convertible 180 spin-cast with spare spools, loaded with 12-pound test. My lures are the same as in trolling, only in weights of ½ to ¾ ounce. Weedless spoons are the best, retrieved deep and slowly, because you can get them deep into the weeds where the big fish cruise. I vary the action: sometimes a slow, steady, wobbling retrieve; at other times a bottom-bouncing retrieve that looks like a feeding baitfish. Then perhaps a faster retrieve—jerking the rod tip, then stopping so that the spoon can flutter down before resuming speed again. Other lures should also be retrieved in a variety of ways. One of them just might stir a lounging muskellunge into striking.

My spinning rod is a two-handed 8-foot medium-action Coho Spinner which I use in concert with either a Mitchell 302 or 406 spinning reel—both surf-casting models and plenty stout for the toughest muskie. The monofilament is again 12-pound test, and the lures the same as used on the spin-cast rod.

Fly fishing for muskellunge is altogether another sport, and not for the uninitiated. My rod is the same one I use for big pike and salmon—a 9-foot Garcia fiber-glass rod and 4-inch Garcia Beaudex fly reel with as much backing as the reel will take. I use both floating and sinking lines, weight-forward taper, with a 12-pound-test tippet. If muskies are in the mood to take a fly, any colorful bucktail streamer will do—the big white-and-red and red-and-yellow patterns universally being the most effective.

Once you've hooked your muskie and have survived that awesome first surging strike, the powerful spray-tossing leaps, the bottom-hugging refusals to budge, the line-shredding runs, and he's alongside ready to take—how to bring him on board? Carefully—*very* carefully! A sturdy, wide-mouth, deep-bodied net is fine for fish up to 30 pounds. Beyond this, the gaff is the best method—unless you want to try beaching him to make sure. Then a weighted billy or a length of lead pipe applied stoutly between the eyes for good measure. A big muskie can be an extremely unfriendly addition to a fishing boat.

A primary lure for big muskies and pike is live bait—the bigger the better. Big sucker minnows or suckers are the best, up to 12 inches long if you can get them. Hook them right under the dorsal fin just above the backbone, and set them on a bobber to control their depth. Then put a heavy lead sinker about 2 feet above the bait to guarantee that it will swim around at the depth where you expect your big muskies to be cruising. I recommend hanging them in 10 to 20 feet of water and off a point of land.

Start in 10 feet of water with the minnow set about 2 feet off the bottom. Then work your way into deeper water, changing the length of line between bobber and bait to keep the minnow 2 feet off the bottom. The rod you use can be your trolling, spinning or spin-cast, depending on how sure you want to be of your fish should you hook him and how much action you're looking for.

A cruising muskie looking for food will travel 5 miles or more in a day. If your suspended minnow is set up in the right spot, you'll have a good chance at some exciting action. First, your bobber will likely disappear violently as the muskie hits it. Relax, if you can; give him plenty of time to savor the tidbit, swallow it and move on. When he has the bait well into his maw and starts to move, lay the good wood to him. Hit him five or six times in a row, hard. That fish has a tough, bony mouth and you'll have to really hit him solidly to sink a barb so it won't pull loose. Then, brace yourself for the explosion. You've got a tiger by the tail—the great muskellunge!

The Northern Pike

The second-largest fish in the pike family (Esocidae) is the northern pike (*Esox lucius*). The current world record is a 46-pound-2-ounce pike caught in New York's Sacandaga Reservoir in September, 1940, by Peter Dubuc. The Canadian record, 42 pounds 12 ounces, was caught at Stony Rapids, Saskatchewan, by Willard Terry in 1954. Minnesota's top fish to date is a 45-pounder caught in Basswood Lake in 1929, and Michigan's best is a 33-pound-8-ounce northern taken in Bond Falls Basin in 1969. In 1920, I. Garfin landed a 53-pound pike in Lough Conn, Ireland, but the fish is not recognized as a world record because of a lack of documentation.

With a wide range historically through the British Isles and Europe, the pike acquired its name and numerous legends from antiquity. From its malevolent eye and evil temper, it gained the name Luce, the water wolf—hence *Esox lucius*. Because of its

Northern pike are aerial acrobats, especially in Northern waters. Not too many New Hampshire fishermen are aware that their Spofford Lake produces northern pike action this dramatic.

droop-tailed attitude in the water, similar in shape to a medieval weapon, the Anglo-Saxons gave it the name "pike." Among its many other names are great northern pike, jackpike, jack, jackfish, northern, hammer handle and pickerel.

The northern pike's appearance is quite similar to that of the muskellunge, with its elongated body and duckbill nose. The dorsal and anal fins are set well back on the body. The tail of the northern is more rounded and less forked and pointed than the muskie's. The key identification features are the cheek scales and the sensory pores on the lower jaw. The pike has small scales over the entire cheek and larger scales on the upper half of the gill cover. The muskie has no scales on the bottom half of the cheeks. Five or fewer sensory pores on each side of the lower jaw distinguish the pike from the muskie, which has six or more on each side. The northern's mouth is well armed with long, sharp teeth along the jawline and the entire roof of the mouth is studded with short, rear-pointing teeth.

The coloration of the northern pike blends from a dark green (almost black) dorsal surface to greenish-toned or olive-gray sides which shade into yellow tones on the lower sides, and then a white belly. The sides are profusely marked with cream or yellow bean-shaped spots, and the fins are dark-spotted.

There are several species and subspecies of pike. The widest distribution is recorded for *Esox lucius*, found in North America and Europe. *Esox reicherti*, a black-spotted pike similar to the muskellunge, roams the Amur River region along the borders of Manchuria and Siberia. A subspecies, *Esox lucius baicalensis*, is found in eastern Siberia and in the Ob River in western Siberia.

A mutation of the northern pike, discovered first in Lake Belle Taine, Minnesota, in 1930, has been named the silver pike. The body is generally a dark silver or gray, and the scales are sometimes flecked with gold. This fish is rarely caught over 10 pounds. The silver pike is apparently a true breeder, mating with its own kind and not with the northern pike and muskellunge that live within its environs. It is a very hardy fish, hardier than other pike. It has been found as far north as Beaverlodge Lake, east of Great Bear Lake; in three lakes in Manitoba; in one near Ottawa and in one lake in Sweden.

Northern pike territory is in the northern regions of the Northern Hemisphere (Europe, Asia and North America). In North America it is found from Alaska to Labrador and south to northern New England, the Hudson River drainage of eastern New York, the northern reaches of the Ohio Valley, the Great Lakes District, Missouri, eastern Nebraska and northern Manitoba, but not west of the Great Plains regions. Northern pike are widely distributed in Canada.

Excellent waters for northern pike include Savant Lake, Lake of the Woods and Ogoki Reservoir in northwestern Ontario; Sioux Lookout and Lac Seul in the White River, Ontario, area; Dog Lake, Kesagami Lake and the Trent Canal in eastern Ontario. Minnesota's best include Basswood Lake, Leech Lake and Mille Lacs. In Michigan, Bond Falls Basin; and in New York State the Saint Lawrence River and Sacandaga Reservoir.

Northern pike spawn in marshy areas along lakes or streams. Often their spawning grounds are fields and other grassy lowlands that are usually dry in the summer. In Ireland, a favorite spring sport of the local farmers is spearing with pitchforks the huge pike that come up over the lake banks to spawn in the hayfields. Northerns start spawning soon after ice-out, when the waters reach 40 degrees. In the southern regions of their range, northerns occasionally spawn as early as their second summer. In Minnesota the average spawner is 3 to 5 years old. One female will lay upwards of 200,000 eggs. One 32-pound fish yielded 595,200 eggs. Pike usually spawn in the late afternoon. Their eggs differ from those of the muskie in that they are very sticky and will adhere to anything they touch.

Pike fry hug the bottom for several days after birth. They remain in shallow water for several weeks, and their first food is tiny water fleas and other small aquatic organisms. They soon graduate to microcrustaceans, fish larvae and insects such as mayflies; then eventually to young salamanders and other small amphibians. Avid cannibals, they also dine vigorously on any of their brethren unlucky enough to be about two-thirds their size or smaller.

Pike have relatively low weight-maintenance requirements and relatively efficient conversion of food to growth. Above their basic maintenance requirement, 1 pound of food equals about ½ pound of growth.

One recent Canadian study developed the following growth statistics from a sampling of eastern Ontario pike:

Age (years)	Length (inches)	Weight (pounds)
1	12.3	0.5
2	19.5	1.5
3	22.9	2.4
4	25.3	4.5
5	27.8	5.8
6	30.7	9.0
7	33.2	9.11
8	35.8	11.5
9	37.1	12.75
10	39.2	16.3
11	41.8	19.0
12	45.0	21.0
13	49.5	24.0

Northern pike are now considered an important game species by fisheries biologists. They grow rapidly, are relatively easy to catch, are acceptable table fare and are excellent for controlling overpopulation and crowding, which leads to stunted fish. In the summer, with plenty of forage fish available, a northern will consume one-fifth of its own weight daily. It's an enemy of any fish or other aquatic creatures that inhabit shallow waters. It will eat crayfish, frogs, mice and other rodents, ducklings and any other bird that will fit into its maw—even a sea gull!

For fishermen interested in action, there are hundreds of lakes that will afford steady activity with fish in the 1-to-4-pound class. However, if you are looking to improve your chances at hooking into a trophy-class fish, you should be aware of a Minnesota study that revealed that fishing pressure as low as two or three fishing trips per acre per year is enough to reduce the size of the northern pike caught to a 2-pound average. Large pike are present in these overfished lakes, but their percentage of the total is much lower than it is in unfished or seldom-fished lakes.

In unfished waters, the northern's aggressive, cannibalistic traits serve as a natural selector for trophy northerns, since smaller pike are eaten and thereby eliminated as competitors for other available forage fish.

The northern pike is considered the dominant predator over the muskie, the walleye or the bass. He is a more successful predator than the muskie from birth because the pike spawn two to three weeks before the muskies, and their fry, being bigger, feed heavily on the younger muskellunge. But if, in turn, the pike is too heavily preyed upon by fishermen, even this king of the predators suffers.

The message is perfectly clear. If you want bigger pike, go to those remote lakes where few people fish. Anglers who take advantage of the fly-in tent-camping opportunities offered now by a number of Ontario and other flying services are making a good move for bigger pike. They're usually the only fishermen on the lake. The prices are generally quite reasonable—often $60 or $70 apiece for a party of two for a week's fly-in which includes tent or cabin, boat, motor and all beds, cots and cooking and lighting equipment necessary to spend a comfortable week. Ten- to 20-pound pike are not uncommon on many of these fly-in lakes, and there's the usual bonus of walleyes, bass or trout.

Big water is the other best bet for lunker pike—waters like Basswood Lake in Minnesota, Dog Lake in Ontario, Mistassini in Quebec and the Saint Lawrence River. Plenty of room for pike to roam, plenty of forage fish and huge waters with a great variety of cover.

A number of northern pike larger than the existing records—fish either speared, netted or taken by other means—have been reported over the years by reliable witnesses. In 1969, in an inn near

Lough Erne in Northern Ireland I saw a mounted 38-pound pike taken in Lough Erne's Kesh Bay, and was told 50- to 60-pounders taken by commercial fishermen on Erne were reported by the local newspapers once or twice a year. The inn owner told me that a Belgian fisherman had taken a 56-pound pike in 1952 on Lough Erne, and the catch had been reported in a number of local papers. Farther into Northern Ireland, on Lough MacNean, I took a 30-pound northern and lost another, much larger, fish I fought for half an hour but never saw. My guide, Pat Stewart, told me that the long-line eelers fishing on MacNean occasionally used to hang onto monster pike in the deep waters off the islands on the northeastern waters of the lake. They'd be running their lines in 70 feet of water and hang a huge fish. Some they hooked were so big they couldn't even get them up. The fish would just shake their heads and hang on the bottom. Occasionally they'd get one to the surface and see how huge and mean-looking a pike it was, and they'd cut it loose. Pat said they estimated that some of the fish were at least 80-pounders.

Another guide I met while in Ireland, John "Roddy" Flanagan, had quite a story to tell. A British medical officer from Belcoo, a Colonel Flood, whom Roddy used to guide, saw a huge pike take a cygnet (young swan) on Lough MacNean one year. Many islanders carry binoculars wherever they go, and the Colonel was using his to watch the young swan fly into a small bay and land. Suddenly there was a huge swirl of water and the swan was gone. Moments later it reappeared on the surface, struggling, but unable to fly. Another huge swirl of water and the head of a monster pike appeared, taking the swan down for good this time. Colonel Flood has seen many 30- and 40-pound pike in his life, and he estimated by the size of the head he saw that the pike was at least a 100-pounder. The men who report these events are longtime fishermen and know their pike. They're not subject to hallucinations.

On Lake Mistassini, in northern Quebec, several years ago I landed an 18-pound northern. He fought a powerful fight, and when I landed him I discovered one reason why. Across his back were fresh tooth marks where another pike had hit him while he was fighting my lure—attacked him the way a shark will hit a hooked game fish in trouble. The tooth marks extended 11 inches across the widest span. That's a 70-pound-plus pike.

With me on the Mistassini trip was André LaChance, public re-

Teeth marks 11 inches across on the back of this big northern pike convinced author Knight that Mistassini Lake in Quebec supports world-record-class fish.

lations director for Quebec's Parks Department. André knows his northern pike pretty well; he took the fly-rod world record (6-pound tippet) northern pike on Mistassini in 1971—a 28½-pounder. André tells numerous stories of Mistassini pike so huge they've towed boats backward and of one that hit and scarred a 30-pound northern, leaving tooth marks 12 inches across on its back. That's mute evidence of the tremendous size of the attacking fish. André is certain that there are more than several world-record-breaking northern pike lying in 118-mile-long Mistassini. In water that huge, it's not too hard to believe that there's ample forage to produce fish of such tremendous size.

Dog Lake in eastern Ontario, where I fished in 1972, has produced a number of pike in the 40-pound class and stories of even larger fish lost. Charlie was a master church-bell hanger and enjoyed his lifelong vocation. That is, until the summer of 1971 when he took a vacation to Dog Lake and went fishing one day. He'd never fished much before, so he made several mistakes. One of them was hooking a northern pike so huge, he reported later, that it was almost half the length of the boat. It took him an hour to get the fish close enough to estimate its size. He guessed it weighed at least 100 pounds. Charlie had no way to get the fish into the boat, so he tried to tow it to shore—mistake number two. The line broke.

No one quite believed the story. But when Charlie went out and spent $15,000 on a fiber-glass fishing boat, bought all the right heavy tackle, and then *quit his job* to spend the whole summer of 1972 fishing for that big fish or his twin, the local townspeople began to believe Charlie had seen something pretty impressive on Dog Lake that day.

George Brown, part owner of Pioneer Lodge on Dog Lake, saw a northern take a sea gull one day. "A fish at least ten inches across the back," he told me. "It wasn't more than ten yards from the boat." (The gull had landed to take some sandwich crust that George's daughter had thrown into the water.) A 10-inch beam makes a pretty fair pike. I measured across the widest part of the back of a 47-inch-long Michigan pike at Higgins Lake Conservation School last summer. The notation indicated the fish was only 8 years old. It was 5 inches across and weighed 36¼ pounds. Ten inches across the back has to be better than a 70-pound fish.

George's partner, Ernie Frick, hung onto a fish so big it towed his 18-foot boat all around the bay across from camp. He never saw the fish, but figured it was a pike from the savage strike it made. It stayed right on the bottom, fighting a submarine battle. When he tried to winch it up, all it would do was shake its head from side to side. When he bent the rod double and "twanged" on the line with his fingers, the fish would take off. It finally broke the line. Two other guests have hooked enormous fish in the same bay with similar results. George has fished Dog Lake much of his life and has taken many big pike. He figures this fish would have gone well over 50 pounds.

For fishermen interested in lots of excitement with pike in the 2-to-5-pound class, a 7-foot medium-action spinning or a 5½-foot spin-casting rod will be the best bet. Each will work equally well with bait or spinning lures. An 8- or 10-pound-test monofilament line will work well with ½- to 1-ounce lures. A 10-inch braided-wire leader, plastic-coated, will do a fine job of parrying the northerns' razor-sharp teeth.

If you're expecting lunker northerns in the 8-to-20-pound class, you should move up to a 6½-foot heavy-action spinning rod or a 5- or 5½-foot heavy-action spin-casting rod with 12- to 15-pound-test monofilament line and the same 10-inch steel leader.

This tackle will handle fish heavier than the listed test strength, as the various line-class records for muskies and northern pike will show. However, for the average fisherman who has yet to take his first 15-pound-or-larger northern pike, some of the chances for error should be removed. Big fish seldom permit even one mistake. Better heavy tackle at first. Sophistication comes later as skill, experience and confidence build.

Just as northerns will take a full spectrum of natural baits, they'll also take almost any spinning lure you'll offer them. My pike-fishing tackle box always includes the Red Eye Wobbler spoon in nickel, brass and copper tones; Dardevles in red-and-white, orange-and-black and gold; the jointed Pikie Minnow and Rapalas in gold and silver, both the sinking and the floating varieties. Squirrel-tail tandem spinners are also very effective, as are a variety of Abu spinners.

You'll find your northerns in the same waters where you'd expect to find bass—in weed beds, under lily pads, around underwater obstacles. Where you think baitfish will hang out, that's where the northerns with hunger pangs will also be cruising. They prefer temperatures in the 50-to-70-degree range. The smaller pike usually cruise in 60-to-70-degree waters, the larger pike holding to the deeper, cooler waters—especially after feeding.

Average-size northern pike are relatively easy to take. *Big* northern pike are tough to entice to hit, tougher to beat with a rod and a challenge to land at the end of a tough battle. I've found to my satisfaction where the largest northern pike hang out once they leave the spawning beds in the cool 40-degree waters of the spring thaw. They head for *deep* waters. Early in the morning and late in the afternoon as the day cools, they may move in to hunt the weed beds if they're hungry. But the largest fish hang out in the deep waters and let other deep-running fish provide their free meals. Many's the time I've set up two trolling rigs from my boat. One is a mediumweight spin-casting rod trolling 8-pound-test monofilament with a 10-inch steel leader and a 4-inch red-and-white Dardevle. I fish this lure back about 30 yards and down about 3 to 4 feet. The other rod is the same one I use for muskies, a 5-foot stainless-steel-wrapped Heddon sturdy-action boat rod with an Ocean City reel boasting a star drag. This is running with lead-core line 25 yards out and 25 feet down, trailing an 18-inch stainless-steel leader and the largest Dardevle spoon made. Using

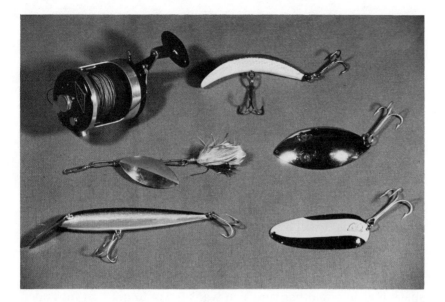

Note how large the lures are compared with the saltwater reel. These are the tackle items that enable the author to consistently boat lunker northerns.

sonar gear such as that which was covered in the muskie section, I look for underwater points of land off bays and islands where the echoes show me big fish at 20, 30 or 40 feet, and that's where I troll my big lures.

I'll catch fish at 4 feet—northerns up to 7 and 8 pounds that are cruising the 60-to-65-degree upper waters. But every so often, one of those big blips I see on the screen at depths of 30 feet or more will move up behind that big, lazily wobbling, deep-running spoon and inhale. The result is some mind-boggling action and, quite often, a huge pike brought up alongside.

Fly rodders have great fun with pike. I use a 9-foot salmon-action Garcia fiber-glass rod with a 4-inch Beaudex reel, torpedo-taper line and leader tapering to 12-pound-test tippit. In the spring an Air Cell floater line and a red-and-white bucktail streamer are a deadly combo.

Later in the season—June through late August—I use a Wet Cell line. The pike are down deeper, and when the fly hits the water I just wait until it sinks as much as 10 or 12 feet before I start retrieving. The retrieve is a tantalizing, darting movement that seems to really agitate the pike into striking. Yellow-and-black or yellow-and-red streamers or bucktails are also effective for pike.

The color of the fly should be bright. A few strands of bright silver plastic tinsel (from your Christmas tree) tied to lie along the sides of the fly will add sparkle and allure to your bait. I've found this has greatly improved my results with pike *and* other fish. The tinsel is very easy to add to a streamer—just a matter of a few more wraps of thread to hold it on and a touch of clear lacquer.

A frog popping bug used over a good northern weed bed will produce almost constant action from 2- to 5-pound pike. Occasionally a lunker will hit and you'll really have to handle him with care, especially if he sticks his head down in the weeds and sulks. Often, if you get the rod tip right over him, put stress on the line and then "plink" the taut line or leader with your finger you can spark him into another run. You want to try to get him into open water because otherwise your leader may get hung up in the weeds. A hair mouse bug is equally effective; but instead of the "pop!-and-rest" action you impart to your frog, you should move the mouse in tiny, steady jerks to simulate the swimming action of a rodent. It should stop and rest after each 5- or 6-foot swim.

Many successful northern pike fishermen use live bait—minnows and suckers. If you check their bait cans, you'll see their minnows are generally 3 to 5 inches long. I'm after big pike, so I try for the largest baitfish I can get; sucker or flathead minnows 7 to 10 inches long are very good. I expect fewer strikes, but those I get usually mean larger pike. I use a 12-inch braided steel leader (plastic-coated) and a large bobber to keep the height of the bait off the bottom constant. The lead weight is attached to the line about 2 feet above the minnow. I use a weight that can be locked around the line, not the dangling loop kind. It should be just heavy enough to keep the minnow down to the depth the bobber is set for—no heavier. Figure to keep the bait about 1 to 2 feet off the bottom. Your sonar depth finder will help you determine that with accuracy.

Try to fish along the deep-water edges of the weed beds, perhaps 2 or 3 feet out from the weeds. Don't worry if your bait floats away. It might just float over a cruising northern. Every once in a while, bring it back and toss it out to the edge of the weeds again.

Many good northern bays are all weeds. If so, adjust your bait to float about 1 foot above the thickest weeds (not 1 foot above the stray, longer tendrils). Channels and rivers with weeds lining both sides are very productive. Again, fish one edge of the weeds or the other and let your bait float with the water flow, but try to keep it along the weedy edges.

Your landing net should have a wide mouth and a deep belly, with a sturdy handle. You may want to insert a wood dowel about the same diameter as the inside of the aluminum handle to give it more strength. If you wipe the dowel well with epoxy resin before inserting it, the epoxy will waterproof the dowel and lock it permanently into the handle for solid, long-term strength. I've seen 20-pound northerns break the handles of unreinforced nets. Once you have your big pike in the boat, the prompt application of an 8-inch length of lead pipe between the eyes should quiet things down.

The Pickerel

Pickerels are the smallest members of the pike family; the chain pickerel (*Esox niger*) is the largest of the pickerels. When caught on sporting tackle, it is a fine, scrappy game fish and a tasty addition to any sportsman's dinner table.

Big at 5 pounds, the largest chain pickerel are usually found in Georgia and Florida lakes where food is abundant and they can feed most of the year. The world-record pickerel—31 inches long, weighing 9 pounds 6 ounces—was taken in Homerville, Georgia, in 1961. In defiance of geography, however, a 9-pound-5-ounce pickerel (not caught on rod and reel) was taken from Pontoosuc Lake in Massachusetts. And in 1938, on Panther Pond in Maine, I was fishing with my father when we caught a deep-bellied 32-inch pickerel that would have pushed the records if it hadn't broken off our stringer. (Taking big fish is a function of all of the links of your fishing gear, even down to the stringer. That fish is not a record until he's swinging from a scale back on shore.) The average pickerel runs from 1 to 3 pounds, with 4- and 5-pounders relatively hard to find.

Across his range, the pickerel has collected a number of aliases, including banded pickerel, barred pickerel, black pike, eastern pickerel, grass pike, green pike, jack, Old Chainsides, pike, jackfish, red-finned pike and snake.

The chain pickerel has an elongated body, duckbilled head and set-back dorsal and anal fins similar to those of its larger pike relatives. Its cheeks and gill covers are completely scaled, distinguishing it from the northern pike and the muskellunge. The lower half of the northern's gill covers is without scales, and the muskie has no scales on the lower halves of either the cheeks or the gill covers.

Coloration of the chain pickerel starts with a dark, greenish-black back which shades into a brownish green along the upper portions of the sides. It gets its name from the black, chainlike markings along its light green sides. The belly shades from greenish yellow on the lower sides to white. The fins are unmarked, and there is usually a vertical black mark below the center of the eye on the front part of the cheek.

Besides the eastern chain pickerel there are two other pickerel subspecies. They are often referred to as "little pickerels." The first is the redfin, or barred, pickerel (*Esox americanus americanus*). This fish is a dark green in color and has curved black bars on its sides. It rarely exceeds a pound in weight. The reported maximum length was a 19-inch specimen suspected to be a hybrid between the redfin and chain pickerels.

The grass pickerel (*Esox americanus vermiculatus*), also called the mud pickerel, has a dark green body marked with long, wavy lines. It seldom exceeds 15 inches in length or a pound in weight.

Both "little pickerels" can be distinguished from the young of the muskellunge and northern pike by the fact that their cheeks and gills are completely scaled. Both of the adult little pickerels differ from the chain pickerel in that their sides are marked with vertical bars. They also differ in that the little pickerels have eleven to thirteen branchiostegals (throat bones beneath the gill covers), whereas the chain pickerel has fourteen to sixteen. The key visible differences between the little pickerels themselves is that the grass pickerel does not have the red fins of his miniature cousin.

The chain pickerel's range is chiefly east of the Alleghenies from Maine to Florida and from the Gulf of Mexico drainage north to southern Missouri and west to eastern Oklahoma. The redfin pickerel is found in streams and lakes in the Atlantic drainage from southern Maine to Florida, and in the Lake Champlain drainage and areas of the Saint Lawrence River. The grass pickerel's range

Chain pickerel are abundant throughout the state of Maine. This angler is fishing in the eastern part of the state near the Canadian border.

runs from the Saint Lawrence River at Montreal through the Great Lakes region, Wisconsin, Nebraska and the Mississippi drainage system and on into Texas. Redfins are often found in sluggish streams and backwaters and less commonly in lakes and ponds, where chain pickerel are more common. The grass pickerel is found mainly in slow-moving, heavily vegetated streams and lakes.

The pickerels spawn in the early spring, just after the northern pike, which are the earliest spawners of the pike family. There is some evidence the grass pickerel may occasionally spawn in the fall as well. The pickerels select shallow waters in swampy, weedy areas for spawning. They also spawn in flooded areas with abundant vegetation. They seem to like a quiet, open piece of water over a soft bottom. The eggs are scattered across the bottom by the female and fertilized by the male as they swim along side by side. The eggs are adhesive and fall in a glutinous string that sticks to whatever it touches. A mature chain pickerel female may lay as many as 30,000 eggs. The average female redfin, a much smaller fish, lays from 185 to 550 eggs. Depending upon water temperatures, the fry hatch in one to two weeks and soon are following in the same predatory path as their larger pike-family relatives. The young pickerel usually stay in the spawning area for the first year of their lives.

The diet of the pickerels starts with insect larvae, then advances to small fish, dragonfly nymphs and young crayfish. Surprisingly, they seem to ignore tadpoles even where they are abundant. Larger pickerel feed on newts, golden shiners, mice, sunfish, white and yellow perch, snakes or anything else that moves and is of the proper size. The larger the pickerel grow, the lazier they become. Big pickerel show a preference for crayfish and slower-moving fish such as small carp, suckers and bullheads. Pickerel are also cannibals at all ages and sizes. One 19-inch pickerel was found to have successfully ingested a 13-inch pickerel.

Several studies have indicated that in the summer active pickerel feeding occurs in the weed beds at depths where the temperatures range between 44 and 59 degrees. Most of this feeding is early in the morning to midday in the summer and in the afternoon in the winter. Where the weather is warmest, feeding usually reaches a peak in the late afternoon and is at a minimum at night.

The chain pickerel, like all of its pike relatives, is a solitary fish. The larger fish move into shallow water at night and return to deeper water during the day. They grow poorly in high-acid waters. Chain pickerel can live in brackish waters up to 1.5 percent salt and in waters to 98 degrees; however, they prefer temperature ranges of 45 to 70 degrees. Studies have shown that little feeding takes place when water temperatures are above 68 degrees.

I have caught and eaten the pickerel over much of its range and have found it to possess sweet, white, easily flaking meat of excellent flavor. There is little resemblance between pickerel and pike meat in flavor or texture. Northern pike is excellent fare if properly prepared. I have found pickerel tasty regardless of how it has been prepared.

You will find your pickerel in a variety of waters. Anglers after other game fish often discover a pickerel on the end of their line. Pickerel, when they're in a feeding mood, will take almost any lure. You'll find them in lakes, rivers, streams and ponds in water where the flow is gentle or nonexistent. They'll lie in wait in weed beds and hide around logs and under lily pads. They tend to spurn open waters, but are often found in river and stream mouths. Because they avoid open waters, the best technique for catching pickerel is to make your casts parallel to shore rather than perpendicular to it. Casting straight in will force the fish to follow your lure across open waters toward your boat, and this the bigger fish are loath to do.

Most effective fishing methods are discovered accidentally, and that's how many fishermen, including myself, have taken our largest pickerel—by accident. A typical pickerel-catching accident can come by way of the backlash on an old level-wind reel. The lure sails out, you get a backlash and while you're straightening it out, the lure has settled to the bottom of the weed bed. By the time you have worked out the tangle, one or more nearby predator pickerel have had time to slowly cruise over and check out all the commotion. About that time, guess what? You begin to reel in for another try; up flies your lure from the bottom, sparkling and shiny, obviously trying to escape . . . Bang! Action!

There are two important points here. Important for all fisherman after denizens of the weed bed, be they muskie, pike or pickerel. You make a long cast with a weedless spoon. Let it sink to the bottom and sit for a couple of minutes. Then start a rapid retrieve to make the lure jump out of the weeds. After a few feet, let the lure stop to flutter down again, as if injured. Then retrieve again, as if your lure "sees" some approaching predator.

The other key item is the bright, sparkling lure. It can be seen from a distance and often sparks a reflex-action strike from a predator that has been in a drowsy state. Those old lures in your tackle box that have lost their luster can be easily buffed clean of lacquer, dipped in a fast-acting brightener such as Vin-Rock CQ-3 and sprayed with a pressurized, fast-dry lacquer. Of course, be sure your old hooks are sharp to match your new-looking lures. Sharp new treble hooks and split rings to attach them are easy to pick up from any tackle supplier.

In selecting your pickerel-fishing tackle, emphasize *lightness*— light, flexible-action rods; lightweight reels and low-test lines. Garcia makes 4-to-5-foot ultralight spinning rods that pair up with a pint-sized Mitchell reel. With 2-pound-test line and ¼-ounce lures, you'll have equal fun with 1- and 2-pound pickerel and the occasional bass you'll pick up, for bass like the same lures and much of the water in which you'll pursue Old Chainsides.

In fishing, the fun and challenge are relative to the balance

The pickerel prefers to lie in wait for food to pass by. When you use one of these popular pickerel lures, cover as much water as possible.

between tackle size and fish size. You'll have fine sport with the pickerel if you'll use tackle that tests him and doesn't horse him in.

Lure patterns that are bright or flashy or colorful will usually attract the pickerel. The Abu spinners, Meppses and double-flashers like the Heddon Hep with a squirrel-tail hook end are steady producers. The Johnson silver spoon with a pork-rind tail is always good. The smallest Rapala minnow, the floater, worked like a crippled minnow on the surface will bring a savage strike from any Old Chainsides anxious for an easy meal. Because the lure floats, it works very well over submerged weeds. After the initial splash-in, you let the minnow lie, the ripple rings spread and die. Then twitch the lure. More rings. Then bring it in several feet and let it rest again. Then a twitch. No pickerel can long refuse such temptation unless he is full to the gills already.

A fly rod is the ultimate fishing tool to use on the pickerel. A light 7-foot rod with an equally light, balanced reel, working a bright fly or streamer, will provide very rewarding action. Parmachene Belle, Royal Coachman, Mickey Finn and Yellow or White Marabou are all excellent patterns. The silver-tinsel sides I mentioned for northern pike will work equally well for their smaller pickerel cousins.

Hair frogs and mice are excellent early and late in the day when the larger fish move in from the deeper waters to search for food. Be aware that the pickerel is a sandbagging forager. He lies in wait for his food, so you'll have to cover plenty of water before you uncover the big one's hiding place. Only when the day begins to fade will he move silently out of his lair in search of the food that failed to come to him. Now's the time when surface commotion will attract the big fish to see what is going on.

Casting live bait is an excellent way to fish for pickerel, especially the lunkers. However, here's a good time to move up a size in fishing tackle. The 7-foot medium-action spinning rod and 6-pound-test line will be sturdy enough. Or you can use a long cane pole with 8-pound-test line. Either way, when that big one hits, you're guaranteed plenty of sport!

A crayfish or a good-sized minnow on a bobber fished along the deepest edges of the weed beds will often lure the over-5-pound pickerel out of their hiding places. If your bait doesn't attract a strike in fifteen minutes, move it. Eventually you'll lop it down right in front of that big one you've been looking for and you'll be wishing that you'd ignored my advice to use light tackle!

The Walleye

The walleye (*Stizostedion vitreum vitreum*) is the largest member of the perch family (Percidae). The present world record is a 25-pound, 41-inch-long lunker taken on Old Hickory Lake, Tennessee, in August 1960. The previous record was a 22-pound-4-ounce walleye taken at Fort Erie, Ontario, in May 1943. One of the more popular sport fishes because of its excellent flavor and scrappy tenacity on the end of the line, the walleye is also extremely valuable commercially as a food fish. The average walleye caught by fishermen runs from 2 to 5 pounds. A fish in the 10-to-15-pound class is considered a trophy.

The most prevalent name for this fish is walleyed pike. However, it is not a pike at all, but a perch, very closely related to the yellow perch. The walleye has a number of other aliases, including pike

perch, yellow pike perch, green pike, gray pike, blue pike, yellow pickerel, doré, dory, pickerel, walleyed perch, jack, jackfish, jack salmon, glasseye, marble-eye, sauger, Susquehanna salmon, wall-eyed pickerel and white-eye.

The name doré, common in Canada, was used by the early French settlers in Quebec. It derived from the fact that they identified the fish by its color—the color of gold. Its scientific name is additionally descriptive: *Stizostedion*, meaning pungent throat, and *vitreum*, meaning glassy—describing the strange white eyes.

The walleye's body is an elongated oval with a forked tail, spines on the first dorsal and anal fins and sharp caninelike teeth on the jaws. It is distinguished from the true pikes by its two dorsal fins; the pikes have only one. The walleye received its name from its large, white, glassy eyes, which give it the appearance of being blind. The upper jaw extends to a point beneath the rear margin of the eye.

The fish's back is crossed with six or seven narrow, dark bands blending into olive-brown or dark brown scale coloration that is mottled with brassy yellow tones. The belly is light in color, blending into the darker tones of the sides.

A close relative, the sauger (*Stizostedion canadense*), is often confused with the walleye. The walleye is most easily distinguished from the sauger by the very distinct white or cream-colored margin on the lower lobe of its tail. The forward dorsal fin of the walleye is often streaked or blotched with dark markings. The sauger's forward dorsal, on the other hand, is marked with small, dark spots aligned in definite longitudinal rows. The walleye is known to inhabit only larger bodies of water, but the sauger inhabits only the *largest* bodies of water. This is a phenomenon that no fisheries biologists have been able to satisfactorily explain to date. With the advent of the huge hydroelectric-dam empoundments, the sauger has come into its own. In the past, saugers were rarely caught over 2 or 3 pounds. Now, stocked in these huge new reservoirs, saugers have been taken up to 8 pounds. Other names for the sauger include sand pike, jack, river pike, spotfin pike, horsefish, eastern sauger and pickering.

The walleye's range extends from New Brunswick southward into a number of the South Atlantic States, where it has been widely stocked, through the Great Lakes region and upper Mississippi Valley, westward to the Saskatchewan Valley, northward to the Mackenzie River region and the Hudson Bay drainage. It is found throughout Ontario. Its range is constantly being extended by stocking. The walleye prefers clear, cool water and gravel or sandy bottoms. It is rarely found in muddy waters.

Saugers are found mainly in the Great Lakes and other very

Michigan has plenty of reason to be pleased with the quality of its walleye fishing, as this 8-pounder proves. Spin-casting gear and a small, heavy spoon run deep produced the action.

large lakes in the Northern United States and Canada. Many large specimens are taken in the Mississippi, Missouri, Ohio and Tennessee rivers and some of their major tributaries. Excellent sauger waters in Minnesota include Lake of the Woods, Rainy, Kabetogama and Lake Saint Croix.

In Minnesota, the walleye is considered the "king of fishes" and has been designated the official state fish. There are a number of natural walleye waters in Minnesota, the best being Winnibigoshish, Leech, Mille Lacs, Basswood, Upper Red Lake, Lake of the Woods, Rainy, Kabetogama and Vermilion. The Mississippi River, especially in the Hiawatha Valley area, is an extremely prolific walleye ground.

Top Canadian walleye waters include the Kawartha Lakes, the Trent River and the Moon River Basin of Georgian Bay, in southern Ontario. Farther north in Ontario, Parry Sound to French River on Georgian Bay, Lake Nipissing, Lake Temiskaming, Lake of the Woods, Kesagami Lake, Hornepayne (Cochrane area), Wabigoon Lake (near Dryden), Ogoki Reservoir, Whitewater, Whiteclay and Shebuiskwia lakes, Lac des Mille Lacs, Dog Lake and the White River area.

Walleyes spawn soon after the ice goes out in the spring when the water temperatures reach a range of 38 to 44 degrees. They may run up tributary streams in great numbers to spawn in the riffles. However, many do not leave the lake but deposit their eggs on gravel reefs or stony shoals in shallow water. The walleye is not a nest builder. The males precede the females to the spawning areas, spawning usually taking place at night. The female discharges the eggs on the gravel bottom and the male immediately fertilizes them. The eggs are very sticky and adhere to the gravel downstream from the spawning area.

Walleyes are very prolific spawners. A 3-pound female will produce about 75,000 to 85,000 eggs. The eggs are small, measuring approximately 120,000 to the quart. Average counts of eggs in the ovaries show that a female walleye can produce about 26,000 eggs per pound of fish. Observation by fisheries biologists indicates that walleyes do not eat while spawning.

Incubation takes about two or three weeks. Up to 20 percent of the eggs hatch, depending on water temperature and oxygenation. The walleye fry is about ½ inch long when hatched and practically invisible to the naked eye. After several days it has absorbed its egg sac and starts to feed on small plankton organisms. As it increases in size, the young walleye graduates to aquatic insects and their larvae. As walleyes are early spawners, the fry of later-spawning fish soon fall prey to them. Soon the walleye will graduate to meals of yellow perch, minnows, suckers and ciscoes.

By the end of their first summer the walleyes are from 3 to 7 inches long, depending on the fertility of the water, its acidity or alkalinity and the forage fish available. The farther south walleyes are found, the longer the growing season and the faster the yearly growth. Interestingly enough, the slower-growing Northern fish live longer than their faster-growing Southern relatives. A Canadian walleye typically lives fourteen to fifteen years; the Southern fish are rarely recorded over 8 years of age. A study of growth characteristics in Ontario water produced the following statistics:

Age (years)	Length (inches)	Weight (pounds)
2	7.4	.18
3	10.6	.62
4	12.3	1.0
6	15.3	2.18
8	20.3	4.9
12	24.1	8.9
13	25.1	10.8

Walleyes rank close to whitefish and lake trout as a valuable food fish. They are popular sport fish because they are plentiful, they willingly take lures and bait, they are courageous scrappers and they are excellent eating.

The walleye is primarily a nocturnal feeder, leaving deep water as night approaches to move closer to the shore to feed on other shoreline fish. Anglers will usually find them in moderately deep, clear-flowing water with sand, gravel or rocky bottoms, where they tend to congregate in schools. Where you catch one, there are likely to be others in the vicinity. The larger fish like deep holes in rivers and lakes. Pools below falls and rapids are usually excellent places to find a gathering of walleyes. I've found many good walleye grounds around underwater ridges and submerged points of land. They normally hang close to the bottom whenever they're cruising, so your lures should be bottom runners and your bait should always be either on the bottom or not too far above it.

The walleye is a cool-water species, often lying beneath the thermocline. If sufficient dissolved oxygen is available, the biggest walleyes will lie as deep as 50 feet or more during the day, moving into shallower water to feed as darkness approaches. Generally walleyes prefer water temperatures from 55 to 67 degrees.

In Canada and the Northern states, the best walleye fishing is May through June and October through November. Because they pretty much stop eating during spawning, the walleyes come off the spawning beds with rapacious appetites, and some of the largest total catches and biggest fish are caught then, while they are still in shallow water. Walleyes are taken all summer, of course, but the best fishing luck seems to come during the shorter daylight hours of spring and fall. The largest fish are harder to come by in the summer. They hold to deeper waters and are very difficult to locate. Summer fishing is often good if the day is calm and overcast, with perhaps a light rain falling.

Tackle is varied, but your regular bass-fishing gear will work fine on the walleye. A 7-foot medium-action spinning rod with 8-pound-test line plus a 12-inch braided steel leader to protect the line from the walleye's sharp front teeth will serve you well. A 6-foot spin-casting rod of medium action, again with 8-pound-test line and 12-inch leader, is a fine rig for fishing bait or lures.

If you're using lures, deep-running plugs with those diving-plane noses are excellent. My best luck has come with the Bomber, Creek Chub, Arbogast, Flatfish and Rebel 2 deep-divers in light-colored patterns. The deeper you go, the less light there is, so the brighter the lure must be to catch the attention of those deep-water fish. If it bounces on the bottom, all the better. You'll rarely catch weeds in good walleye water. Jigs are also effective for walleyes.

Yellow is a good color, perhaps because it looks like a yellow perch or another, smaller walleye. Just bear in mind that you'll get more walleye strikes from a slowly retrieved, deep-running lure than by any other means.

Even fly rodders can have fun with the walleye with an 8-foot bass fly rod and a Wet Cell sinking line. Bass streamers in bright colors are effective, especially the old faithful Mickey Finn.

Minnow-pattern streamers are very effective. Just make certain your fly is at or near the bottom before you begin your retrieve. A small single or double fly-rod spinner mounted just in front of your fly will give you both extra weight to get down to the fish and the added dazzle of the spinner.

However, the largest stringers of walleyes are usually brought in by the bait fishermen. Because of the depths he ordinarily feeds at, the walleye is more of a scent feeder than a sight and sound-wave hunter. Minnows, worms, crayfish and frogs are all effective baits and emit natural scents. Minnows, though, are the best in 1½-to-3-inch lengths. They must be lively. Just enough split shot to get them down to the bottom is placed about 18 to 24 inches above a No. 8 or 10 hook. One of the most effective walleye fishermen I know, Don Beland of Ely, Minnesota, impales two minnows on a single hook. One he hooks through the tail just behind the anal fin; the other he hooks through the lips. His split shot are about 12 inches above the bait. Don likes to fish the pools off to the sides of fast water. He casts to the edge of the moving stream, then lets the bait sink. After a reasonable waiting period, Don starts his re-trieve—slowly, with plenty of stops in between. The walleye is slow and methodical about taking his food, so Don doesn't want to hurry him. When the walleyes are in and feeding—usually early in the morning or late in the afternoon—Don has action on just about every cast.

Many walleye fishermen get their best action from dark until 1 or 2 o'clock in the morning. Some anglers find good luck in the summertime by trolling a flashing spoon or a set of spoons ahead of several hooks loaded with night crawlers. A small plastic trolling keel mounted about 3 feet in front of the rig is weighted with an eyelet sinker on about 6 inches of light leader material. This lets your rig travel about 6 to 8 inches off the bottom, right where the walleyes should be lying. Every time you get a strike, mark the spot on your map. Keep working those X marks over and over and you should soon pick up your limit of the finest-eating freshwater fish I know.

BY CHARLES F. WATERMAN

BECAUSE everyone knows that the farther you travel the larger the fish you're supposed to catch, panfishing is usually done around home by anglers who lack time to go after *real* fish. This makes for a lot of local experts, but world travelers are likely to splash past a lot of bluegills and crappies on the way to marlin or Atlantic salmon.

All of this takes some of the dignity out of panfish expertise, and the author of a panfish chapter is generally recruited from the unlearned peasantry. He is supposed to be a dozing bucolic with a sedentary love of nature, and with crude tackle unsuited to more exotic pursuits. Very few Payne fly rods are bought for yellow perch, and panfishing expeditions are the last stop for old clothes. Having passed up bonefish for bream on a few occasions, I fit the panfish mold to perfection, and you are reading the right guy.

To get scornful brown trout anglers into the tent, I like to tell about the time I was fishing for bluegills in California twenty-five years ago. It was on a little backwater of the Tuolumne River, and I had already found the black bass weren't interested in popping bugs or surface plugs. It was dusk when I got around to the bluegills, and I was nursing the skiff along a shore with a few over-

266

hanging grass sweepers when I heard one of those bluegill *plops* that generally mean business at that time of evening. Over against the bank I saw a little disturbance on a shelf where the water couldn't have been more than 8 inches deep. I put on a little dry fly, since I didn't see any rubber-legged bugs in the box. I got it into the general area of the little surface curlicues, and a bluegill took it as if he were beating out his friends. I tossed the fly back in there and another bluegill struck. Then I caught a couple more and figured I had the place and the method.

By that time the little fly was fish-slimy and unwilling to float; but I supposed it wouldn't make any difference, so I slapped it back on the water and saw a couple of wakes moving toward it—but this time nothing happened to the fly, so I tried it again and fifteen or twenty more times. All I produced was a series of confused swirls, and I decided the picnic was over at that spot. But I thought the fly might as well float, so I blew on it, doped it and laid it back in there, playing that I was after a smart trout instead of a bluegill that would eat anything. When the fly floated high, the bluegills took it. When it sank, even a little, nothing happened. It had to float, and it had to float high and dry.

Since bluegills often prefer something soggy, and since many bluegill experts will tell you that getting a fly down to the fish is the only requirement for success, it was jarring to learn that these fish, operating in water that barely covered their dorsal fins, insisted on finesse, even as the frogs tuned up and night came on. Like any other game fish, they can be doggoned particular sometimes.

There are other times when they can be just as insistent that the fly sink, and there are days when it has to sink to an exact depth. That's one of the things bluegills are particular about.

A couple of years ago I was fishing with Al Klemack on a canal just off Lake Okeechobee in Florida. On the previous day the bluegills (better call them bream in that country) had shown no restraint at all concerning rubber-legged popping bugs. It was spawning time for Okeechobee bluegills, and all you had to do was stand up in the boat and locate round light spots on the sand bottom next to the bank. Each light area was a bream bed, and there would be a burly guardian finning above each nest. Then you'd just flip the bug over there, shake it a little and give your

The small, lightly weighted green nymph shown here is highly effective when bluegills aren't working on top.

fish time to get to it. But on this occasion nothing happened, and Al was getting a little fidgity. He's a guide who has had much experience with brook trout of the Northeast, and on this occasion he was running the boat for me while I made a fool of myself.

He hinted about a little green nymph he had tied and sold by the thousands, and tactfully suggested I try it instead of the little bug. Just to please him, and hoping to get back to my favorite after a few casts, I let him tie on one of his pets.

This nymph, Klemack explained, has just a little lead on it. Not enough to hamper the casting, you understand, but enough to get it down to where the fish are. The water there was just a little deeper than what I'd been fishing, he said, and since it was a hot late-spring day, the bluegills weren't at all anxious about coming up for a suntan. So I false-cast it a time or two and laid it over there where Al kept telling me the bream were nesting. He told me just how long it should sink and I counted to 7 or 8 to make sure it was down there. I started to move it—but it wouldn't move very well because there was a half-pound of bluegill hanging on it. In fact, the fish had pretty well eaten it and was starting the digestive process. After that, I was a little quicker on the strike and we caught most of them in the mouth. By the time I had the count just right, the fishing had turned into a production line. I was leading the bluegills back to Al, and he was unhooking them, tossing the little fly into the air and letting me get back into action with a single false cast. Since we were putting the fish back, it got a little ridiculous for grown men, but we had gotten into a fishing contest with some other folks and we kept it up until we had drifted past the row of beds.

I believe the depth was most important in that day's fishing, although I've found green about as effective as any color in nymphs. For panfish, a nymph needn't be ornate. You can call it an "impression lure" if you want to, but there are many kinds of greenish worms that the sunfishes like. Black nymphs or Woolly Worms seem to be better at times. These green nymphs are in hook size 10 or 12 and haven't done much for me on bass. I think you'll get more incidental bass strikes on surface flies or bugs.

Dry-fly fishing for bluegills produces well at times, but most of the highly effective patterns are tied on such tiny hooks that it's a major operation to get the thing back after the fish gulps it. My rule is to use as large a hook as the fish will take consistently, as that culls out the really small ones and is sometimes more attractive to the big ones.

Year in and year out, I believe the best surface lure has been the sponge-rubber spider, or "bream killer." It barely floats in soggy fashion, and the slightest twitch causes the rubber legs to wave seductively. Bluegills have such small mouths that they often do considerable nibbling before actually eating a good-sized bug, and the soft body with its rubber legs still feels like something alive, even though the fish may gum it gently for two or three investigations. He just fools around until he gets hooked. Tiny bluegills often tug on the individual legs, and this in itself often attracts better fish. Many times I've simply let the bug lie while 3-inchers worried it, only to have a determined wake arrive on the scene and the bug disappear with a *plop* that meant a worthwhile fish.

I am going into a little extra detail about the methods and tackle for bluegills, partly because they are among the most popular of panfish and partly because the tackle, with minor variations, is good for other fish.

You can pretty well divide the sunfishes into two classifications —those with small mouths like the bluegill's, and those with bass-like mouths such as the green sunfish, the crappie and the warmouth possess. The rock bass has a good-sized mouth; the pump-kinseed, a very small one. Presented at the right time and place, the same lures and flies will take all of them.

Generally speaking, the fly rod does its best work in shallow water or when the fish are very near the top. Spinning gear usually does better when the fish are deep, even though sinking lines will put a fly down there. Bait fishing is at its best when the fish are deep, usually unwilling to move very far to strike. Of course, most panfishermen have caught fish on the surface with bait, but this is fly rod territory, and the flies are generally more fun. Besides, it's difficult to keep a natural bait in good condition for long if you're slapping it around on top.

Bob Budd, who has won national casting championships, is one of the very best panfishermen I know, and he employs ultralight spinning gear almost exclusively. He uses about 4-pound line most of the time. The light stuff gives the little lures a chance to work, and it's necessary for easy casting. He sticks to short rods, be-cause they're highly accurate. Frankly, the rods he uses tend to be slightly stiffer than I'd prefer, but he throws flat casts with the accuracy expert's snappy wrist action. In spinning for any of these fish it is seldom necessary to present the lure gently, and the lure is so small it doesn't make much of a splash anyway.

Budd's fishing is nearly always against a lake or river shoreline, and there are plenty of obstacles in the form of logs, grass, rocks or bank sweepers—small branches or very long grass. I suspect that part of his preference for the shoreline is a matter of having something to cast at, but the cover concentrates the fish, and as you learn to interpret it you don't waste much time on sterile water.

Most of the panfishermen who work shorelines do so with cane poles, using monofilament line. A very light cane pole that can be managed well with one hand is highly efficient, for most of the casts are quite short. There is a useful outfit that comes very close to fly fishing but uses a light cane pole. You take a piece of fairly heavy level fly line, use a short, light leader and flop the thing along with one hand. The piece of fly line, generally about the length of the pole, gives you some weight to make the casting easy, and such an outfit will work well with light spinners, small plugs, popping bugs, wet flies or even bait.

Bob Budd, casting champion, runs a small gasoline outboard with his feet to be able to cast for crappies along a shoreline.

There isn't much need for a reel in this kind of fishing. Fastening a reel to a cane pole is usually more trouble than it's worth, and it is very rarely that you need to give much line to any of the panfishes. You play them, all right, but it doesn't take very long. You can dip the cane pole a little to give the fish a short run, and then bring him to the surface. Only the larger fish are likely to get down again after being brought upward once. The long pole is good for the lifting action, since the tip will be almost over the fish as he tires and a fish is decidedly weak on the diving business if his head is being pulled skyward.

There are times when a small bobber can be used with artificials, especially small jigs or "darts," but the bobber is generally a bait-fishing device, giving you a chance to let the worm or minnow hang suspended at a predetermined depth. It is at its best when you're drift-fishing in wind or current.

You can use a bobber or casting bubble with spinning tackle, but unless you're very careful the casting procedure is hard on natural baits, especially minnows or small frogs. Fishing with live frogs never appealed to me, although they have caught plenty of panfish.

We divide spinning lures into three classifications—surface and subsurface plugs, underwater spinners and small spoons, and jigs or weighted flies. The small jigs are especially good for crappies in fairly deep water and have been deadly in ice fishing for perch. If I had to choose a single spinning lure for all panfish, I'd go for a small spinner that turned very easily and a treble hook dressed with some sort of hair or a feather that works freely as the lure is retrieved. Marabou, squirrel hair, bucktail, polar bear hair and soft nylon are good. Bob Budd, who specializes in this kind of fishing, uses a No. 8 treble hook much of the time. He has to use a gentle touch when he hooks an especially large fish, but the small hook is good on the nibblers, especially bluegills. There are times when brass spinners are better, but nickel is most popular. These are free-swinging spinners. Airplane-type spinners work too.

It's essential that the spinner be light and that it turn very freely, for a slow retrieve is essential in much panfishing. There are times when you want the thing to sink a considerable distance before beginning the retrieve, and if you have a balky spinner it goes down like a piece of scrap iron. If it's light and loose, it wobbles and gives off all kinds of glints as it sinks. Many fish are hooked during the descent. When you start your retrieve you want the spinner to begin work instantly. Examine it frequently to make sure there are no moss or weed particles clogging the shaft. Inspection is especially important if you troll rather than cast, as you could go a long way without noticing that nothing is working.

As a callow youth throwing panfish spinners on hollow steel bait-casting rods that preferred lures weighing half an ounce or more, I used to attach a big sinker ahead of an unweighted spinner —preferably several inches ahead. The casting efficiency was about what you'd expect, but that was before the days of light spinning tackle in this country. You'll do better if your casting weight is an integral part of the spinner/fly combination. Some of the best are beads between the spinner and the skirt, although there are some good lures with the weight ahead of the spinner. With a small twirler, the weight up ahead changes the water flow and makes it tougher for the spinner to get started. Remember, we're dealing with very small stuff. Don't interpret this as a criticism of some excellent bass lures.

Don't be scared off by the weight of these little things. I find that you can cast very accurately for short distances with spinner/fly combinations that weigh less than $\frac{1}{16}$ ounce, using 4-pound

This is a good design for a panfish spinner/fly combination, with beads between fly and spinner providing casting weight. The offbeat spinning outfit features a plastic fingering device for added accuracy.

line and a light rod. And don't worry about the little hook's doing a job on big fish if you use sufficient care. A number of 10-pound bass have been landed on these rigs.

I often fish for crappies on a Southern river where the black water moves gently against undercut banks festooned with brush piles, fallen logs and living cypress. Most of that water is several feet deep, and it is no place for a timid soul with only one jig. You make a short cast of about 25 feet and let the little jig go all the way to the bottom (if it doesn't hang up on the way down). Then you pick it up very gently and retrieve it slightly, possibly a foot, letting it back to the bottom again. After two or three such maneuvers, you crank it in slowly with a little rod-tip manipulation.

The strike is usually a gentle twitch, or the jig simply stops. There are many cases in which the bait simply doesn't get back to the bottom after one of the gentle lifts. Since the hook is generally larger and the type of strike is different, you'll need to set it more briskly than with the spinner/fly, and on many occasions you find you've simply driven it securely into a log down there somewhere. The amount of junk waiting to collect your lures is one of the reasons why jig bouncers often make a hobby of constructing their own.

Crappies are school fish, even more so than the bluegills, and once you've had a strike you may be in business for several more. When I'm drifting past a good spot and something happens, I ease over the anchor and try some more. Oars or a paddle are satisfactory propulsion, but the boatman doesn't get to fish much that way. An electric motor is excellent, and there are even good anglers who idle a small gasoline outboard constantly. In water as deep as that where crappies are usually found, a small motor seems to have little effect on them. On the days when they're caught in a foot of water along a shoreline, the motor gives you only one or two shots at a spot.

Like most game fishes living in moving water, the river crappie prefers to hold in a spot where it can get to food brought by the current and doesn't have to expend too much effort. Eddies are excellent if they're near good cover. There's a good spot right below a log or bush, and the slow-moving cushion of water backed up just above an obstacle is most frequently ignored by casters. Casting upstream of obstacles and letting the current swing your jig under them is productive of fish but conducive to even more hangups.

A spinner/fly combination can sometimes be just as efficient as a jig when fished in the same manner. Small sinking plugs, generally improved by addition of a small spinner, work very well at times. Little spoons are fine too, and addition of small strips of pork rind helps the score occasionally. As with other panfish, frequent changes in technique are important. Having caught all he wanted with a certain lure on a previous trip, a fisherman is reluctant to try anything else. The preferences definitely change from day to day, but panfishermen are not the lure changers you find among trout and bass anglers.

Where I have fished, the most prevalent fly and jig colors are yellow and white. There are times when one far outdoes the other. Black has not been so good for me except in imitation worms or nymphs. Natural squirrel tail has been very good. Thin strands of Mylar on an underwater fly help sometimes, and some flies are made up entirely of Mylar. I guess if I had to use only one spinner/fly it would be white, but I'd rather not argue about it.

Fly equipment for panfish should be fairly light, but we run into compromises, for most panfishermen also fish for bass. There's much more overlap between bass and panfish than between trout and panfish. Using a dry fly for bluegills or other sunfish, it's hard to come up with an outfit that's too dainty; but more bluegill fishing is done with small bugs or rubber spiders, both of which require a little more rod to be cast easily. Full-size bass bugs are too much for the light trout sticks, and some of the larger bream bugs get up there in weight and wind resistance. On some Ozark waters I have preferred No. 6 bugs with rubber legs—big enough to take both large- and smallmouth bass as well as green sunfish, bluegills and rock bass ("goggle eye" or "redeye" to most of those fishermen).

The very smallest panfish bugs have caught very few sizable bass for me. If the hook is size 6 or larger, there'll be more bass action. One of the finest combinations of all is a medium-size popping bug with rubber legs, and the approved method of working it is to let it lie for a time after casting, then move it slightly to activate the rubber legs, then pop it a few times before picking up. If the action becomes progressively more vigorous and noisy, there is little chance of scaring off a customer that doesn't care for much action. A bass sometimes goes for the final loud *plops* before the pickup.

My favorite panfish fly rod is 7½ feet long and takes a No. 6 line, but if I think I'll be using full-size bass bugs on the same trip I often use an 8½-footer with an 8 line. Admittedly, the bigger rod is more than I'd like for bluegills, but it's better for bluegills than the little rod is for bass bugs. Most panfishing is a matter of short casts, so I prefer to overload the rod a little. Thus, a rod that's recommended for a 5 line will work well with a 6. I prefer weight-forward lines for nearly all panfishing, and on those occasions when I use a true dry fly I can get by with the forward-taper, although a double-tapered line would be nicer for the time being. A level line is almost as good as the weight-forward if it's heavy enough.

Most of the wet flies can be handled well with a floating line, and an 8- or 9-foot leader will allow you to get a nymph down in most cases. If you really want to compete with jig fishermen you'll need a sinking line, or one with a sinking tip at least. Of course, the high-floating lines are easy to cast. I did very well on black crappies last year, using the aforementioned slightly weighted nymph and a floating line. Most of those fish were caught in lily-pad water of modest depth. I'd just let the nymph sink for a few seconds and then retrieve very slowly by working the line with my fingers. The "hand-twist" retrieve used by wet-fly fishermen for trout (I think the late Ray Bergman originated the term) proved to be about the right speed.

Most of the fly-rod hardware—tiny plugs, miniature spoons and skirted spinners—can be worked better on light spinning tackle, but there are still those who use the fly rod for them. That was necessary before spinning gear, but all of those things are difficult to cast with anything but a brute of a fly rod. Maybe it isn't even fly fishing if you use those gadgets, although there have been a few paper-thin spoons that cast like streamers.

Some of my earliest "fly fishing" was for green sunfish and blue-gills in some Kansas creeks and ponds, and the "flies" were Pflueger "luminous tandem spinners" that would have gone very well on ultralight spinning gear. But my friend and I had what were called "bass rods" in those days. Mine was 9 feet long—of split bamboo, of course, and weighing upward of 6 ounces. I would wade into a mud-bottomed creek until I could barely keep my elbows out of the water; make a couple of false casts, the double spinners going past my ear like low-level strafers, and let fly. Oh, we caught fish all right, and some of them were bass. There's nothing wrong with those spinners—but I'd rather not use a fly rod with them. It was in one of those creeks that I learned both bass and panfish would eat a hair mouse, and my fishing has never been quite the same since.

Don't shortchange the surface bug. Anyone who has dredged crappies from the bottom of a hill-country impoundment using small minnows is likely to figure such a fish would never want something on top. I have found differently, and although surface fishing for crappies is not reliable, there have been times when a popping bug was better than anything else around. I recall one dusk when I paddled a skiff up to a tinkling run-in along a grassy bank of a Southern river. There were numerous swirls and *plops* around the little creek, and when I threw a full-size bass bug over there it was a big crappie that banged it. His friends were there

Small popping bugs give excellent results on bluegills, especially in late evening. This fish is dark in color, coming from vegetation-stained water.

too, and it has happened since—but most crappies are caught farther down.

Many times a bass fisherman will find his lure isn't coming in just right and finds a 3-inch sunfish hooked on a 5-inch lure. He holds it up and tells his friends that if sunfish grew to 15 pounds it wouldn't be safe to use anything smaller than a 20-foot boat. This pugnacity has not been fully explained, but I think it's often a matter of panfish's using a cooperative attack on some kinds of food. I do know that you can take a large grasshopper, toss it to a batch of undersized bluegills and see them dismember it and then have tugging matches over the pieces. There's no doubt that they will attack lures they have no chance of swallowing.

They are especially intrigued by fuzzy lures that appear fragile enough to take apart. Some forty years ago I was fishing with a young fellow named Johnny Herrell; he was using a big hair mouse that had been in his box for a long time and was a little the worse for wear. He'd caught some green sunfish and other odds and ends and had gotten into some small ones that seemed bent on taking the hair mouse apart. He just left it floating and watched. There must have been half a dozen little fish working on it. Eventually they got some of the deer hair loose, and finally they stripped the hook. Then they continued to worry the pieces, although I doubt if there was much taste to the thing except for a little dry-fly dope.

Cast a big, squishy lure to such fish, let it lie awhile, and sometimes a bunch of them will form a circle around it. Then a bigger or braver fish will come up and give it a tentative tug—whereupon everybody will take hold and try to tear it up. From the fisherman's standpoint this is important, because it shows that it isn't necessary for the sunfishes to get a lure completely into their mouths. They often attack the shiny hooks of plugs simply because those seem to be appendages they can get hold of.

Some of the most effective underwater plugs I've seen have streamers and beads out ahead of them, making a lure 6 inches long that's effective on fish much smaller than that. The theory is they'll chase anything that won't chase them.

The sponge-rubber bugs and worms that work so well are made much more effective by the use of rubber legs. Some bluegill experts I know have found that these "dry" lures that float soggily when thrown on a fly rod will work with small spinners ahead of them when the fish are farther down. The merit of soft lures is that a fish which doesn't get hooked on the first try still isn't convinced it isn't good to eat and will try again. The rubber spider being towed behind a spinner doesn't look like anything that lives, but it has some of the elements of food—waving legs and soft body—and that's enough for many sunfish. Of course, competition is one of the principles of catching fish on such artificials. A fish that might not go for it alone will throw caution to the weeds when his associates show interest.

So far I have spoken mainly of fishing for bluegills and crappies,

Sponge-rubber bugs and spiders are effective panfish lures for light fly rods. Long rubber legs add considerable attraction.

partly because they are about the best-known of the panfishes and partly because it gave me an opportunity to discuss tackle with direct relation to the fish. I'd now like to branch out a little on the various species and how they live.

The bluegill, probably best-known of the bunch, is found in nearly all of the states (they insist there are none in Maine) and is highly prolific. At first glance, management of a fish that reproduces so rapidly would seem fairly simple, but the bluegill population is a touchy thing, prone to explode at any time conditions are right. Most of us have fished bluegill waters where the fish were tiny, ravenous and apparently beyond number. There can be large fish in such places too, but the size level tends downward. Although bluegills can be prime food for larger game species, the balance is risky and the "bream" can actually crowd out the fish they are supposed to sustain. Part of this is a matter of cover, for if the bluegills can escape to areas where they cannot be followed, they can multiply with impunity. And "impunity" is a very mild word when applied to a fish that lays eggs by the multiple thousands and grows rapidly. In some areas fishermen are urged to keep all of the bluegills they can catch to minimize stunting, but once a bluegill population is on the runaway, hooks and lines can't help much.

There have been a few bluegills over 4 pounds, but that's highly unusual. I'd say that half-pound bluegills are very good ones, in spite of the occasional waters that produce them much larger. Generally, the larger the fish the fewer you'll catch—the reverse of stunted overcrowding.

The bluegill varies greatly in color. The back is generally olive green and the sides purplish with darker bands, but I have caught fish in vegetation-stained water that were almost black, and I have caught them in other places where the overall tone was so light that the basic colors were difficult to pick out. Frankly, if you want to make positive identification of the sunfishes with small mouths, you may have to resort to a biologist's technical description in some cases.

As with other species, the larger fish are likely to be more wary, and methods that will attract crowds of runts may not work for the big ones. You'll generally find that the spawning fish run pretty much to a size in a given area. I have seen limit catches, taken off spawning beds, in which thirty-five fish averaged around 8 ounces. None weighed less than 6 ounces, and none more than 10 ounces. The assumption is that the "bed" is made up of fish from a given hatch, but it's sometimes confusing to figure out what becomes of the fish just a little smaller. In warm climates bluegills may spawn any month of the year and the major spawning period is spread out. In the Northern contiguous states it comes in midsummer. In the South it is in midspring. Spawning fish or those guarding the beds are likely to strike well. I have never heard any biologist say that catching spawning fish was harmful to the overall population.

Once hooked, the bluegill puts up one of the hardest fights of any freshwater fish, making short, darting runs with its broad side turned against the pull of the line. It is a very hard fish to lift straight upward, for it turns parallel to the bottom and swings in circles; but constant pressure tires it very quickly.

In warm weather, bluegills feed heavily very late in the evening; in most of the places I have fished them, they seem to begin operations somewhat later than largemouth bass. Dusk is the busiest time during settled warm weather, and they usually slack off at full dark. Surface feeding can be heard in the form of soft *plops* near cover. Where there is floating or emergent vegetation such as lily pads, hyacinths or duckweed, there are often sucking sounds of very small bluegills taking organisms from the underside of the plants. Most of those fish are too small to interest a fisherman, but it's a sign that the bigger ones may be active. There are some good bluegill fishermen who fish deep during the day and then change to surface lures as night comes on. The very shallow edges, only a few inches deep, may be expected to contain fish during late-evening feeding binges. But although I have studied the ideal temperatures for bluegills in given areas, I sometimes find them resting in very shallow water in bright sun, certainly at a temperature above what they're supposed to prefer. I can't explain it.

The green sunfish has a large, basslike mouth and is thus capable of banging a bass-size popping bug. I guess I've caught more green sunfish on outsize bass lures than any other panfish, unless you want to count pickerel in the classification. The green one is tolerant of silty water and can be active when the water is very, very warm. Probably because some of my earliest fishing was for them, I rate the green sunfish high on the list, although a 9-incher is

These bluegills were taken at midday from lily-pad water.

about tops in size. If you want to mix them with bass, just grade the size of the bass lure down a little. My personal experience is that they often take well in bright sun—more so than bluegills. Like other small species, they have plenty of names. We used to call them black perch.

The green sunfish doesn't seem to show up on the East Coast or in most of the Western states, although it's now found on the Pacific Coast and through most of the remainder of the country. The fins generally have yellowish edges. I think it looks more like a black bass than do any of the other panfishes.

Rock bass, like most of the other sunfishes, are cover-lovers, and I've caught more in smallmouth water than elsewhere. They put up with swifter current than the other sunfishes and like clear, rocky water. You can catch them with all sorts of natural baits and they strike spinners readily, but the most I can recall catching were on Ozark rivers during float trips many years ago. I was primarily after bass and used medium popping bugs and streamers. Although there have been rock bass of more than 3 pounds, most of us never saw anything near that size. They have large mouths, red eyes and small, dark spots on a greenish-olive background.

I put the warmouth bass, or warmouth perch, in here with the rock bass because of general appearance, although he's a sort of poor relation—since he doesn't operate in quick streams, preferring quiet water, and he doesn't care if it's muddy or not. Warmouths are frequently caught in very heavily vegetated water. Like the other sunfishes they often overcrowd and become stunted. The worst stunting I've found was in the South in muddy, weed-choked sloughs. I doubt if predator fish were very active there, and the warmouths thrived—and almost starved themselves out. Those taken from clean water taste as good as any other sunfish, but they often live where water is stagnant and cloudy, and taste like it. Warmouths sometimes grow to almost a foot long, but mine have been smaller. They're brassy-colored and have large mouths and little teeth on their tongues. I never figured they fought as hard as the bluegill or rock bass, but that could be a matter of the waters I caught them in.

The pumpkinseed sunfish is an eager striker with a small mouth. This one has a rigid black gill cover with a red or orange spot on the tip. The belly is yellow or orange, and there are bright blue longitudinal lines and plenty of multicolored spots. It takes all sorts of small baits and will strike small wet or dry flies. It doesn't spawn as frequently as the bluegill and is somewhat less prone to stunting, but most pumpkinseeds are pretty small. Many kids begin with them.

The longear sunfish has a long, flexible gill flap and is brilliantly colored. It takes well on top, but runs small. The yellowbreast, redbreast and spotted sunfishes have small mouths, as has the longear. The redear sunfish, or shellcracker, is a burly specimen and grows very rapidly, but is primarily a deep-water denizen and doesn't take artificials regularly. It's mainly a Southern resident and doesn't care much for current. The Sacramento perch is said to be the only sunfish native west of the Rockies and gets quite large, almost 10 pounds, but it isn't very active on artificials except when caught by slow retrieving or trolling across spawning beds. They say it's declining because of competition from other species, and I don't think I've ever caught one.

The crappies, both black and white, are true sunfishes. They run a little larger than most of their relatives and spawn somewhat earlier in the season. Crappie schools can be very large, and a crappie spawning area can be large enough to keep fleets of boats busy for weeks. The black crappie likes clear, cool water and hard bottoms, while the white crappie will live on soft mud bottoms and can make it with little cover. They aren't as easy to tell apart as the names indicates, although the black crappie is generally darker overall. The white crappie is likely to have six instead of seven spines in its dorsal.

White perch aren't perch at all but are a member of the sea bass family. They live in brackish water as well as in fresh, and there is considerable commercial fishing for them along the Atlantic Coast. They have a reputation for being an extremely advanced form of fish, more intelligent than larger and more revered game fishes, but whether this is really advanced intelligence or simply perversity about taking baits and lures I wouldn't know.

The whites are school fish, and the best surface fishing for them usually comes when they move inshore for feeding after lying in deeper water during the bright part of the day. They love nymphs as well as dry flies—sometimes. As evidence of chronic white perch perversity, I once caught them in very shallow water over Maine boulders at midday. I used a very small popping bug and heaved it a considerable distance to no more than 6 inches of water. The perch pushed wakes as they came for it, and there were some occasions when I'd actually sight-cast to individuals. They didn't run very large. White perch prefer small lures for the most part, although I have caught them on big bass poppers, even in Currituck Sound, a place where they aren't noted for taking surface lures.

White perch have unusual spawning habits. They release their eggs and sperm in small tributary streams, where they go in schools. There is no pairing off by the male and female fish, the eggs being fertilized as they cling to almost anything they contact. Since this is a very potent way of building a large population of fish, biologists watch with some apprehension. There's no problem in the perch that migrate along the coasts, but the landlocked populations are increasing and can possibly crowd out other species.

Yellow perch are real perch, as are the walleye and sauger. They are a cool-water fish, preferring water somewhat colder than that of the sunfishes, and they are found over most of the United States. They're popular targets for ice fishermen. They're not good surface takers, and if the oxygen supply is sufficient the perch are generally very near the bottom. Most of the shallow-water fishing is during the spring when the water temperature is around 45 degrees, and at that time they will take artificials, but most yellow perch are caught on bait. They bite small fish, crayfish and worms. The larger yellow perch are generally found at the deepest levels, often at 30 to 50 feet, and locating a school can be a chore on a good-sized lake. Regardless of the time of year, they do most of their feeding in the daytime, and observers report that the schools tend to move into the shallows and break up at night, individual fish lying quietly on the bottom. Good perch waters are fairly clean, often have rocky bottoms and are not heavily vegetated.

White bass and yellow bass belong to the sea bass family and thus, although strictly freshwater residents, are relatives of the saltwater striper and the white perch. The white bass is the better-known of the two and became popular through wide introduction in man-made impoundments. Until these big lakes spread across the Midwest and South, it was primarily found in the Northern United States. Now it's over most of the Eastern two-thirds of the country. It grows larger than other panfish, even up to 5 or 6 pounds.

This is a big-water fish and the schools are often hard to find, sometimes going to considerable depth in hot weather. The lures that work on black bass and other sunfishes work on the white bass, but its greatest claim to sporting fame is its custom of surfacing in large schools to cut up shoals of baitfish, especially shad. "School bass fishing," or "jump fishing," is a specialized sport and sometimes requires pursuit of the splashing and swirling schools by boat and a very sneaky approach for the last few yards. Some fishermen say the black bass learned to "school" on the impoundments by watching the whites. The fishing sometimes involves a small trailer behind a heavier lure that provides throwing weight, and the true school fisherman becomes a top-rank caster, generally using spinning or plugging tackle. Things become most complicated when the schools move rapidly. Early morning and late evening are best for surface feeding. Although often caught around dropoffs and underwater ridges, the white bass doesn't hold to cover. It's a wanderer. There's considerable concentration when the fish ascend rivers for spring spawning. When there's no surface activity, slow trolling sometimes locates them. When they're on the bottom, they take jigs much as crappies do.

The yellow bass, although living in warmer waters for the most part, has similar habits, but doesn't grow so fast or so large. Populations of both yellow and white bass fluctuate wildly. The yellow bass is generally considered a better food fish, but its introduction has been less successful than that of the white. It is found in much of the Midwest and South. There's nothing wrong with the fighting qualities of either fish.

Panfish are occasionally almost too easy to catch, but anyone who has pursued them for many seasons will find a challenge and tough days, and it is very, very hard to outfish a local expert. As a friend of mine said: "If I'd rather catch bream than tarpon, that's my business."

EPILOGUE:
THE FISHERMAN IN CONSERVATION

BY MICHAEL FROME

DURING the summer of 1971 I noted a rather chilling newspaper report concerning an accident at the Dow Chemical Company plant located at Midland, Michigan. A workman there had apparently misread a gauge. As a result, he had released caustic soda into the Tittabawassee River, killing between 2,000 and 3,000 fish.

Such tragic blunders do not happen every day, thank heaven. At least, they're not reported in such a manner as to be part of our daily consciousness. But how widespread are they in actuality? Are they fundamentally "accidents" affecting only fish, or are they inescapable by-products of our highly technological society and our superstandard of living which embrace all species?

Fish kills of significant consequence now occur to an alarming degree in every section of the country. On October 24, 1972, for example, a tank truck overturned in a remote area near Cimarron, New Mexico, spilling about 7,000 gallons of diesel oil into the Cimarron River. According to the New Mexico Game and Fish Department, the oil killed 18,500 fish, mostly brown trout, in a 9½-mile stretch of river, and also destroyed most of the trout food organisms for 84 miles downstream. The trucking company involved agreed to pay compensation for the fish loss and the cleanup expenses. "Unfortunately," commented Ladd Gordon, director of the Game and Fish Department, "money cannot completely correct the environmental damage to the stream and fish habitats. And it will require several years to restore this fishing water to its natural condition."

Meanwhile, more than 100 men already were battling to contain oil from another accident in New Mexico, this time in the northwest corner of the state. A 16-inch pipeline had ruptured on October 10, releasing an estimated 38,000 gallons (but possibly as much as 200,000 gallons) of crude oil into a dry wash in the desert. Then rain had washed the oil through an irrigation canal and down a Utah arroyo into the San Juan River, which flows into Lake Powell, one of the nation's largest recreation areas and the most popular fishing hole in the Southwest. It spread into a slick reported to be more than 80 miles long, threatening a resource where anglers have taken catfish weighing over 20 pounds and largemouth bass, rainbow trout and German browns of 6 pounds or more.

Turning eastward, the Big Piney River once was queen of the Ozark Highlands of Missouri, in the heart of America. It was known as a stream of green-blue beauty, pure enough to drink from, the epitome of the Ozark float river, as restful and rewarding as they come anywhere. By mid-1972, alas, the entire river was afflicted with serious sewage pollution, principally from the communities of Cabool, Houston and Licking and from the Fort Leonard Wood military reservation; all, in fact, were under orders from the Missouri Clean Water Commission to cease discharges by December 31, 1973. Then came an "accident" from quite another source, killing 110,000 fish, as well as all other aquatic life, in a 15-mile section below Cabool. The cause was seepage from the saturated soil around a chemical/bulk-oil complex. Heavy rain and snow had forced highly toxic materials into the stream; the major killing ingredient was pentachlorophenol, a chemical which is mixed with fuel oil and used to treat fence posts and telephone poles. Included in the kill were many minnows and sunfish, carp and small bass; suckers, always sensitive to contaminants, were among the quickest to die. When it was over, state biologists foreclosed any chance of early fishing on the Big Piney; it would take a rise of several feet of water, they said, to flush the oil off the rocks and clean out the stream so that it could begin rehabilitating itself.

Perhaps the most massive fish kills in America occur in Florida's lakes, canals, rivers and estuaries and on both coasts, almost summer after summer. The causes are principally pollution from sewage and industrial "wastes" discharged into public waterways. South Florida cities along the Gold Coast dump 116 million gallons of virtually raw sewage into the ocean every day. Beaches at such playgrounds as Miami Beach often are so contaminated that they are unsafe for body contact (though rarely, if ever, posted). Ocean game-fish populations have been drastically reduced— partyboat skippers say they must now travel 50 miles from Miami to find good fishing. Annual sailfish catches have dropped from an average of 4,000 fish in the years before 1948 to only 900 in those since 1962. Even more disturbing, sick fish with cancers, tumors, lesions and fin and tail rot have been showing up in Biscayne Bay; but sick fish have also been increasingly observed in the Florida Keys, Tampa Bay and Escambia Bay at Pensacola, and doubtless are present in other grossly polluted waters.

"Every year it seems to get worse," a Florida sportsman wrote to the editors of *Field & Stream* magazine in the fall of 1972. "Not only are fish dying in old areas, but they are turning up in new areas as well. I've seen beautiful game fish—sheepshead, mullet, speckled trout, croakers, redfish and black drum—that any angler would give his right arm to catch lying rotten on the beaches."

This fisherman expressed his despair soon after the latest tragedy had struck. In the period from August 26 to September 15, 1972, a 22-man municipal crew working along Bayou Texar had carried off more than 40 tons of dead fish, averaging more than 2 tons per day. The whole area was pervaded by the stench of dead and decaying fish. Most were menhaden drawn to the bayou waters by prolific algae blooms, where they soon exhausted the oxygen supply of the water and died. The algal growth resulted from an overflow of raw sewage into the bayou from inadequate sewage lines in an area of accelerated real estate development and construction. On September 15 the bayou was closed to swimming and water skiing, but three days later another major kill struck East Bay, site of major oyster beds and the last relatively unaffected estuary of Escambia Bay. The dead menhaden stretched five miles long in a strip one-half mile wide, and more were still dying by the millions. Fish of different species were seen floating in distress, swimming in circles upside down.

Still, some of the worst disasters escape attention because they're not immediately self-evident. They deal with tragedies of a deteriorating environment shared by fish and fishermen, and therefore are the most frightening of all. This was plainly revealed in the case of Lake Apopka, in Orange County, Florida, in early 1971. Sixteen alligators were found dead; so were many fish, snakes and fish-eating birds such as egrets and gulls. A study team from the University of Georgia arrived on the scene with expectations of investigating illness and mortalities of wildlife populations.

But the team found something else instead: that Lake Apopka was paying the toll of uncontrolled effluents from municipal sewage, muck-farming operations, citrus groves and citrus-processing industries. Moreover, organic debris from water hyacinth and "trash-fish" control programs—promoted in the name of better fishing—had added to the excessive enrichment of Apopka's waters. The team concluded the dead and dying animals were sounding an alarm. The evident catastrophe was essentially a symptom of something much deeper. What needed study and treatment was the sickness of the lake itself.

There is little time to lose, for people can be afflicted too. After all, when birds, or fish, or any living species, succumb to an unhealthy environment, how can man be expected to prosper or survive? Within a three-year period, at least five persons died from a newly recognized disease, amebic meningoencephalitis, contracted from swimming in the central-Florida lakes. Authorities concluded that some unknown factor in polluted waters causes virulent strains of a certain organism, *Naegleria gruberi*, to develop suddenly, then to strike, most typically, young swimmers. The organism enters the nose, then eats its way up the olfactory nerves into and through the brain. Each of the five recorded victims perished in agony.

In order to save the fish, we must save the fishing environment. If the fisherman wants to enjoy his sport, and to be sure that there will be sport for his sons to enjoy, and for their sons following them, he can no longer devote himself solely to the techniques and pleasures of fishing, but must also concern himself with the protection and perpetuation of the fishery against the harsh challenges of a technological age.

The degradation of aquatic systems, including the fisheries, is under way everywhere in the world—caused by industrial pollution, pollution from human and livestock "wastes" and pollution from inorganic-fertilizer technology. The sickest aquatic systems, quite paradoxically, are found in the richest, most advanced, most civilized nation on earth, where rivers and lakes have been severely impacted by dams; channelization; herbicides and pesticides; erosion from uncontrolled logging, mining and road building and thermal pollution. All this in the name of progress, profitability, "increasing the tax base," attracting industry and a thousand other explanations that essentially serve a few and go unchallenged by the many. We need to reassess our equation of values, to weigh more closely losses against gains within our supercivilization, then to incorporate values based on the quality of life as part of the process of doing business.

For example, the blessings of the motorcar are indisputable. All America moves on wheels. Nevertheless, highways constructed to the highest technical standards have been endowed with culverts that block fish passage. Siltation resulting from dredging and filling for new roads has destroyed fish habitat on a broad front. The widening of stream channels by highway builders has created warmer, shallower water—a condition that prevents the growth and movement of desirable game species, notably trout, and completely alters the stream ecosystem. Is it really worth the price?

Dr. George Cornwell, professor of wildlife ecology at the University of Florida, has pointedly discussed the question of values with reference to production of food. "Which do you want, fishing for fun or food for life?" demand proponents of herbicides, pesticides and channelization, all in the name of food for more people. But Dr. Cornwell has written: "With our aquatic systems destroyed, the food we produce becomes valueless. We can't separate one part of our life-style from the others and still have an existence worth living. We are not making any headway if we sacrifice our aquatic systems to produce food. A great many Americans value their aquatic systems sufficiently to place food production in a more realistic perspective."

More than a billion acres of crop-, pasture- and rangeland, plus another 637 million acres of forests, are treated with fertilizers, pesticides and herbicides that drain into our waterways. Normally a large store of humous nitrogen is maintained in the soil by the organic remains of plants and animal manure. But when the soil is intensively cultivated and the natural crop stripped from the land rather than fed to animals, the supply of humous nitrogen declines. The answer of agri-industrial corporations, with vast holdings devoted to single-crop production, is to add artificial inorganic nitrogen to the soil. Once it reaches the lakes and streams, fertilizer stimulates the growth of algae.

Even now, the fertilizer industry is doubling production of artificial nitrogen in the United States about every six years—thereby doubling the load the ecosystem has evolved to carry and process. A surplus of nitrates is definitely harmful to both plants and animals, and this explains the natural cycle of their release into the atmosphere. The alternative, through overloading, is eutrophication—literally the "enrichment" of water. Spread over many centuries, the gradual accumulation of nutrients and sediments ages a lake so that it ultimately changes from an aquatic to a terrestrial ecosystem—or from water to land. In the past few decades, however, the aging process has been accelerated through man's interference, including the use of fertilizers. Ironically, even with the additional applications, agriculture on a national scale is now no longer increasing crop yields; the environment is being overloaded without receiving even the promised short-term returns.

The finest fisheries are being affected by poisons used broad-scale in agriculture and forestry. Pesticides are present today in every major river system in the country. Coho salmon in Lake Michigan have accumulated concentrations of DDT which are believed to be largely the reason for reproductive failure. In December 1969, widespread deaths of immature catfish occurred in Southern and Midwestern states. Analysis revealed contamination by endrin, dieldrin, DDT and toxaphene. Fish life is very sensitive. The poison may enter the body of the fish through the gills. It then may act on the blood, the nervous system or the organs.

Some poisons are transmitted up the food chain from "loaded" insects; others from microscopic aquatic plants eaten by small invertebrates and subsequently by small fish. Small fish are eaten by large fish; large fish are eaten by birds such as the osprey and the eagle, transmitting the poison to the top of the aquatic chain. Pesticides may not kill on the first go-round, but they may appear in milk and eggs or accumulate in animal fat.

Some herbicides and pesticides are used by fish managers themselves in enormous quantities for control of aquatic plants and to kill off carp and other species that are considered undesirable. The theory is to make the waters more productive; yet poisons are scarcely selective, and the total effect on the environment is unknown. Too little effort has been made to understand the flow of plant nutrients and energy in the aquatic ecosystem and food chain, the interdependence of plants and food organisms. The urgent need among resource managers is to "think in ecosystems," relating every decision and every action to the total life community, rather than to a single, isolated component, or to a production of a commodity, even when it's sport fish; the challenge to the sportsman is to encourage them to do so for the long-term benefits.

Federal agencies committed to commodity production have demonstrated a singular inability to "think in ecosystems." This is notably true in the Department of Agriculture, where agencies such as the Soil Conservation Service and Forest Service have spread environmental pollution and ecological disruption over rural America in the name of furnishing food and fiber to a growing nation; in the process, they have diminished the quality of life, and certainly the quality of fishing in particular.

The Soil Conservation Service, under Public Law 566, has "improved" thousands of miles of waterway through channelization and claims that no fewer than 11,000 streams still need to be channeled. The standard treatment involves clearing all vegetation a distance of 100 feet from the bank, then deepening the stream channel and eliminating all natural curves in order to speed the flow of high water. The objective is to drain adjacent wetlands so that they can be used to grow more crops and to reduce local flood damage. These goals are usually achieved (at considerable public cost for private benefit), but channelization is equally liable to shift the flood damage downstream and to induce erosion along the banks.

According to a 1970 study by the Tennessee Game and Fish Commission, a proposed channelization project on the Obion and Forked Deer rivers would result in an annual loss of $3 million in

fish, wildlife and recreational values. Why so? The studious fisherman can look at a stream and appreciate its relation to the surroundings: Trees and other plants along the banks plainly exercise
great effect on the living river by contributing organic matter to its
food energy. Leaves that fall into the river provide the primary
food source for many microorganisms, such as bacteria and fungi,
which are eaten by higher organisms; mayflies, stone flies, caddis
flies and blackflies obtain most of their food energy from dead
leaves, algae, moss and other particles in the stream before they,
in turn, are eaten by fish. Likewise, spiders, crickets, beetles and
grasshoppers either fall, crawl, hop or are blown from trees and
plants into the water, where they too become important food for
fish.

Insects are denied a place by modern farm- and forest-commod-
ity producers, regardless of the roles they play in the food chains
for fish and birds. Entomologists of the Forest Service have directed a major portion of their time to finding ways of eliminating
insects. Their concern has been for timber production. The Forest
Service consequently has sprayed millions of acres with ecologi-
cally crude insecticides—and still has failed to eliminate the pests.

Timber-cutting practices permitted on National Forests have
also been anything but favorable to the fishery resource. Trout and
salmon especially demand clean, cold waters for survival, yet silt
and sedimentation have been widespread as a result of erosion
from logging on slopes that should never have been disturbed. The
South Fork of the Salmon River, as one of many examples, has historically contained Idaho's largest salmon run, composed entirely
of summer chinook, a species endangered in the Columbia River
system. This river runs through steep, mountainous terrain con-
stituted almost entirely of granitic materials in various stages of
decomposition. Such terrain simply will not tolerate modern logging and roading without unleashing havoc on the drainage system. Nevertheless, logging did take place, with the inevitable con-
sequences. In 1971, a Forest Service fisheries biologist, William S.
Platts, conceded very serious devastation of the aquatic habitat—
to such an extent, he said, that it would take the river an estimated
eighty-five years to recover and regain reasonable conditions.

Other Federal agencies—the Army Corps of Engineers, the Bureau of Reclamation and the Tennessee Valley Authority—have im-

pacted classic fisheries with massive dam-building projects in all parts of the country. One has only to look at the Pacific Northwest to recognize the disastrous effects. Once the clear, rushing waters of the Columbia and Snake hosted the finest runs of salmon and steelhead trout in the world. Since the dam-building orgy of the past three decades, all in the name of profit and progress, a chain of more than twenty dams stands between the Pacific salmon and their spawning grounds on the Upper Snake.

The mighty Columbia, once the proudest river on the continent, is only a shadow of itself, almost entirely bottled up by eleven main dams. The Snake has been plugged by twelve major dams of varying sizes, shapes and purposes. Millions of dollars have been spent on ladders to aid adult fish to reach their spawning grounds in the mountains and their offspring to return to the Pacific Ocean, but still the fishery is declining. Many fish cannot make it. Even when they do manage to get upstream, their young have great difficulty in swimming downward to the sea. They follow the bottom contour of a river, not the surface. When they reach the upstream side of a dam, they mill about near the base; they have lost their way, and many die. In recent years, young and adults by the millions have also been killed on the Columbia by nitrogen gas, which is caught from the air and concentrated as excess water falls over the dams. Under great pressure in the basins below the dams, the nitrogen supersaturates the water and blinds, cripples and kills fish swimming in large schools.

Is all this justified by the alleged benefits in terms of progress and growth? A reading of *The Experts' Book of Freshwater Fishing*, I believe, will convince even the most casual observer that the enjoyment of life cannot be measured in material terms alone. What a sterile world it would be without the wonders of the outdoors and the mystery that waits to be solved with each cast over the ripples of a clear natural stream! How inadequate by comparison is the ultimate prospect provided by the endless exploration and exploitation of energy sources for commodity production and growth unlimited. Who needs it all?

Industry and government officials insist we must extract increasing volumes of coal by surface mining. They don't deny that damage to the earth is inevitable, but allege that it can be repaired and the land reclaimed. It scarcely is, in fact, except for public relations purposes. But even if it could be, damage is never limited to the mine site. Strip miners widen streambeds, drain lakes, divert surface flows, bury and remove spawning gravels, cause siltation and sedimentation, bring about chemical changes in soil and water quality. The damage in all cases extends miles downstream from the source. As Bernard T. Carter, Director of Fisheries in Kentucky, reported in 1963, following a comprehensive Federal/state study on the Beaver Creek Watershed in the eastern mountains of his state: "The entire fish population and nearly all the bottom fauna—the little animals fish feed on—were completely eliminated from the stream receiving drainage from the strip cut."

The boomers of strip mining in Washington and on Wall Street are now threatening to devour the surfaces of valuable, productive cattle country of Wyoming and Montana just because coal lies beneath them—to give these states the old Appalachian treatment. The irreplaceable environmental, cultural, scenic and social values of the great Western Plains stand to be scarred beyond recognition, or lost altogether.

"Of initial concern is the nationally famous fish and wildlife resource," as the Montana Department of Fish and Game has protested. "But even more important is the land, air and water on which this resource depends. This high-quality aquatic and terrestrial habitat could disappear forever from Montana's landscape, leaving fish and wildlife as unfortunate victims and Montanans as the 'biggest losers of all.'" This must not happen. When Montana —or any state—is critically affected, we are all losers.

But who can make the losers into winners? Who can reverse the tide of degradation that threatens not only the fisheries but the environment at large? The challenge, as I see it, rests with the people—especially fishermen who care—not to depend on experts, but to mobilize their own forces and to express their concern for the quality of life with vigor, to demonstrate their influence in the body politic and when necessary, to carry the environmental issues before the courts. This, happily, is already taking place. The most promising aspect of the whole scene is the maturing of the American fisherman as an environmental activist.

It's encouraging to observe the aggressive involvement and growth of anglers' organizations everywhere. Trout Unlimited, for one, is gaining influence because it doesn't avoid confrontation on tough issues; its members have learned they must stand up and be counted for the fisheries if they want their share of the fish. TU chapters have been on the firing line to save the free-flowing Delaware River from the Tocks Island Dam; the Little Tennessee from the Tellico Dam; the Middle Snake River as it flows through Hells Canyon from the Hells Canyon Dam and the Teton River from the Teton Dam. TU is an effective advocate of better fishing, encouraging the average angler to "Limit your kill, rather than kill your limit"—in other words, to release most of the fish he catches, in the spirit of true sport.

A key role is also being played by the Bass Anglers Sportsman Society (BASS). In one recent year it filed over 200 antipollution suits in the courts and is carrying the message to the people with fishing and environmental seminars. "The mercury crisis that closed 51,000 acres of fishing waters in Alabama is evidence enough that if we don't have stronger laws and regulate what's dumped into our streams, our fishing will vanish," Ray Scott, BASS president, has declared. "If we do not act now, we can blame only ourselves when our favorite fishing spots die."

I should also mention the Hudson River Fishermen's Association, the essence of grass-roots activism. The meetings, as Robert H. Boyle describes them in his book *The Hudson River*, are something of a cross between a technical seminar at Woods Hole and an old *Duffy's Tavern* program. "I have seen factory workers stand up and put their jobs on the line," writes Mr. Boyle, "by reporting their own employers as polluters. 'Don't check on the company during the day,' one man said. 'They keep the stuff downstairs and let it out after midnight.'" This demonstrates beyond doubt the gutsy character of the American fisherman.

A great deal of progress has been made; or perhaps I should say the foundations have been laid for progress. Congress and state legislatures have enacted a variety of promising protective legislation—the Wilderness Act, the Wild and Scenic Rivers Act, the National Environmental Policy Act, the Water Quality Act—but it's up to the people to make them work.

Water pollution is still worsening; the environment continues downhill. About 500 new chemicals are added every year to the 13,000 "potentially toxic" ones already used by industry. Thanks to its friends in Congress, the petroleum industry can pump its pollutants via injection wells under the soil, threatening to contaminate the most valuable water storage. These trends must be reversed.

"One could be an ecologist regardless of what he calls himself," wrote Paul Sears in 1964. I agree. The true test is in the breadth of perspective—whether one knows what he is up to in terms of the great patterns of life and environment. In this respect, I think of Senator Alan Cranston's heroic proposal to establish a 35,000-acre Pupfish National Monument in the California desert devoted to an inch-long fish which few people have heard of or seen. Except for scientific value, the desert pupfish are useless to man. They're too small to eat, don't make pets and won't survive in home aquariums.

Still, I believe that saving the pupfish would symbolize our appreciation of diversity in God's tired old biosphere, the qualities that hold it together and the interaction of life forms. When fishermen rise up united to save the pupfish, they can save the world as well.

JOSEPH D. BATES, JR., is a fresh- and saltwater fly fisherman who realizes that other angling methods also offer advantages. Immediately after World War II he pioneered the then-new method of spinning, designing and testing tackle for the sport. His three books and numerous magazine articles about spinning earn him credit for popularizing this multibillion-dollar contribution to the fishing-tackle industry and to anglers everywhere.

His books *Streamer Fly Tying & Fishing* and *Atlantic Salmon Flies & Fishing* are internationally recognized as authoritative. His latest and largest work, *The Complete Book of Fresh & Salt Water Fishing*, was published in the fall of 1973. Other books and booklets by Bates teach the simplicity of fishing to novices and young people and are used as instructional texts in fishing classes.

HOMER CIRCLE, the Angling Editor of *Sports Afield* magazine, has covered several continents fishing and writing about fishing. He is renowned as a preeminent specialist in the black bass—the family of the largemouth.

In addition to writing monthly columns and features for *Sports Afield*, Circle writes and narrates an outdoor radio show which is regularly heard over 600 stations in the United States and Canada. He's the author of the books *The Art of Plug Fishing, Guide to Black Bass Fishing* and *Plugging for Bass.*

Circle is a past president of the Outdoor Writers Association of America and has received that association's highest honor for conservation writing. A former Commissioner on the Arkansas Game and Fish Commission, he has also been named to the Fishing Hall of Fame.

CLARE CONLEY is Editor-in-Chief of *True* magazine. Before joining True, he was Editor-in-Chief of *Field & Stream* magazine, where he served for ten years.

Conley came by his steelheading expertise the hardest and best way —pursuing the fish for months at a time, in all weathers, with all manner of tackle, on the rivers of his native Idaho and in Oregon and Washington. And he wrote about steelhead for both *Field & Stream* and *True* before he went East to become a staff editor.

He has also written on outdoor themes for encyclopedias, yearbooks and anglers' guides and has served on fishing and conservation advisory boards and as a consultant to companies manufacturing outdoor products.

MICHAEL FROME, Conservation Editor of *Field & Stream* magazine, has been highly acclaimed for his work. The late Representative John Saylor of Pennsylvania, in a speech before the House of Representatives, called Frome "a courageous editor and crusading all-fronts conservationist." Senator Gaylord Nelson of Wisconsin called him "one of the country's most distinguished environmental writers, both knowledgeable and highly respected in his field." Walter Hickel, former Secretary of the Interior, said of him, "Mike tells it like it is, not necessarily like we'd like to think it is." In 1972, the highly esteemed conservation organization Trout Unlimited awarded Frome its annual "Trout Conservationist of the Year" award.

Among the books Frome has written are *Strangers in High Places: The Story of the Great Smoky Mountains,* for which he won the Thomas Wolfe Memorial Award; *The Forest Service* and the *Rand McNally National Park Guide.*

JERRY GIBBS is Fishing Editor of *Outdoor Life* magazine and was formerly Assistant Outdoors Editor of *True* and Editor of *Camping Jour-*

nal. In addition to these publications, his stories and photographs on outdoor subjects have appeared in such major national magazines as *Field & Stream, Sports Afield* and many others. He is coauthor of the book *Outdoor Tips.*

Gibbs has fished over much of North America, Europe and the Caribbean.

LARRY GREEN, West Coast Editor of *Field & Stream* magazine, began to fish in his native California at the age of 6. Since then he's tramped over most of the Western states in pursuit of both fresh- and saltwater species.

Green began writing after working in the field of fisheries management with the California Department of Fish and Game. In 1962 he sold his first article, to *Salt Water Sportsman* magazine. Today, in addition to holding the *Field & Stream* post, he serves as Conservation Editor for *Western Outdoors* magazine and has written and photographed for seventeen other national publications.

DOUG KNIGHT has been a regular contributor of fishing articles to the major outdoor magazines for many years and has taken trophy-class fish in just about every freshwater category. At one time a fishing guide in northern New England, Knight has switched roles, now traveling the world in search of new fishing adventures. Over the years, his travels have taken him from Alaska to Patagonia and from the West Coast of the United States to the highlands of Scotland and the shores of Ireland.

Knight has a particular interest in the pike family, pursuing trophy-size great northern pike from northern Minnesota through the eastern Canadian provinces and even to the northern borderlands of Ireland. He hasn't yet broken the world record, but twice he's certain he's had fish on the end of his line that would have challenged it.

ALBERT ("A.J.") MCCLANE, Executive Editor of *Field & Stream* magazine, has been writing for that publication for more than twenty-five years, joining it in 1947 and serving as Fishing Editor for many years.

He is Editor of the monumental angling work *McClane's Standard Fishing Encyclopedia.* He has also written three books on fishing—*The Practical Fly Fisherman, Spinning for Fresh and Salt Water Fish of North America* and *The American Angler*—and has edited a number of others. McClane is angling historian for the *Encyclopaedia Britannica* and *The American People's Encyclopedia* and has written articles for such magazines as *Esquire* and *Coronet*. He holds a degree in fisheries biology.

Toм McNally is Outdoors Editor of *The Chicago Tribune*. Before that, he wrote about the outdoors for newspapers in Baltimore. McNally has been a full-time outdoor writer for twenty-five years, author of hundreds of articles that have appeared in *Outdoor Life, Field & Stream* and other magazines, including such general-interest publications as *Reader's Digest, Life, Look* and *Time*. In addition, McNally has written books (among them *Tom McNally's Fishermen's Bible*), starred in angling movies, made countless appearances on television shows and served as consultant to the *Encyclopaedia Britannica* and Rand McNally & Company.

He has established five world fishing records. McNally has matched wits with fresh- and saltwater species all over the United States and Canada and throughout the Caribbean, Central and South America, Europe, Africa, Asia and much of the Pacific.

STEVE NETHERBY was a Navy pilot, with two tours in Vietnam, before he began writing and editing. After leaving the Navy in 1968, he and his wife, Jackie, moved to Colorado, where he sold advertising for a weekly newspaper. He ultimately became Editor of the paper, and shortly thereafter he received Colorado Press Association awards for his work. In 1969 he joined the editorial staff of *Field & Stream* magazine in New York, and in 1972 he became the magazine's Camping Editor. Netherby has been a fisherman since he was a small boy fishing for small trout in California's Sierra Mountains.

JEROME B. ROBINSON, before settling to become a department editor for the magazine *Sports Afield,* was a free-lance writer contributing fishing articles to that publication and also to *Outdoor Life* and *Field & Stream.*

Robinson grew up in the Northeast, where he has fished for smallmouth bass all his life. Before he became a magazine writer and editor, he was a reporter, outdoor columnist and Editor-in-Chief of a newspaper.

Robinson has fished for many species from Ungava Bay, in northernmost Quebec, to the Caribbean, but he reserves his greatest affection for the smallmouth.

NORMAN STRUNG began writing about fishing while teaching writing and literature at Montana State University, his alma mater, and moonlighting as a hunting and fishing guide. He sold his first article in 1966 to *Field & Stream* magazine.

Since then he has left Academia to concentrate on writing and guiding in the Rocky Mountains. He has published more than 150 articles on fishing, camping, hunting and conservation in magazines, anthologies and encyclopedias. Strung is also the author of six books dealing with the outdoors.

CHARLES F. WATERMAN has been writing about the outdoors since 1934. He had been catching panfish on everything from worms to dry flies even before that.

A full-time newspaperman who became a full-time free-lance writer, Waterman taught journalism at Stetson University. During World War II he was a combat photographer with the Steichen Group.

Among the four books he has written are *The Fisherman's World* and *Modern Fresh and Salt Water Fly Fishing*. Waterman contributes regular columns to the *Florida Times-Union* in Jacksonville and to *The Salt Water Sportsman, Fishing World* and *Florida Wildlife* magazines.

LEE WULFF has written articles for leading magazines and is the author of six books, including *Fishing with Lee Wulff, The Atlantic Salmon, Leaping Silver* and *Handbook of Freshwater Fishing*.

Wulff was a pioneer in the use of ultralight fly rods for big fish and was among the first anglers to take bonefish on a fly.

He created the Gray Wulff and White Wulff, dry flies often used on trout and salmon, and has designed many salt- and freshwater tackle items. He is a former conservation adviser for the Province of Newfoundland and for the U.S. Air Force.

In addition to these talents, Wulff is an award-winning maker of outdoor films (serving as producer and expert commentator for ABC-TV's *The American Sportsman*) and lecturer. He has also been cited by Winchester as Outdoorsman of the Year.

Abu spinners, 250, 258
Adams fly, 63, 88, 97, 104, 202
Agriculture Department, U.S., 292
Air Cell floater line, 251
Alaska
  lake trout in, 133
  Pacific salmon of, 214
Alewives, in Lake Michigan, 132
Amebic meningoencephalitis, 289
American Food and Game Fishes
    (Jordan and Evermann), 231
Amur River, 244
Anadromous fish, 184, 225, 228
Anchovies, as salmon bait, 224
Angelina River, 161
Anglers' organization, ecology and,
    295–96
Angling, vs. float fishing, 106–07
Aquatic plants
  herbicides for, 292
  in mountain lakes, 72
Aquatic systems, degradation of, 290
Arbogast lure, 264
Arctic grayling, 133
Artificial nymphs, for brook trout, 50
Atlantic salmon, 184–211
  air temperature and, 203
  angler's pressure on, 204

Atlantic salmon (*cont.*)
  in Canadian rivers, 208
  cycle of, 188–92
  dams and, 208
  darkness and, 196
  decline of, 208–09
  dry flies for, 195, 198, 202
  farming of, 210
  flies for, 184–87, 195, 198, 200–02
  as game fish, 210
  goading of with flies, 186–87
  grilse stage in, 185–86, 191
  growth of, 190, 192
  hooks for, 200, 207–08
  Icelandic, 209–10
  as leaping fish, 204
  life history of, 188–92
  low-water flies for, 201–02
  night travel of, 202–03
  as parr, 185, 188
  playing of, 204–06
  pools of, 199–200
  releasing of for spawning, 193–94
  respect for, 207
  resting of, 206
  rising of, 184–87, 196, 200
  rods for, 192, 197–98
  safety and comfort of, 199–200

Atlantic salmon (*cont.*)
    spawning of, 186–94, 204, 207
    speed of, 199
    strength of, 188
    wet flies for, 194–95
    see also Salmon
Attractor patterns, in wet flies, 62
Au Sable River (Mich.), 108
Ausable River (N.Y.), 93
Automobile, ecosystem and, 290

Backpacks, in mountain areas, 81–82
Bailey, Dan, 92
Bait
    for lake trout trolling, 144
    live, 67, 241
    for muskellunge, 241–42
    for pickerel, 259
Bait-casting equipment, 16–18, 22,
        30–33, 67
    for largemouth bass, 156–57
    lines in, 32–33
    wrist freedom in, 29
Bait fishing, 67–68
    wet flies for, 60
Bannack, Mont., 93
Barred pickerel, 254
Bass, 15
    largemouth, *see* Largemouth bass
    red, 284
    rock, 281
    smallmouth, 169–83
    warmouth, 281–82
    white, 284
    yellow, 284
BASS (Bass Anglers Sportsman
        Society), 296
Bass boats, 166
Bass fly, 105
Bass plugs, 118
Basswood Lake, Minn., 242, 246, 262
Battle River, 104
Beartrap Canyon, 92
Beaudex reel, 251
Beaver Creek Watershed, Ky., 295
Beaverhead River, 93, 97
Beaverlodge Lake, N.W.T., 244
Beland, Don, 265
Bergman, Ray, 276
Big Brownies, *see* Brown trout

Big Hole River, 93, 97
Big Mantrap Lake, Minn., 234
Big Piney River, 287
Bird's stonefly, 97
Bitterroot Range, 93
Bivisible dry flies, 202
Black bass, 152, 169–83
    see also Largemouth bass; Small-
        mouth bass
Black Creeper, 53
Black Dose fly, 202
Blackfoot River, 43
Black Lake, N.Y., 134, 234
Black pike, 253
Blond Wulff fly, 104
Blue Charm fly, 202
Blue Dun fly, 88
Bluegills, 266–67, 274
    dry-fly fishing for, 269
    feeding of, 280
    habitat of, 279
    popping bugs for, 277
    weight and color of, 279–80
Blue pike, 233
Blue Quill fly, 94
Blue Upright fly, 94, 104
Boats, in Western trout fishing, 106–
        107
Bobber, for panfish, 271
Bodega Bay, Calif., 225
Bogachiel River, 128
Bomber lure, 264
Bond Falls Basin, Mich., 242
Book of the Black Bass (Henshall),
        169
Borovicka, Bob, 107
Bottom fishing, for largemouth bass,
        155–56
Boyle, Robert H., 296
Bream, 285
British Columbia
    Pacific salmon of, 214
    steelhead fishing in, 127
Brooks
    fishing of, 58–60
    meadow, *see* Meadow brooks
    meandering, 75
Brooks, Joe, 92
Brook trout, 9, 47–51
    in alpine environment, 78
    anadromous, 51

Brook trout (*cont.*)
  artificial nymphs for, 50
  brushy, 60
  Eastern, 48
  food of, 50–51
  migration dates for, 49
  mountain, *see* Mountain trout
  "salters" and, 51
  water temperatures for, 48–49, 55
Brown, George, 249
Brown trout, 9, 53–55, 287
  mouse bait for, 67–68
  water temperature for, 53, 55
Brushy brooks, techniques for, 60
Bucktail Caddis, 97
Bucktails, 60, 62
Budd, Bob, 270–72
Bugs, as lures, 44, 278
Bureau of Reclamation, U.S., 129,
    293

Caddisworms, 73
California
  Rocky Mountain area in, 69
  steelhead rivers in, 129
Canadian lakes, trout in, 133
Canadian rivers, salmon in, 192, 208
Cane-pole technique, 75
"Cannonball," for lake trout trolling,
    141
Carlson, Herb, 114
Carter, Bernard T., 295
Casting
  in brooks, 59
  double haul in, 125
  for largemouth bass, 162–63
  see also Bait-casting equipment;
    Fly casting
Casting bubble, 271
Chain pickerel, 254–55
  tackle for, 256–58
Channelization, of rivers, 290, 292
Chautauqua muskellunge, 234
Chemical spills, fish kills from, 287–
    288
Cherry Bobber, 119, 122, 124
Chetco River, 227–28
Chinook salmon, 214, 219
  as endangered species, 293
  playing of, 228–29

Chinook salmon (*cont.*)
  in tidewater, 222
  in upper rivers, 227–28
  see also Atlantic salmon; Salmon
Chippewa Flowage, Wash., 234
Circle, Homer, 151–68
Cirque, 71
Clark Fork River, 93
Clinch-on sinkers, 21
Clock, Phil, 103
Clothing, for mountain areas, 83
Club Foot George, 93
Coal, surface mining of, 294–95
Cochrane River, 134
Coho salmon, 214, 219
  flies for, 223
  see also Salmon
Coho Spinner, 241
Color, for lures, 45
Colorado
  fishing in, 9
  Rocky Mountain area of, 69
Columbia River, 113, 123–24, 216,
    225, 293–94
Committee on the Atlantic Salmon
    Emergency, 209
Compleat Angler, The (Walton),
    105
Cone sinkers, 21
Conley, Clare, 109–30
Connecticut River, 170, 180, 208
Cooking gear, for mountain areas,
    83–84
Cornwell, George, 290
Corps of Engineers, U.S. Army, 129,
    167, 293
Cotton, Charles, 105
Cowbells, in lake trout trolling, 142
Cowichan Bay, B.C., 214
Cranston, Alan, 297
Crappies
  casting for, 271
  as school fish, 274, 282–83
Cravens, Willard, 114
Crayfish, as salmon bait, 224
Cree Indian guides, 136
Creek Chub lure, 264
Cree Lake, Sask., 133
Crickets
  as bait, 67
  for mountain trout, 70

Cross-stream casting, 107
Current flow, in trout streams, 56–58
Custer, Gen. George A., 93
Cutthroat trout, in mountain lakes, 77–79

Dacron lines
    for bait casting, 32
    for fly casting, 35
Dale Hollow Lake, Tenn., 183
Dams
    Atlantic salmon and, 208, 294
    steelhead and, 129–30
Dapping, in brooks, 59
Dardevle spoon, 66, 116, 237, 250
Dark Buck Caddis, 97
Dark Hendrickson flies, 94
Darwin, Charles, 189
DDT, in river systems and lakes, 291
Dead drifting
    of flies and nymphs, 61–62
    for rainbow trout, 51–52
Deer-hair flies, 52, 60, 97
Delaware River, 180, 296
Depth finder, electronic, 147, 166–167, 238–39
Deschutes River, 107–08, 128
Desert pupfish, 297
Dipsey sinkers, 21, 140
Dog Lake, Ont., 246, 248, 262
Donnelly, Roy, 98
Doré (walleye), 260
Double-ender boat, 106
Dow Chemical Company, 286
Downriggers, for lake trout trolling, 141–42
Dragonflies, 101, 103
Drifting
    for smallmouth bass, 173
    for steelhead, 120–21
    see also Dead drifting
Dry flies
    for bluegills, 269
    for brown trout, 54
    light-wire hook and, 98
    nymph and, 62–63
    for salmon, 198
    types of, 63, 201–02
    unsinkable, 52
    variants of, 99–100

Dry flies (cont.)
    walking vs. dragging, 101
    Western, 97–98
Dry-fly fishing, 63–64
    hackles in, 63, 104
    high-water, 100–01
    for rainbow trout, 52
    "realness" in, 101
    turbulence in, 100–01
    "walking" in, 101, 103
    in West, 95
Dry Muddler, 96
Dubuc, Peter, 242
Dusty Miller fly, 200, 202

Eagle Lake, Ont., 138, 234
Ecosystem, fish life and, 292
Eel River, 129
Egg bait
    for steelhead, 120, 124
    terminal rig for, 122
Electronic fish finders or depth readers, 147, 166–67, 238–39
Ephemerids, 100
Escambit Bay, Fla., 288
Esocidae (pike family), 231, 242
Esox americanus americanus, 254
Esox americanus vermiculatus, 254
Esox lucius, 242, 244
Esox lucius baicalensis, 244
Esox masquinongy, 231
Esox masquinongy immaculatus, 233
Esox masquinongy ohioensis, 234
Esox masquinongy masquinongy, 234
Esox niger, 253
Esox reicherti, 244

Fall Favorite streamer fly, 126
Field & Stream, 11–12, 288
Firehole River, 100
Fish
    pesticides and, 290–92
    stunting in, 74
Fishback lure, 226
Fisherman, conservation and, 286–97
Fishing, gearing up for, 14–45
Fishing environment, conservation of, 289–90

Fishing rods, types of, 16–19
  see also Fly rod; Rod
Fishing tackle, freshwater, 16–22
  see also Fly-casting tackle
Fishing vest, for mountain fishing, 89
Fish kills, 286–88
Fish locators, electronic, 147, 166–167, 238–39
Fixed-spool principle, 26
Flambeau Flowage, Wis., 234
Flanagan, John "Roddy," 247
Flashers, 142
Flatfish lure, 66–67, 226, 237, 264
Flathead River, 93
Flies
  for brook trout, 60
  dry, *see* Dry flies
  "horse-size," 94–95
  for mountain fishing, 87–88
  for northern pike, 252
  for panfish, 274–75
  for salmon, 184–85
  skimming, 195
  skittering of, 64
  size of, 94–95, 105–06
  stream, 149–50
  with turned-down eyes, 201
  tying of, 63
  types of, 63, 104
  underwater, 79
  wet, *see* Wet flies
  see also Lures; Streamers
Floater-darter lures, 41
Float fishing, 106–07
Florida
  bass lakes in, 161
  fish kills in, 288
  University of, 290
Fly casting
  for Atlantic salmon, 186–87
  slack-line, 103
Fly-casting tackle
  knotted leaders in, 37
  lines in, 35–36
  profile of, 33–40
  rods for, 34–35
Fly construction, innovations in, 53
Fly fishing
  for bass, 158
  for lake trout, 138–39

Fly fishing (*cont.*)
  luck in, 10
  for steelhead, 127
  subsurface, 105
Fly lines, 35–36
  code letters for, 36
  for steelhead, 125
  for mountain fishing, 85
Fly reel
  for lake trout, 149
  types of, 38–39
Fly rod
  for brown trout, 54
  dry-fly fishing with, 63
  for mountain fishing, 84–85
  for pickerel, 258
  for smallmouth bass, 173
  types of, 39–40
Fly-rod fishing
  bait for, 67
  in tidewater, 223
  for walleyes, 264
Fly-rod guides, 17
Fly-rod lures, for largemouth bass, 159
Fly-rod reel seat, 17
Fly tackle, 16
  "difference" of, 34
  for lake trout, 149
  see also Fly rod; Fly-rod fishing
Fly tying, 63
Forest Service, U.S., 293
Forked Deer River, 292
Freeze-out, in mountain lakes, 72
Freshwater tackle, 16–22
  see also Dry-fly fishing; Fly-rod fishing; Hooks; Lines; Lures; Rods
Frick, Ernie, 249
Frome, Michael, 286–97

Gallatin River, 93
Garcia Beaudex fly reel, 241
Garcia fiber-glass rod, 241, 251, 257
Garfin, I., 242
George, Elmer, 94, 106
Georgetown Lake, Mont., 98
Gibbs, Jerry, 14–45
Ginger Quill fly, 88
Ginger Variant fly, 104

Glacial moraines, 71–72
Glaciers, lakes and, 71
Glassy water, flies for, 98
Gods Lake, Manitoba, 134–35
Gods River, 135
Golden trout, in Sierra Madre mountains, 80
Goofus Bug, 52, 95–97
Gordon, Ladd, 287
Grand Lake, Maine, 170
Grand Traverse Bay, Lake Michigan, 234–35
Grant, George F., 53
Grass pickerel, 254
Grasshoppers
    artificial, 50, 60
    live, 67
    for mountain trout, 70
    for smallmouth bass, 180
    in Western fishing, 101, 103
Grayling
    Arctic, 133–34
    in mountain lakes, 81
Great Bear Lake, N.W.T., 133, 139, 150, 244
Great Lakes, 141
    lake trout in, 131–32
    saugers in, 261–62
    steelhead in, 113
Green, Irving, 103
Green, Larry, 212–30
Green Butt fly, 202
Greenheads (flies), 106
Greenland, salmon off, 208
Green River, 96–97, 136
Greers Ferry Dam, Ark., 161
Grey, Zane, 110
Grey Sedge fly, 88
Grey Wulff fly, 202–03
Grilse, Atlantic salmon as, 185–86, 191
Grubs, as bait, 67

Hackles, for dry flies, 52–53, 98–99
Haggis fly, 202
Hair hackles, 52–53
Hairy Mary fly, 202
Hardwicke, Bob, 103
Hatch, "matching" of, in dry-fly fishing, 63–64

Hawaii, smallmouth bass in, 171
Hayes, D. L., 183
Heddon Hep lure, 258
Heddon rod, 237, 240, 250
Hellgrammites, 67, 177
    for smallmouth bass, 180, 182
Hells Canyon Dam, 296
Hendrickson fly, 63
Henry's Lake, Mont., 97-98
Henshall, James A., 169
Herbicides, fish ecology and, 290–91
Herrell, Johnny, 277
Hip boots, for steelhead fishing, 121
    see also Waders
Hog-line fishing, for Pacific salmon, 216–18
Hoh River, 128
Hooks
    for dry-fly fishing, 104
    fine-wire, 20
    light-wire, 98
    for mountain fishing, 86
    stainless steel, 20
    weedless, 163
Horner Deer Hair, 97
Hot Shot lures, 226
Hudson River, 180
Hudson River, The (Boyle), 296
Hudson River Fishermen's Association, 296
Humptulips River, 128

Iceland, Atlantic salmon off, 209–10
Idaho Power Company, 130
"Imitator" patterns, in wet flies, 62
Insect netting, for bait catching, 90
Intermediate Lake, Mich., 231
Ireland, northern pike in, 242, 247
Irresistible fly, 96, 103–04
Isaacs, Bill, 94

Jackfish, 243, 253
Jack pike, 233
Jackson Hole, Wyo., 97
Jefferson River, 92–93
Jigging, in lake trout trolling, 146
Jigs
    for crappies, 271–72
    as lures, 42
Jock Scott fly, 200, 202

Joe's Hopper fly, 96–97, 104
Jump fishing, 284

Kawartha Lakes, Canada, 262
Keels, for lake trout trolling, 141
Keel sinkers, 22
Kennebec River, 208
Kesagami Lake, Ont., 262
Klamath River, 216
Klemack, Al, 267–68
Knight, Doug, 231–42
Knives, for mountain fishing, 90
Knotted leaders, in fly casting, 37
Kreider, Claude, 99

La Chance, André, 247–48
Lac La Ronge, Sask., 133–34
Lady Joan fly, 202
Lake Apopka, Fla., 289
Lake Athabasca, Sask., 133
Lake Belle Taine, Minn., 234, 244
Lake Champlain, N.Y., 170
Lake Chautauqua, N.Y., 234
Lake Court Oreilles, Wis., 234
Lake Erie, bass in, 166
Lake Kissimmee, Fla., 161
Lake Michigan, 113, 131–32, 235,
    291
Lake Mistassini, Quebec, 246–48
Lake Montgomery, Ga., 152
Lake Nipissing, Ont., 236, 262
Lake of the Woods, Ont., 234, 236,
    262
Lake Okeechobee, Fla., 267
Lake Powell, Wash., 287
Lakes
    freeze-out in, 72
    mountain, see Mountain lakes
    for muskellunge, 234–35
    types of, 74
Lake Sam Rayburn, Tex., 161
Lake Simcoe, Ont., 134–35
Lake trout, 131–50
    cowbells and flashers for, 142
    electronic fish finders for, 147
    flesh of, 136–37
    flies for, 149–50
    fly fishing for, 138–39
    habitat of, 131
    hook sizes for, 150

Lake trout (*cont.*)
    leaders for, 140–41
    lures for, 137
    monofilament line for, 140
    oxygen and, 132
    rocky shores and, 148
    size of, 136–37
    spoons for, 143
    tackle for, 137–48
    terminal rigging for, 140–41
    ultralight spinning tackle for, 138
    water characteristics for, 132–33
    see also Mountain lakes; Trout
Lake trout trolling, 137–39
    bait for, 144–45
    wind and, 145–46
Lake Wentworth, N.H., 170
Lake Winnibigoshish, Minn., 234,
    262
Lake Winnepesaukee, N. H., 170
Largemouth bass, 15, 151–68, 287
    bait-casting equipment for, 31,
        156–57
    casting for, 162
    deep cover for, 154, 163–64
    diet of, 154
    feeding habits of, 153
    fly fishing for, 158
    habitat of, 152–54
    identifying of, 152
    live bait for, 163
    lures for, 154–55, 160–63
    plastic worms for, 163–64
    playing of, 166
    setting hook in, 165–66
    spinning for, 157
    spring rods for, 29
    strength of, 152
    terminal tackle for, 160–62
    water temperature for, 152
    world record for, 152
Law, Glenn, 166
Lead, for mountain fishing, 86
Lead-core lines, for lake trout, 139
Leaders
    with dry flies, 64
    in fly casting, 37–38
    for wet flies, 62
Lead strips, as sinkers, 22
Lead weights, for salmon lures, 226
Leech Lake, Minn., 234

Lewis and Clark expedition, 93
Lewiston, Idaho, spawning grounds, 225
Life vests, in steelhead fishing, 121
Light Buck Caddis, 97
Light Cahill fly, 63, 97
Line control, thumb riding in, 32
Line
    braided, 32, 140, 148
    for deep trolling, 139
    for lake trout trolling, 148
    monofilament, 32, 39, 64–65, 115, 125, 140, 148, 270
    for mountain fishing, 85
    sinking-tip, 105
    for spinning, 158
Little Vermilion Lake, Ont., 234
Live bait, 67, 241
    see also Bait
Livingston, Mont., 93
Longear sunfish, 282
Lough Conn, Ireland, 242
Lough Erne, Northern Ireland, 247
Lough MacNean, Northern Ireland, 247
Lures, 40–45
    "bream killer," 269
    in brooks, 59
    bugs as, 44
    colors for, 45
    finishes for, 87
    floating-diving, 155
    fly-rod, 159
    for lake trout, 137
    for largemouth bass, 154
    for light spinning, 64–65
    for mountain fishing, 86
    for muskellunge, 237–38
    for Pacific salmon, 217
    plastic, 44
    for spinning, 64–67
    for steelhead, 115, 117–20, 124
    types of, 40–44, 64–67, 160–63
    for walleyes, 264
    weedless, 156
    see also Flies; Spoons
Lyons, Haze, 93

McCaulay Lake, Ont., 183
McClane, A. J., 92–108

McKenzie River, 97
McKenzie River boat, 106
McMahon, Malachi, 122
McNally, Tom, 131–50
McNally Magnum streamer flies, 135–36, 149
McNally Smelt streamer, 149
McPhadrain, Willard, 147
Madison, Larry, 94
Madison River, 93, 95–97
Mad River, 129
Magnum Rapala lure, 237
Mallard Quill fly, 100
Manitoba, lake trout fishing in, 134
Marabou Muddler fly, 105
Marabou streamers, 258
Mar Lodge fly, 202
"Matching the hatch," in dry-fly fishing, 63–64
Mayfly lure, 101–02
Meadow brooks
    hot spots in, 76
    meandering, 75
    sneaky approach to, 76
    spinning in, 77
    technique for, 59
Mepps spinner, 65, 258
Merrimac River, 208
Mice, as bait for brown trout, 67–68
Michigan Department of Natural Resources, 132
Mickey Finn streamer, 258, 264
Midges, for mountain fishing, 87
Minnesota, walleyes in, 262
Minnow lure or fly, Muddler type, 97–98, 102, 104, 202
Miramichi River, 190
Mississippi muskellunge, 233
Mississippi River, 152, 170
Missouri Clean Water Commission, 287
Missouri River, 92–93, 97
Mitchell reel, 257
Monofilament line
    for bait casting, 32
    for fly reels, 39
    for lake trout, 140, 148
    for light spinning, 64–65
    for panfish, 270
    for steelhead, 115, 125
Montana, rivers in, 93, 97

Montana Department of Fish and Game, 295
Montgomery Lake, Ga., 152
Mooching, for Pacific salmon, 220
Mosquito fly, 97
Mountain brooks, 75–76
Mountain fishing
bait catching in, 90
fishing vest for, 89
waders for, 90
Mountain lakes
characteristics of, 70–72
clothing for, 83
cooking gear for, 83–84
fishing gear for, 84–87
freeze-out of, 72
hot spots in, 78
lures for, 86–87
transportation and, 81–82
Mountain streams, fish in, 74–75
Mountain trout, 69–91
binge feeding of, 77
flies for, 87–88
growth rate for, 70
nymphs for, 89
size of, 88–89
size stratification in, 73
streamers for, 88–89
stunted, 73–74
Muddler fly or lure, 97–98, 102, 104, 202
Multicolor Marabou fly, 105
Multi-Wing streamer, 149
Muskellunge, 231–42
appearance of, 233
feeding period of, 239–40
flies for, 237–39
growth of, 235–36
habitat of, 234–35
live bait for, 241
lures for, 237
rod for, 237, 240–42
size and weight of, 236
spawning of, 235
subspecies of, 233
trolling gear for, 237–38
water temperature for, 240

Naegleria gruberi, 289
Namaycush trout, 136–37

Natural Environmental Policy Act, 296
Netherby, Steve, 9–13
New Brunswick, N.S., salmon run in, 190
New Fork River, 97
Newfoundland, Atlantic salmon off, 197
New Mexico Game and Fish Department, 286
Nicolet River, 235
Night crawlers, for steelhead, 120
Night Hawk fly, 202
Nokomis Lake, Manitoba, 147
Northern Ireland, northern pike in, 247
Northern pike, 134, 242–53
cannibalistic traits of, 246
characteristics of, 243
in deep water, 250
flies for, 252–53
fly rodding for, 251–52
habitat of, 244
life cycle of, 244–45
lines for, 251–52
lures for, 250–51
size and weight of, 231–32, 245, 247–49
subspecies of, 243–44
tackle for, 249–50
trolling for, 250
in weed beds, 252
world records for, 242, 247–49
Norway, salmon farm in, 211
Nymphs and nymph fishing, 62–63
for bluegills, 268
for brown trout, 54
dead drift of, 62
innovations in, 53
for mountain fishing, 87–89
for rainbow trout, 51–52
Nylon line
in bait casting, 32
for steelhead, 115
see also Monofilament (nylon) line

Obion River, 292
Ocean City reel, 237, 250
Ohio River, 170, 180

Oil spills, fish destruction from, 286–287
O'Neill, Lucky, 122, 124
Oncorhynchus species, 213–14
Ontario
    lake fishing in, 134
    muskellunge in, 234
Oregon
    deer-hair flies in, 97
    steelhead rivers in, 128
Outdoor Life, 11–12
Oxygen, for lake trout, 132
Ozark bass fly, 105

Pacific salmon, 191, 212–30
    baits for, 224–25
    fingerlings of, 229
    fly fishing for, 227
    habitats of, 215
    hog-line fishing for, 216
    hooks for, 228–29
    life cycle of, 212–13
    lures for, 226, 228
    migrating, 217–18
    mooching for, 220
    in river mouths, 216–20
    rolling and porpoising of, 222
    short life of, 228–29
    shrimp fly for, 219
    spawning of, 212–13, 230
    species of, 213–14
    sport fishery and, 214
    in tidewater, 220–25
    in upper rivers, 225–30
    see also Chinook salmon; Salmon
Pack rods, 19, 84
Packtrains, in mountain areas, 81
Pal "sturdy-action" rod, 237
Panfish, 266–85
    bugs for, 275, 278
    casting for, 271–72
    monofilament line for, 270
    spinner/fly combination for, 272–274
    spoons for, 274
    surface bugs for, 275–76
Panther Pond, Me., 253
Parmachene Belle streamer, 258
Parr, Atlantic salmon as, 185, 188
Penobscot River, 208

Perch
    warmouth, 281–82
    white, 283
    yellow, 283
Percidae (perch family), 259
Perry, George, 152
Pesticides, effect of on fisheries, 291
Phillips' Bead-Head streamer, 149
Pickerel, 253–59
    bait for, 259
    chain, 254–55
    diet of, 256
    fly rod for, 258
    lures for, 258
    spawning of, 255
    world record for, 253
    see also Northern pike
Pickup arm, in spinning tackle, 27–28
Pigeon Lake, Quebec, 235
Pike
    muskellunge, 231–42
    northern, 134, 242–53
    walleyed, *see* Walleyes
Pikie Minnow lure, 237, 250
Pink salmon, 214
    in tidewater, 222
Pipeline ruptures, fish kills from, 287
Planers, for lake trout trolling, 141
Plastic lures, 44
Plastic stringer, 90
Plastic worms, 21, 30
    fishing with, 164–65
    for largemouth bass, 163–64
    for smallmouth bass, 176
Platts, William S., 293
Plug-casting equipment, 16–18
Plugs
    for lake trout trolling, 144
    as lures, 41–42
    miniature, 66
    for walleyes, 264
"Plunking," for steelheads, 120–21, 124–25
Pollution, fish kills from, 286–88
Pontoosuc Lake, Mass., 253
Pools
    in brooks, 59
    salmon, 199, 203, 228
Pork rind, for light spinning, 66
Potomac River, 180

Pumpkinseed sunfish, 282
Pupfish National Monument, pro-
    posed, 297

Quebec, muskellunge in, 235
Queets River, 128
Quill Gordon fly, 63, 88, 94
Quinault River, 116, 128

Rainbow trout, 51–53, 287
    in mountain lakes, 80
    steelhead variety, 111
    water temperature for, 55
    Western, 98
Rainy Lake, Ont., 134
Rapala lures, 250
Rat-Faced MacDougall fly, 202
Rebel lure, 226, 264
Red Ant fly, 88
Red Eye Wobbler spoon, 237, 250
Redfin pickerel, 254
Red Quill fly, 63
Reel(s)
    balance in, 23
    for lake trolling, 140, 143
    for mountain fishing, 85
    revolving-spool, 31
    spin-cast, 17, 22–25
    wide-frame, 32
    see also Spinning reels
Reel handle, position of in casting, 24
Reindeer Lake, Sask., 133
Revolving-spool reel, 31
River bass, 180–81
Rivers
    channelization of, 290, 292
    toxic chemicals in, 287–88
River salmon, 216–20
River trout, see Stream trout; see also
    Steelhead
Robinson, Jerome B., 169–83
Rock bass, 281
Rock Creek, Mont., 102
Rockworms, 73
Rocky brooks, technique for, 60
Rocky Mountain area, lakes in, 69–
    71, 95
Rods
    balance in, 23
    for deep trolling, 139

Rods (cont.)
    for fly tackle, 34–35
    for mountain lakes and streams, 84
    for muskellunge, 237, 240–41
    for pickerel, 258
    for salmon, 192, 197–98
    see also Fly rods
Rogue River, 97, 128, 216
Royal Coachman fly or streamer, 63,
    88, 104, 258
Royal Ontario Museum of Zoology,
    233
Royal Wulff fly, 202–03
Ruby Mountains, 93
Ruby River, 93
Ruminski, Tom, 135–36

Sacandaga Reservoir, N.Y., 242
Sacramento River, 226–27
Sailfish, decline of, 288
St. Clair River, 234
St. Lawrence River and Seaway, 132,
    170, 172, 180, 231, 234–37, 246
Salmon
    Atlantic, see Atlantic salmon
    biological degeneration of, 213,
        225
    biting reflex in, 185
    chinook, see Chinook salmon
    chum, 214
    coho, 214, 219, 223
    dams and, 208, 294
    life cycle of, 212–13
    as "overgrown trout," 226
    Pacific, see Pacific salmon
    short lives of, 228
    sockeye, 214
    spawning of, 186–94, 204, 207,
        212–13, 230
    trout flies for, 201
    see also Atlantic salmon; Pacific
        salmon
Salmon Creek, Calif., 225
Salmon eggs, as steelhead bait, 120
Salmon farms, 210–11
Salmon fishing, 192–98
    "rules" of, 203–04
    vs. steelheading, 113
Salmonfly hatch (July), 95
Salmon lures, 226–27

Salmon pools, 199, 203, 228
Salmon River, 109, 113, 127, 129–130, 293
Salmon rods, 192–93, 197–98
Salmo salar, 213
Saltwater reel, for lake trout trolling, 140, 143
Salvelinus namaycush, 131
Sam Rayburn Lake, Tex., 161
San Juan River, 287
Saskatchewan, lake trout in, 133–34
Saugers, 260–62, 283
School bass fishing, 284
Sea bass, 284
Sears, Paul, 297
Shark-fin sinkers, 22
Shooting-head line, for salmon, 228
Shrimp fly, for Pacific salmon, 219
Shrimps, for steelhead, 120, 224
Sick fish, pollution and, 288
Silver Doctor fly, 200, 202
Silver Gray fly, 202
Silver Wilkinson fly, 200
Sinkers
    for lake trout, 140
    for lures, 42
    types of, 20–22
Sinking lures, 105, 155
Sinking-tip lure, 105
Skaters (dry flies), 202
Skeena River, 214
Skimming fly, for salmon, 195
Skykomish River, 128
Slack line, casting of, 103
Smallmouth bass, 169–83
    baits for, 172–73, 182
    cannibalism among, 175–76
    fly rod for, 173
    habitat of, 170–72
    hooking of, 177
    identifying of, 172
    lures for, 175
    nests of, 174
    plastic worms for, 176
    in rivers, 180–81
    season for, 174
    silent approach to, 173
    spawning of, 174–75
    spinning reels for, 177
    water temperatures for, 182
    world record for, 182–83

Smelt
    in lake trout trolling, 143–44
    for steelhead, 120
Smith River, 227–28
Snake River, 92, 97, 99, 113–14, 130, 225, 294, 296
Snap swivels, for mountain fishing, 86
Snoqualmie River, 128
Sockeye salmon, 214
Sofa Pillow fly, 97
Soil Conservation Service, U.S., 292
Solitude Lake, Mont., 77
Spanish Peaks Wilderness Area, Mont., 77
Spin casting vs. spinning, 64
Spin-cast tackle
    antireverse mechanism in, 24
    disadvantage of, 25
    profile of, 22–25
    reel drag in, 24
    reel-handle position in, 24
    rods for, 17
    vs. spinning gear, 23
Spin/fly rods
    for mountain fishing, 84
    for panfish, 272–74
Spinners, as lures, 43, 65
Spinning
    bait for, 67
    for largemouth bass, 157
    light, 64–67
    lines for, 85, 158
    in mountain brooks, 77
    pork rind for, 66
    vs. spin casting, 64
    worms for, 66
Spinning lines, 85, 158
Spinning lures, 160–61
    types of, 64–65
Spinning reel
    antireverse lock on, 28
    balance in, 23
    drag in, 28
    fixed-spool principle in, 26
    pickup in, 27
    for smallmouth bass, 177
Spinning rods, 158
    balance in, 29
    for smallmouth bass, 177

Spinning tackle
    fixed-spool reel and, 16–18
    hand position in, 27
    lightweight, 29–30
    for panfish, 271
    profile of, 25–30
    vs. spin-cast types, 22, 25–26
    ultralight, 29
    see also Spinning; Spinning reel;
        Spinning rods
Split shot, 20–21
Spoons
    for lake trout, 143–44
    as lures, 43–44
    for panfish, 274
    for steelhead, 118, 122
    wobbling, 66, 218, 220
Sports Afield, 11–12
Static lines, for mountain streams, 75
Steelhead eggs, 120
Steelhead streams, 113
Steelhead rivers, 128–29
Steelhead
    bait for, 120
    dam building and, 129
    "drifting" bait for, 120–21
    eggs for, 124
    fly fishing for, 127
    as "freight-train" strikers, 123–24
    lines for, 116–17, 125
    lures for, 117–20, 124
    playing of, 110–11
    "plunking" for, 120–21, 124
    range of, 113
    spawning grounds of, 225
    spoons for, 118, 122
    tackle for, 114–15
    technique for, 114
    warm water and, 128
    weights of, 112, 114
    wind and, 126
    world record for, 112
    worms for, 124
Stizostedion canadense, 260
Stizostedion vitreum vitreum, 259
Stone fly, swimming of, 101–02
Stonefly Creeper, 53
Stone fly hatch, Madison River, 95
Streamer flies or streamers, 60, 62
    for brown trout, 54
    for lake trout, 149

Streamer flies or streamers (cont.)
    for mountain trout, 88
    for pickerel, 258–59
    for walleyes, 264
Streams, technique of fishing in, 57–
        58
Stream trout, 46–68
    see also Brook trout; Mountain
        trout
Stringer, plastic, 90
Strip mining, pollution from, 294–95
Strung, Norman, 69–91
Stunted fish, in mountain lakes, 73–
        74
Subsurface fly fishing, 105
Sunfish, 269–70, 277, 280–81
    pumpkinseed, 282
Super Popper lure, 160
Surface Stonefly, 202
Swing, C. P., spinner, 65
Swivels, for lake trout fishing, 141

Tarpon, 109, 285
Tellico Dam, 296
Temperature probe, brook trout and,
        48–49
    see also Water temperature
Tennessee Game and Fish Commis-
        sion, 292
Tennessee River, 180
Tennessee Valley Authority, 157, 293
Tents, types of, 83
Terminal moraine, lakes and, 71–72
Terminal tackle
    for largemouth bass, 160–61
    tie-up for, 122
Terry, Willard, 242
Teton Dam, 296
Teton River, 108, 296
Thermocline, for smallmouth bass,
        182
Thomson River, 108
Thousand Islands, St. Lawrence
        River, 235
Tidewater
    fly rodding in, 223
    Pacific salmon in, 220–21
Timber cutting, fisheries and, 293
Tittabawassee River, 286
Tocks Island Dam, 296

Toxaphene, 291
Treble hooks, for spinning, 66
Tree River, 133
Trent River, 262
Trolling
  cowbells for, 142
  for lake trout, 137–39
  lures for, 155
  terminal rigging for, 140–41
  see also Lake trout trolling
Trolling gear, for muskellunge, 237
Trout
  bait fishing for, 67
  big-water, 92–108
  brook, *see* Brook trout
  brook fishing techniques for, 58–
    60
  brown, *see* Brown trout
  compared with salmon, 226
  lake, 131–50
  mountain, 69–91
  rainbow, 51
  steelhead, 109–30
  stream, 46–68
  types of, 46–47
  of Western rivers, 92–108
  see also Brook trout; Brown trout;
    Lake trout; Mountain trout;
    Rainbow trout; Steelhead
Trout flies, for salmon, 201
Trout streams, 46–68
  current flow in, 57
  rocks in, 56
  see also Mountain trout
Trout Unlimited, 295–96
True, 11
Trueblood, Ted, 103, 109–10, 116,
  123, 127–28
Turle knot, for fly tying, 63

Ultralight rods, for smallmouth bass,
  177
Ultralight spinning tackle, for lake
  trout, 138
Umpquah River, 128
Union River, 93

Vancouver Is., B.C., 214
Virginia City, Mont., 93

Waders
  for mountain fishing, 90
  for steelhead fishing, 121
Wading
  in boat fishing, 107–08
  casting and, 61
  in dry-fly fishing, 101
Walleyes, 259–65, 283
  bait for, 265
  characteristics of, 260–61
  feeding of, 263
  lures for, 264
  range of, 261–62
  size and weight of, 263
  spawning of, 262–63
  tackle for, 264–65
  water temperature for, 264
  world record for, 259
Walleyed pike, 259
Wapata Lake, Sask., 143
Warmouth bass, 281–82
Washington State, steelhead rivers
  in, 128
Water
  depth readers for, 147, 166–67,
    238–39
  "edge" in, 56
  "reading" of, 56–57
Waterman, Charles F., 266–85
Water pollution, 287–97
Water Quality Act, 296
Water temperature
  for brook trout, 48–49
  for brown trout, 53
  importance of, 55
  for largemouth bass, 152
  lures and, 58
  for muskellunge, 240
  for walleyes, 264
Weedless hooks, for largemouth bass,
  163
Weiser River, 130
Western flies, 94
Western trout fishing, 92–108
  boats in, 106
  see also Mountain lakes; Mountain
    trout
West Yellowstone, Mont., 93
Western waters, big-water trout in,
  92–108
Wet Cell line, 251, 264

Wet flies, 60–62, 202
  for Atlantic salmon, 194–95
  "attractor" and "imitator" patterns
    in, 62
  dead-drift fishing with, 61
  innovations in, 53
  nymph-bodied, 51
  for panfish, 275
Whiskers fly, 202
White bass, 284
White perch, 283
White River, 262
White Wulff fly, 198, 202–03
Whitlock, Dave, 105
Wide-frame reel, 32
Wild and Scenic Rivers Act, 296
Wilderness Act, 296
Wilkinson fly, 202
Willamette River, 97
Willow River, 92
Wind, steelhead fishing in, 126–27
Wind trolling, 145–46
Wire, for sinkers, 22
Wire line, for lake trout, 139

Wobble-Rite spoon, 66
Wobbling spoons, 66, 218, 220
Wollaston Lake, Sask., 133–34
Wolverine River, 135
Woolly Worms, 105
Worms
  for brook trout, 10, 67
  for light spinning, 66
  for mountain trout, 70
  plastic, 21, 30, 163–65, 176
  for steelhead, 124
  for walleyes, 265
Wulff, Joan Salvato, 192
Wulff, Lee, 184–211
Wyoming, rivers in, 94, 96

Yellow bass, 284
Yellowstone National Park, 100
Yellowstone River, 93, 97

Zern, Ed, 92